The Assembly of Gods:

OR

The Accord of Reason and Sensuality in the Fear of Death.

Early English Text Society.

Extra Series, LXIX,

BERLIN: ASHER & CO., 13, UNTER DEN LINDEN.
NEW YORK: C. SCRIBNER & CO.; LEYPOLDT & HOLT.
PHILADELPHIA: J. B. LIPPINCOTT & CO.

The Assembly of Gods:

OR

The Accord of Reason and Sensuality in the Fear of Death

BY

JOHN LYDGATE.

EDITED FROM THE MSS. WITH INTRODUCTION, NOTES, INDEX
OF PERSONS AND PLACES, AND GLOSSARY,

BY

OSCAR LOVELL TRIGGS, M.A., Ph.D.

LONDON:
PUBLISHED FOR THE EARLY ENGLISH TEXT SOCIETY
By KEGAN PAUL, TRENCH, TRÜBNER & CO.,
PATERNOSTER HOUSE, CHARING-CROSS ROAD.

OXFORD
UNIVERSITY PRESS

Great Clarendon Street, Oxford OX2 6DP
United Kingdom

Oxford University Press is a department of the University of Oxford.
It furthers the University's objective of excellence in research, scholarship,
and education by publishing worldwide. Oxford is a registered trade mark of
Oxford University Press in the UK and in certain other countries

© The Early English Text Society 1896

The moral rights of the authors have been asserted

Database right Oxford University Press (maker)

First Edition published in 1896

All rights reserved. No part of this publication may be reproduced,
stored in a retrieval system, or transmitted, in any form or by any means,
without the prior permission in writing of Oxford University Press,
or as expressly permitted by law, or under terms agreed with the appropriate
reprographics rights organization. Enquiries concerning reproduction
outside the scope of the above should be sent to the Rights Department,
Oxford University Press, at the address above

You must not circulate this book in any other form
and you must impose this same condition on any acquirer

Published in the United States of America by Oxford University Press
198 Madison Avenue, New York, NY 10016, United States of America

British Library Cataloguing in Publication Data
Data available

Library of Congress Cataloging in Publication Data
Data available

Extra Series, 69

ISBN 978-0-85-991985-2

NOTICE.

THE Society's lists have, for the last three or four years, containd a notice that two Professors in the English Department of the University of Chicago—Dr. Oscar Triggs and Mr. McClintock—had, with the assent of their Principal, Dr. Harper, agreed to edit and print for their University two Early-English Texts, to be issued jointly by that University and the E. E. Text Society, the Society paying only for electrotypes of the editions. Dr. Oscar Triggs brought out in 1895 his edition of Lydgate's *Assembly of Gods* as No. 1 of the *English Studies* of the University of Chicago, with the Title-page given on the next leaf. It is this book, on the Society's smaller page, which is now issued as No. LXIX in our Extra Series for 1896, and for it the Society is much indebted to Dr. Triggs.

It is hoped that Mr. McClintock will soon proceed with his edition of the theological collection of John Lacy of Newcastle, dated 1434.

F. J. F.

28 April 1897.

The Department of English Language and Literature and Rhetoric of the University of Chicago will publish, as an organic part of its work, a series of monographs, written from time to time by its Instructors and Students.

Of this series the present study, Lydgate's *Assembly of Gods*, edited by Dr. O. L. Triggs, Docent in English Literature, is the first number.

The work is published by the University of Chicago, in conjunction with the Early English Text Society, of London, and will constitute one of the regular issues of the English Society.

The University of Chicago

ENGLISH STUDIES
(No. I.)

THE ASSEMBLY OF GODS:

OR

THE ACCORD OF REASON AND SENSUALITY IN THE FEAR OF DEATH

BY

JOHN LYDGATE.

EDITED FROM THE MSS. WITH INTRODUCTION, NOTES, INDEX OF PERSONS AND PLACES, AND GLOSSARY.

BY

OSCAR LOVELL TRIGGS, M.A., PH.D.

CHICAGO
The University of Chicago Press
1895

DEDICATED TO MY MASTER
CHANCELLOR GEORGE EDWIN MacLEAN
WITH HUMBLE AFFECTION.

MEDIÆVAL FIGURES OF DEATH (DRAWN FROM ANCIENT PRINTS).

PREFACE.

This edition of Lydgate's *Assembly of Gods* serves a double purpose. It is, first, a study in literature conducted at The University of Chicago, a part of the work having been first offered in candidacy for the degree of Doctor of Philosophy; it is, second, a study of an English text undertaken for the Early English Text Society of London. The two institutions are associated in the publication.

The critical and linguistic parts of the work and the notes are as accurate and comprehensive as I am able to make them with the materials at hand. The hardihood of venturing to work upon ancient and foreign matters in a land that has no past at its back, that neither possesses antiquarian materials nor engenders antiquarian enthusiasms, will be appreciated by those who, like myself, have made the endeavor without what one may call a traditional training for the event.

The literary discussion of the Introduction maintains the general interest that any work of literature is wont to arouse. This portion represents the reaction which the poem made upon my mind with its own knowledge of mediæval life and art. While this part is necessarily somewhat pedantic I have tried to maintain my natural interest in literature as an exponent of life, as the expression of the imagination. The study of Allegory is a selection and condensation of materials that I have gathered for an extended history of Allegory.

Every one who works in Lydgate will find himself indebted at every turn to the investigations of Dr. Schick, now of Heidelberg, who edited the *Temple of Glas*—indebted not only for matters of fact but also for judgments of critical and literary insight. Workers in the same field will bear witness to the value of the edition of Lydgate and Burgh's *Secrees of Old Philisoffres* by Mr. Robert Steele, of London. For the facts relating to Lydgate's life and works, reference may be made to the very accurate and complete article on Lydgate by Mr. Sidney Lee in the Dictionary of National Biography.

At home I have every reason to be grateful for the encouragement and assistance given by Dr. George E. MacLean, formerly my teacher in the University of Minnesota; also for kindly help rendered by Professors McClintock, Blackburn, and Tolman, of the Department of English in The University of Chicago. Dr. Klaeber, of the University of Minnesota, has performed the offices of a friend in reviewing the proofs. My brother, Mr. Flloyd W. Triggs, has drawn from old prints the figures of Death for the frontispiece.

To Dr. Furnivall, the veteran Director of the work of the Early English Text Society, every one is indebted.

OSCAR LOVELL TRIGGS.

THE UNIVERSITY OF CHICAGO,
    October 2, 1895.

CONTENTS.

PREFACE	iii–iv
INTRODUCTION	vii–lxxvi

CHAPTER I.

A. The Manuscripts—Texts A and B	vii
B. The Prints—Texts C and D	ix

CHAPTER II.

A. The Title	x
B. The Authorship and Date	xi

CHAPTER III.

The Metre—The Types A, B, C, D, E, F, G, H	xiv
The Mixture of Free and Regular Stress	xix

CHAPTER IV.

The Rime—(1) End-Rime	xxi
(a) Identical Rimes	xxi
(b) Imperfect Rimes	xxi
(c) Feminine Rimes	xxi
(d) Medial *gh*	xxii
Rime-Index	xxii
(2) Alliteration	xxix

CHAPTER V.

The Rime and the Final *e*	xxx
(1) The -y -ye Rimes	xxx
(2) The Infinitives among the Riming Words	xxxii

CHAPTER VI.

The Language	
A. Vocabulary	xxxv
B. Grammar	xxxv

Chapter VII.
The Poem

- A. Literary Analysis - - - - - - - xxxvii
- B. Literary Studies - - - - - - xl
  - (1) The Religious Character of the Poem - - xl
  - (2) The Fear of Death and the Scorn of the World xliii
  - (3) The Conventional Materials - - - l
  - (4) The Season *motif* - - - - - liii
  - (5) The Vision - - - - - - - lv
  - (6) Proverbial Phrases - - - - - lvi
  - (7) The Painted Wall - - - - - lvii
  - (8) The Admixture of Pagan and Christian Traditions - - - - - - lviii
  - (9) The Allegorical Type - - - - - lx
  - (10) The Relationship between the Allegory and the Moral Play - - - - - lxi
  - (11) The Allegory of the Vices and Virtues - - lxiii

TEXT - - - - - - - - - - 1–61
NOTES - - - - - - - - - - 77
INDEX of Names and Persons, and Glossary - - - 77

INTRODUCTION.

CHAPTER I.

A. THE MANUSCRIPTS.

1. *Text A=R.3. 19, Trin. Coll. Camb.*—This is a quarto volume, in paper, in handwriting of the second half of the fifteenth century. It contains poems by Chaucer, Lydgate and others (v. Skeat, *Chaucer's Minor P.* p. xliv. Trin: *Legend of Good Women*, p. xl. T. Skeat dates the MS. before 1500). The earliest possible date for the volume is fixed by a poem written by Geo. Ashby, entitled *Prisoner in the Fleet*, and dated 1463. The present poem occupies fols. 68a–98a. A table of *Interpretations* (v. Text p. 1) precedes the poem. The volume belonged formerly to John Stowe and was the source of most of Stowe's additions to Chaucer (Skeat).

This is the earliest and the only authoritative MS. known to me, and its readings are followed with but a very few emendations in the present text. The following are the textual changes made: Eolus is printed for the Colus of the MS.; Morpheus for Morpleus; in feere 166 for feere; Phebe 243, 566 for Phebus; foom 104 for from; presse 256 for preef; she 412 for he; best 634 for bost; ther 635 for the; hys 815 for was; be 875 for he; comparyson 891 for a form not clear in MS.; with 976 for without; fly 1185 for sty; macrocosme 1420 for macocrosme; omnipotent 1467 for omnipotens. The punctuation and the capitalization of proper names are mine.

The orthography is highly unphonetic, the most marked characteristics being the confused uses of *y* and *i*, and the arbitrary doubling of vowels. *Y* is either long or short: wys, whyle, myne; but ys, hys (also his), yn (also in), hyt (also hit), wyth (also with), tyll, wyll, lytyll, shyp, fysshe, sylvyr, knyghtes, syttyng, begynne, etc.; *i* is used in king, philosophres, scisme, idylnesse, Diana, Cirus, Virgyle. The scribe wrote indifferently se or see, fle or flee, fre or free, so or soo, do or doo, wo or woo, mo or moo, whos or whoos, none or noon, hope or hoope, hole or hoole, sore or soore, holy or hooly, wordes or woorde, god or good, ost oost or hoost, blood or blody, sone or soone; regularly—deere, leede, seene, seere, reepe, roote, poore, aboorde, stoode, goold, roode, woode, broode, stoon, Ioob, etc. Final *e* (inorganic) is written with no regularity, occurring after short as well as long vowels. The consonants generally follow the rule of doubling after short vowels.

2. *Text B = Bibl. Reg. 8.D. II, Brit. Mus.*—This is written in color on vellum and in two parts. The first part, in a 15th century hand, contains Lydgate's *Siege of Troy* (5 books) and *Siege of Thebes* (illustrated). The second part, beautifully written and illuminated, is early 16th century work and contains a *Treatise between Trowthe & Enformacion* by Will Cornish, an Elegy by John Skelton, Stanzas by Lydgate, his *Testament* and *Assembly of Gods*. The latter poem is indexed in the MS. as *Discord between Reason and Sensualitie*. This MS. does not differ materially from the Camb. MS. except in its omission of the table of Interpretations. It is, however, most probably a copy of the print by Wynken de Worde (G.11587), since it follows that print most closely in orthography and in the omission of line 812.

The chief variations of this text from A are given in the following collation. A few variants are given from Print D. To indicate the differences in orthography the variations of the first fifty lines are recorded complete.

---

1. hys | his. 2. toward | towarde; iourne | iourney. 3. speere | spere; begonne | begon. 4. syttyng | sittinge; solytary | solitary; alone | allone. 5. musyng | musinge; myght | might. 6. sensualyte | sensualite; oon | one; acorde | accorde. 7. cowde | coude; nat | not; bryng | bringe; about | aboute. 8. long | longe; myght | might; oppresse | oppres. 9. cowde | coude. 10. heede | hede; heuynesse | heuynes. 11. myn | myne; habytacle | habitacle. 12. pylow | pilow. 13. dyssese | disease. 14. anone | anon; came | cam. 15. so lay | soo laye; traunse | traunsse. 16. slepyng | slepinge; wakyng | wakinge. 17. seyde | saide. 18. gret | grete; court | courte; iustyse | iustice. 19. auaylyd | auayled; sylogyse | silogyse. 20. hit | it; ys | is; seyde | saide. 21. nedys | nedis. 22. when | whan; sy | see; bettyr | better; must | muste. 23. seyde | saide; hys | his; commaundment | commaundemente. 24. whedyr | wheder; wold | wolde; leede | lede. 25. forthe | forth. 26. tyll | till; parlyament | parliament. 29. thedyrward | thederward. 30. hys | his. 31. seyde thow | saide thou. 32. seyd | saide. 33. heuen | heuyn; outher | either; elles | ellis. 34. seyde | saide; myn | myne; abydyng | abidinge. 35. ys | is; lytyll | litill; corner | cornoure; eallyd | callede. 36. these wordys | thes wordes; sayd | saide. 37. hys | his. 38. raggys | raggis; arayd | arayde. 39. agayn | agayne; whom | whome; Diana | Dyana. 40. seying | sayenge; thow | thou. 41. yeue | gyue; ageyn | ayen; soo | so.

42. preyse | preise; lord | lorde. 43. proclamasion | proclamacioun. 44. Plutoys
Plutos; co*m*maundyd | commaundede. 45. vppon | vpon; peyne | payne;
strayte | straite. 46. Diana | Dyana; myght | might. 47. greefe | gref; gret |
grete. 48. theym | theyme; done | do; they | *þ*ei; compleynyd | co*m*pleyned.
49. begyn | begynne; Diana | Dyana; constreynyd | constreynede. 50. whyche
| whiche. 56. yef | yf. 57. howe | hou. 70. thorough | thorugh. 71. syngler
| synguler. 72. shuld | sholde; world | worlde. 73. dyspleser | displeasure. 77.
yeue | omitted. 94. yow | you. 98. thorough | thrugh. 99. furst | first. 102.
ferre | fer. 103. merueyle | meruaill. 104. from | come. 107. ebbe | eb. 109.
dykes | dyks. 117. oo | one. 130. perysshe | perish. 132. pepyll | people.
135. requyreth | req*u*iret. 155. vs | hus. 166. feere | infeere. 183. togedyr
| togider. 186. alther | alder. 210. owne wele | one well. 216. pyne |
payne. 217. grogyng | grutching (D = grutchyng). 228. eft | oft. 233. lak | lacke.
234. cese | sease. 235. mery | mercy. 248. compaygnably | companably. 256.
preef | presse (D = presse). 269. good | god. 283. fawchon | fawcon. 325. frese
| frele (D = frese). 337. was then | than was (D = than was). 348. sythe | shithe.
355. chase | chose. 361. Phebus | Pheby. 434. forthe | for. 449. sewerte |
suerte. 462. smete | smote. 473. cosdras | coldras. 480. owther | eyther. 513.
leyte | lightnynge. 520. woll | will. 535. drowthe | drought. 569. I hope shall
| I hope I shall. 587. defaute | the faute (D = the faute). 607. at | omitted
(D omits at). 634. bost | best. 648. foule rybaudy | foule and rybaudry (D has
and). 673. braggars | kraghers. 721. for sowght he | forsoth it. 753. to do a | to
a. 763. row | route (D = rowe). 773. wore | were. 812 | omitted. 815. was |
and. 825. standardes | standartis. 875. he | be. 966. haue ye lost | haue lost
(D omits ye). 970. guytornes | guytors. 974, 981. dubbyd | doubled (D = doubled).
1094. rerewarde | reward. 1113. meryt | might (D = myght). 1161. she | he. 1185.
sty | fly. 1201. as they came by Conscience | as thei to C. cam (D follows B).
1243. bende | ben (D = ben). 1358. kept | kepe (D = kept). 1373. menetyme
whyle | meanewhill. 1467. omnipotens | omnipotent. 1516. singlerly | sy*n*gulerly·
1537. awter | aulter. 1538. Osee | Ozee (D = Ozee.) 1539. Sal*m*on | Salamon.
1591. brayne | barayne. 1701. shall | sall. 1705. nouelte | newelte (D = newelte).
1744. deuyacion | deuocyon. 1806. gnawyng | knawi*n*ge. 1854. tryfyl | triphells.
1858. sauns | sauns (D = sanuz). 1975. a a | aha. 2020. dowtys | doubtes. 2062.
accusacion | actuacyon. 2103. descendyd | desce*n*deth.

B. The Prints.

3. *Text C = G. 11587. Brit. Mus.*—This is the first print of the poem by Wynken de Worde, a folio dated 1498. It is an unique copy. It contains the *Canterbury Tales* and Lydgate's *Assembly of Gods.* Lydgate's "treatyse" is printed in double columns on the last 15 leaves without pagination. On the recto of the first leaf is a woodcut of the Canterbury pilgrims seated around a table. This print is especially valuable in that it assigns the work to Lydgate in the colophon: "Thus endeth this lytyll moralized treatyse compiled by dan Iohn Lydgat somtyme monke of Bury on whose soule

have mercy." The print has commonly the readings of MS.B. It omits line 812 but has the table of Interpretations.

4. Text D=C. 13. a. 21. *King's Collect. Brit. Mus.*—This print is also by W. de Worde and of about the same date as the first. The Catalogue of the Brit. Mus. and Mr. Lee (*Dict. Nat. Biog.* Vol. XXXIV, p. 313, v.) give the date 1500, but Dr. Schick, on the authority of Mr. Gordon Duff (Brit. Mus.), says it is earlier, perhaps 1498. It contains Lydgate's *Story of Thebes, Assemble de dyeus* and *Temple of Glas* (v. Hazlitt, *Bibl.* p. 358, No. 3 under Lydgate; Schick, *Temp. of Glas*, E. E. T. Soc., p. xxvi, 9). This print exhibits no notable changes in the text. It follows most closely MS. A.

5. Later reprints by Pynson and Redman, under the title "The Interpretacyon of the Natures of Goddys and Goddesses," show no important textual differences (v. Hazlitt, *Bibl.* p. 358, No. 4 (b) (c) (d). Redman's last edition is dated 1540).

CHAPTER II.

A. The Title.

W. de Worde's second print (D above) has the colophon: "Here endeth a lytyll Tratyse named, *Le Assemble de dyeus*." This is followed by de Worde's imprint and, on the following page, by the cut of the Chaucer pilgrims seated about a table, also entitled *Le Assemble de dyeus*. Redman's late reprint (1540) ends with the colophon: "Here endeth a lytyll treatyse named *the assemble of goddis and goddesses*." The catalog of Lydgate's works, probably made by John Stowe for the Chaucer-Lydgate volume, printed by Adam Islip in London in 1598 and 1602, includes the *Banket of Gods and Goddesses with a discourse of Reason and Sensualitie* by Lydgate (ed. 1602 fol. 376; ed. 1598 fol. 394).

In the Camb. MS. the title, in the handwriting of Mr. Beauprei Bell (Camb. c. 1727), is given as *Assembly of Gods and Goddesses by Lydgate*. The Brit. Mus. MS. is cataloged as *Discord between Reason and Sensualitie*. Lowndes (*Bibl.* Bohn Lib., p. 1419) uses the title *Banquet of the Gods*. Ritson (*Bibl. Poet.*) lists the poem apparently twice, as *The interpretation of the names of goddes and goddesses* (No. 13) and probably confusing it with *Reason and Sensuality* (Fairfax 16), as *Banket of gods and goddesses with a discourse of reason and sensualitie* (No. 113). Bale, probably noticing the list of *Interpretations* prefixed to W. de Worde's print, enumerates among Lydgate's writings, *De Nominibus Deorum*. Collier (*Hist. of Dram. P.* I., p. 30) refers to the poem under the title, *Interpretation of the names of Goddes and Goddesses*. Schick, in his chronology of Lydgate's works (*Temp. of Glas* cix.), adopts the title, *The Assembly of Gods;* and so, following him, Dr. Furnivall in the Early Eng. Text Society's Announcements, Sidney Lee in the *Dict. of Natl. Biog.* (Vol. XXXIV., p. 313, V., 18) and Mr. Courthope in his *History of English Poetry* (I. p. 322). We may suppose, on the authority of W. de Worde's print, that this was Lydgate's own title. It is not, however, a sufficient title as titles go, inasmuch as it does not express the central moral of the story. A truer name would be the *Accora of Reason and Sensuality*.

B. THE AUTHORSHIP AND DATE.

1. *The authorship*. The external testimony is in itself quite sufficient to establish the fact of Lydgate's authorship. W. de Worde's first print (C) ascribes the work to our monk of Bury in the colophon: "Thus endeth this lytyll moralized treatyse compiled by dan Iohn Lydgat somtyme monke of Bury on whose soule have mercy." All the early lists (of Bale, Dibdin, etc.) agree in the assignment. Collier, in his *History of Dramatic Poetry* (Vol. I., p. 30), printed, for the first time since the black-letter copies, a few stanzas of the poem, referring the work to Lydgate. Dyce, in his notes on Skelton's works (p. 144), makes the same reference. The MS. was not known to Warton or Morley. A definite reference to our poem is found in Hawes's *Pastime of Pleasure* (Chap. XIV.). Hawes was a pupil of Lydgate and recounts as the works of his master, the *Life of St. Edmund, Falls of Princes, Chorl and Bird, Court of Sapience, Troy Book, Temple of Glas*:

> "And betwene vertue and the lyfe vycyous
> Of goddes and goddes[ses] a boke solacyous
> He did compyle."

This must refer to the *Assembly of Gods*.

That Lydgate's name was associated with the battle of the vices and virtues is further indicated by the "extemporal play" of the *Seven Deadlie Sinns*, contrived by Richard Tarleton and performed before King Henry VI. (v. description by Collier, *Hist. Dram. P.*, III., p. 198). Our monk Lydgate (here spelled Lidgate) is supposed to regulate the performance, to deliver the prolog and epilog and to explain the dumb shows.

As to internal evidence Lydgate's finger marks are all here:. the monkish piety, the moralization, the allegory, the way in which he dwells upon the themes of death; then his stock words and phrases, especially those repeated to fill up the lines (v. notes and *Temp. of Glas* p. cxxxvii.) the irregular lines (cf. *Secrees*), the rime-forms, and the peculiar Lydgatian metre (type, C. p. xvi; v. Schick, *Temple of Glas*, lviii); further, the saying of things as if "undir correccioun" (cf. *Secrees*, p. 1, 2), the self-depreciation in confessing his thin brain (text, l. 1591) and thin wit (text, l. 1997) and the request to take the very little wheat from the much chaff of the poem (text, l. 2071-2; cf. *Secrees*, p. xx. and *Temp. of Glas*, p. cxl). Lydgate is one of the easiest poets to detect for his conventional manner.

2. *The Date.* So far as I am able to determine from a study of the contents there is nothing to indicate the exact date of the poem's composition. The allegory of the poem is wholly removed from historical place or time. Dr. Schick conjectures the date 1403. In consideration of the general temper of the work, quite prosaic one must allow, the nature of the allegory, and its dominant note of death, I am inclined to assign its writing to Lydgate's second period, that is, after 1412 (the date of the first lines of the *Troy-Book*), as far removed as possible from the genial influence of Chaucer which is so distinctly traceable in the monk's early works. As a youth Lydgate was loath to enter the monastic life, and the poems of his first period have a freshness, a humor, and a love of nature, that belong to the world outside the cloister. But we have the proof of the *Legends* and *Secrees* and the *Testament* that, as he approached age, he grew more pious and more prosaic. The *Assembly of Gods* is the work of a thorough Benedictine both in theory and in practise. And there is a positive lowering of the poetic tone. There are no plaints of lovers, not a word about the "floure of womanhede," not a happy thought of nature. Life is grown serious, and the monk, anxious concerning the battle with Vice and earnest to direct sinners to the Lord of Light, writes in the repentant prayerful temper of the *Testament*.

In arguing for an earlier date it would be true to say that the influence of the *Romaunt of the Rose* is somewhat evident in the allegory, and that the work is rather more original and creative than his late riming histories, and it appears in the classification of his works by

Sidney Lee (*Dict. Natl. Biog.*, Vol. XXXIV, p. 313, 314) that most if not all of the poems under the head of "Allegories, Fables and Moral Romances" were written before 1412.

On the other hand the decline in the *Assembly of Gods* in poetic power is, as noted above, very marked, judging from his known early works. In poetic conception and phrasing the poem is in every way inferior to the *Chorl and Bird* and the *Temple of Glas;* the one written before 1400 and dedicated to "his maister with humble affeccioun," the other written about 1403 in imitation of Chaucer's *Hous of Fame*. There is not a line so poetic as these verses from the *Temple of Glas*:

> "A world of beaute compassid in hir face
> Whose persant loke doþ þurugh myn hert[e] race" 755-6;

nor a maxim so unworldly wise as these from the *Chorl and Bird:*

> "Songe and prison have noon accordaunce," Min. P., p. 183,

and

> "Bettir is fredom withe litelle in gladnesse
> Than to be thralle withe al worldly richesse," Min. P., p. 193;

not a moral so manly as

> "When wo approcheþ lat myrþ most habound,
> As manhood axeþ; and þough þou fele smert,
> Lat not to manie knowen of þin hert."—*Temple of Glas*, 1177-9.

The theme also, notwithstanding its place among the allegories, seems to indicate a late date. While Lydgate was always familiar with the thought of change and death, it being his frequent opinion that "all do but show a shadow transitory" and that "all stant in chaunges like a midsomer rose," it is fair to assume that the dread of death would be most dominant after the period of his youth. The *Dance of Macabre*, which is descriptive of the painting of Death's procession on the walls of St. Paul's, belongs to the second period, perhaps to the year 1425 (Schick, *Temple of Glas*, cxii); likewise his translation of De Deguileville's *Pèlerinage de l' Homme*, representing life as a pilgrimage somewhat in the manner of Bunyan's *Pilgrim's Progress*, belongs to this period, the year 1426.

The proof from the metre and from the language is also, I think, on the side of a late date. The measure, very broken and irregular at one's best mending, is nearer the long lines of the *Secrees* than the very good verses of the *Temple of Glas*. There is also a change in the poetic phraseology, as will be seen by a study of the riming words, which change compels a date as near as possible to the time when the final *e* ceased to be spoken. Though, as to this, it is not impossible that Burgh or some other of Lydgate's pupils rewrote the poem as we have it in the text. Still it is not probable that anyone would alter the riming words.

On the whole I should wish to assign the composition of the *Assembly of Gods* to about the year 1420 or perhaps, the *Story of Thebes* being finished, to 1422 or even later. In the absence of direct testimony, any more exact statement of the date must wait the publication of Lydgate's other works, which will furnish a surer basis for poetic, metrical and linguistic tests.

CHAPTER III.

THE METRE.

In the MS. the metre is very irregular. Of course little dependence can be placed upon MSS. of the fifteenth century, written after the final *e* ceased to be sounded. We know that many little words were inserted by the scribes, who regarded the lines as imperfect. So whether Lydgate himself failed in this poem in his measures or whether the fault is due to the scribes can not be determined. However, it does not appear that Lydgate in any of his poems was especially skillful in the mechanism of his art. He was himself aware of the imperfections of his verse, and in the *Troy-Book* he confessedly "sette asyde" truth of metre and took "none hede nouther of shorte nor longe." Moreover, none of Lydgate's pupils exhibit any especial grace of form. Burgh, his nearest pupil, readily acknowledges in continuing the *Secrees* that he is unable to keep his measures in time and proportion (*Sec.* st. 219). If we take Chaucer's line as the standard of melody, it is probable that Lowell's estimate of Lydgate's verse, a "barbarous jangle," is the correct one. Old French verse with its great variety of lines and measures (no less than sixteen — Skeat's *Chaucer*, Vol. VI, p. lxxxvii) and indeed Chaucer's own verse forms, may have given Lydgate his license to vary his metres at will. If we forego a fixed metre and read the lines with their natural accentuation, a fairly good rhythm is secured.

Our present poem, *The Assembly of Gods*, is written in the common seven line stanza, which came to be known as the Rhyme Royal, riming *ababbcc*. The scheme of the Chaucerian stanza cannot be rigidly applied. Every liberty in respect of length of line and character of measure is taken by Lydgate. Some lines are bald prose.

Type A. In the first place examples will be given of lines which seem to have five iambic measures with the cæsural pause after the second measure. This may be called the standard-line form.

    43: Then was | there made || a proc | lama | sion.
    45: Vppon | the peyne || of strayte | correc | cion.
    57: Remem | bre furst || howe I | a godd | esse pure.
  163: For hys | excuse || came yn | a mess | ynger.
  750: And bade | hem come || in all | the haste | they myght.
  816: He semyd | a lorde || of ryght | gret ex | cellence.
  980: To wynne | theyr spores || they seyde | they wold | asay.
1026: Whyche made | the grounde || as slep | yr as | an yele.
1086: But all | the tyme || whyle Ver | tew was | away.
1146: And fro | thens forth || to Sat | ysfac | cion.

1. The cæsura in the standard line falls generally after the second measure, but Lydgate shifts its position at liberty. He has more freedom than Chaucer in this respect, though the latter is by no means regular in his pauses (v. Skeat's *Chaucer*, Introd. sec. 107). The examples here given to illustrate this variation include lines of different types (see below). The pause may fall

                (*a*) after the first measure:
  566: To compleyn || than Phebe styrt vppon her fete.
1504: Sate || & Scrypture was scrybe to theym all.

                (*b*) after the third:
  18: To the gret Court of Mynos || the iustyse.
782: But the felde was clene defaute || fonde he none.

                (*c*) after the fourth:
621: Pryde was the furst þat next hym roode || God woote.
879: And made hem be caryed toward Vyce || y wys.

                (*d*) twice or thrice in a line:
  603: Wherfore || þow Cerberus || I now the dyscharge.
1231: Ys he soo || quod Vertu || well he shall be taught.
1210: Well || quoth Feythe || for hys sake || I shall do that I may do.
1377: Now Prayer || efte Fastyng || & oftyn tyme Penaunce.

Type B. An extra syllable may occur before the cæsura and at the end of the line. Two such syllables may also occur before the cæsura (v. ll. 38, 390, 808).

(*a*) Before cæsura:

  38: Brought theder Eolus || in raggys euyll arayd.
 160: Shape vs an answer || to thyne accusement.
 305: Rewler of knyghthode || of Prudence the goddese.
 390: There was sad Sychero || and Arystotyll olde.
 456: Thus haue I dewly || with all my dilygence.
 808: Next whom came Pacyence || that nowhere hath no pere.
 908: Well menyng merchauntes || with trew artyfyceres.

(*b*) At end of line:

The form is comparatively infrequent (v. Chap. IV, c).

   9: So ponderously || I cowde make noon obstacle.
  12: To rowne with a pylow || me semyd best tryacle.
  60: Thys traytour Eolus || hath many of my places.
 946: In thys mene tyme || whyle Vertu thus preuyded.

Type C. The thesis may be wanting at the cæsura.

   8: For long er I myght || slepe me gan oppresse.
  68: So that the deere || shall haue no resort.
  85: Thow knowest well || that I haue the charge.
  87: No shyp may sayle || keruell boot ner barge.
 233: For lak of shade || I dar vndyrtake.
 279: And next by her || sate the god Saturne.
 600: No maner of thyng || can hym hurt nor dere.
 618: Hard as any horn || blakker fer then soot.
 806: Roody as a roose || ay he kept hys chere.

1. This is a form almost peculiar to Lydgate (v. Schick, *Temp. of Glas*, p. lviii. C.), though Chaucer occasionally employed it (Skeat, *Chaucer*, Vol. VI. Introd., sec. 110). It is easy however to read some of these lines with four accents; thus line 85 may read: "Thou knówest wéll that I háue the chárge." Other lines, however, as 618, 87, etc., can have no other reading than that given.

Type D. A thesis may be wanting in the first measure.

  17: For he seyde || I must yeve attendaunse.
 106: Secundly || whereas my nature ys.
 124: That to theym || shuld fall opon the see.
 197: Madame ye shall haue all your plesere.
 251: To be had || wherfore ye may nat let.
 557: Walewyng with hys wawes || & tomblyng as a ball.
 640: Malyce || Frowardnesse || gret Ielacy.
 645: Wrong || Rauyne || sturdy Vyolence.
 654: Heresy || Errour || with Idolatry.

Type E. A trochee may take the place of an iambic in the first measure. These measures are best read, however, with "hovering accent," as Ten Brink (*Chaucer's Sp.*, p. 182, sec. 316) and Gum-

The Metre. xvii

mere (*Handbook of Poetics*, pp. 186, 187, 206, 224) read similar lines in Chaucer and other English poets.

    5: Musyng | on a maner ‖ how that I myght make.
  374: Cryspe was | her skyn ‖ her eyen columbyne.
  418: Seying to | her sylf ‖ that chere should þey repent.
  472: Iason ne | Hercules ‖ went they neuer so wyde.
  631: Slowthe was | so slepy ‖ he came all behynde.
  648: Boldnes | in Yll ‖ with Foule Rybaudy.
  747: Pepyll | to reyse ‖ hys quarrell to menteyn.
  760: Gaderyd | to Vertew ‖ in all that they mowte.
 1174: Hauyng | in her hande ‖ the palme of vyctory.

Type F. There may be a double thesis in any measure. In many cases the extra syllable may be slurred over. But the trisyllabic measure was without doubt an accepted poetic form (v. Ellis, *Early Eng. Pron.*, ch. iv, p. 334; ch. vii, p. 648. Ellis cites 69 examples in the Prolog. See Skeat, ed. of *Prioresses Tale*, etc., Introd. p. lxiii).

    7: But I cowde | nat bryng | about | that mon | acorde.
   66: He breketh | hem asondre ‖ or rendeth | hem roote | & rynde.
   98: For hurt | of my name ‖ thorough | thys gret | offence.
  126: With a sod | eyn pyry ‖ he lapp | yd hem | in care.
  139: The more gre | uous peyne ‖ and hast | y iug | ement.
  199: But furst | I yow pray ‖ let me | the mat | er here.
  361: And ones | in the moneth ‖ with Phe | bus was | she meynt.
  383: That he ther | with glad ‖ yd all | the com | pany.
  410: But there was | no rome | to set | hyr in | that hous.
  472: Iason | ne Hercules ‖ went | they neu | er so wyde.
  487: To the dynt | of my dart ‖ for doole | nor des | tyny.

Type G. Lydgate frequently expands the normal pentameter line to six measures. Mr. Steele, the editor of the *Secrees*, remarks that the greater part of that poem might be scanned on a six-beat basis. If such lines were of sporadic occurrence they might be slurred over, but there are so many lines with the longer rhythm that the acceptance of the Alexandrine is rendered imperative. It is possible, of course, to read some of these lines with four accents, as if they were formed on the model of the alliterative four-beat measures as found in the Mystery Plays (v. *York Plays*, ed. by Smith, Introd., p. li), certain ballads (v. *King John and the Abbot of Canterbury*) and the contemporary alliterative poems. The long doggerel lines in Shakespeare may be reduced to this form (v. *Quell. u. For.*, vol. 61, p. 119, 3). But the use of the Alexandrine was now established both by itself and in association with other metres (v. Schipper, *Engl. Met.*, I, Kap. 5, 8, 13, and cf. its later usage by

Wyatt, and see *Mirror for Magistrates*, ed. by Haslewood, p. 123, for mixture of pentameter and Alexandrine), and Lydgate would naturally adopt the form at a time when every irregularity in verse was permissible. He himself was most attracted to the French forms, though the English alliterative principle still had some force in his verse. I think there can be no question about Lydgate's Alexandrines.

Mr. Ellis (*Early Eng. Pron.*, ch. vii, p. 649) thought that Chaucer made use of this variation and noticed four instances in the prolog of the *Canterbury Tales* of what seemed to him to be a six-measure line (ll. 148, 232, 260, 764), all of which have the justification of the best MSS. Zupitza and Skeat in their critical texts of the *Prologue* reduce these lines to the normal (l. 764 by slurring).

    4: Syttyng | all sol | ytary ‖ alone | besyde | a lake.
   54: Accord | yng to | the offence ‖ that he | to me | hath do.
 161: And ellys | I most | procede ‖ opon | thy iug | ement.
 253: And when | Apol | lo sy ‖ hit wold | noon oth | er be.
 267: Lyke | as she | had take ‖ the man | tell & | the ryng.
 298: The pal | eys ther | of shone ‖ as though | hit had | be day.
 325: Clad | in rus | set frese ‖ and brech | ed lyke | a bere.
 327: A shepe | crook in | hys hand ‖ he spar | yd for | no pryde.
 340: Aboute | hym in | hys gyr | dyll stede ‖ hyng fyssh | es man | y a score.
 347: She lok | ed eu | er about ‖ as though | she had | be mad.
 359: Fat | she was | of face ‖ but of | complex | yon feynt.
 364: And on | hyr hede | she weryd | a crowne | of syl | uyr pure.
 367: He had | a gyld | yn tong ‖ as fyll | for hys | degree.
 372: By | hym sate | Dame Venus ‖ with col | our crys | tallyne.
 385: In sygne | that he | was mastyr ‖ & lord | of that | banket.

So I read lines 401, 404, 420, 421, 422, 462, 476, 490, 495, 496, 497, 500, 504, 525, 542, 560, 634, 656, 817, 864, 937, 949, 952, 962, 995, 999, 1048, 1050, 1093, 1097, 1106, 1113, 1120, 1167, 1204, 1210, 1225, 1239, 1240, 1267, 1344, 1589, 1792, 2099, 2100, 2106, 2107. Lines 61, 102, 128, 130, 131, 338, 343, 578, 672, 856, 1000, might be read either as Alexandrines or as pentameters of type F.

Type H. There are occasional four-measure lines.

 232: So that | your game | shall nat | dyscrese.
 307: Safe on | her hede ‖ a crowne | ther stood.
 444: All ye | gret goddys | yeue at | tendaunce.
 693: Getters ‖ chyders ‖ causers | of frayes.
 758: To Ver | tews frendys ‖ thus all | aboute.
 979: These four | tene knyghtes ‖ made Vyce | that day.
1659: Wherfore | ar chyl | dren put | to scoole.
1834: Of eu | ery mans | oppyn | yon.

In this manner may be read lines 16, 17, 22, 27, 28, 47, 50, 94, 134, 182, 204, 530, 550, 703, 722, 916, 1065, 1243, 1506, 1654, 1655, 1740, 1839, 2004, 2035, 2046.

2. Of course many lines can be scanned in more than one way. Other prosodists will probably not agree with the scansion of the examples given. It is difficult and often impossible to determine the pronunciation of many words. I think the final *e*'s are often, if not generally, mute. The rhythm of many lines would be broken by the requirements of the Chaucerian scheme of inflections. It is evident that during Lydgate's lifetime the language was undergoing transformation. The general irregularity of the metre, the intrusion into Chaucer's carefully constructed seven-line stanza of the four and six-beat lines, and the frequent alliteration, suggest the influence of the older English metrical forms. But it is further obvious that Lydgate used in composition the principles both of metre and of stress.

This mixture in his measures of free and regular stress, seems to confirm the opinion[1] of Professor Gummere (v. *Amer. J. of Phil.* Vol. VII, I, p. 46) that the English iambic is not merely the French measure introduced by a *tour de force*, but a "harmonizing of two great systems, the Germanic and the Romance, the rhythmic and the metric, on the basis of two representative measures," the heroic pentameter line being the "result of forcing the iambic movement upon some late form of our old four-stress verse." The conditions are thus stated by Professor Gummere: "On the one hand, four stresses, fixed pause, indeterminate amount of light syllables; on the other, five stresses, shifting and slighter pause, strict ordering and number of light syllables." Proofs of such compromise are furnished by Chaucer, the majority of whose pentameter verses are formed, to some extent, on the plan of the O. E. line of four stresses; by the Mystery and Morality Plays, whose irregular measures very plainly display the continuance of the English traditions; by Skelton, whose peculiar metre seems to be due to the splitting of the O. E. long line and the riming of the parts; by Spenser in his

---

[1] Little attention has been given hitherto to this view of Professor Gummere, but the trend of opinion now seems to favor it. See Courthope's treatment of Lydgate's verse in his recent *History of English Poetry*, I., pp. 326-33. Cf. the statement of Mr. I. Gollancz in his edition of Cyn. *Christ*, p. xvii: "The secret of Marlowe's discovery (the secret of blank verse) lies in this that he Teutonized the 'versi sciolti' imported from Italy."

Shepherd's Calendar, which combines free and regular stress in a remarkable manner; and again by the heroic verses of Shakespeare and Spenser and of Dryden and Pope, many of which have rhetorically but four stresses.

On the whole Lydgate followed his French models, or more strictly his Chaucer. The many alliterative phrases in his poem illustrate, however, the traditions of the older poetry; such a line as 66b

"or *r*endeth hem *r*oote & *r*ynde"

indicating the "*rum ram ruf*" principle of composition. The variable measure and line reveal the confusion into which English verse had fallen after Chaucer, it being still uncertain whether free or regular stress would prevail. Had Lydgate been favored with Chaucer's literary environment and gifted with his genius and ear for rhythm it is probable that he might have maintained the master's delicate Normanized literary English, but the influence of the vulgar Suffolk tongue with its accentual principles of verse and its rapidly disappearing inflections was too strong for the monk. Chaucer's regular measures—regular because artificial—were given over to confusion. The oral, in the rude times of the fifteenth century, superseded the literary. From Chaucer to Spenser no one was able to give permanency to the forms of English verse.

That the metre is at best extremely irregular is shown by counting the syllables. In the first one thousand lines, slurring wherever possible and omitting, except where forbidden by the rhythm, the final *e*'s, the following result is given:

2	14-syllable lines.	See 66, 340.
5	13 " "	See 404, 525.
47	12 " "	
210	11 " "	
546	10 " "	
179	9 " "	
11	8 " "	See p. xvii, Type F.

Types B and F make up the 11-syllable lines and D and C the 9-syllable lines. G has frequently but 11 syllables (v. line 359).

CHAPTER IV.

THE RIME.

1. *End-rime:*—The rime is generally pure throughout. Correct masculine rimes are the rule. The most numerous rime-endings are -ace, -ake, -all, -aunce,- ay, -e, -ence, -ent, -ere, -esse, -y, -yde, -yght, -o, -on, -ore, -ought, -ow, -ure (*v.* Rime Index).

(a) *Identical rimes* occur in a number of cases. By identical rimes I mean here those in which the riming syllables coincide in sound throughout. These syllables may be etymologically different. Acorde 6: monacorde 7; malapert 503: pert 504; dyscharge 603: charge 605; ouerse 772: see 775; take 1388, 1409: vndyrtake 1390, 1411; become 1406: welcome 1407; serue 1408: deserue 1410; goon 1836: ouergoon 1838; before 1871: therfore 1874; hande 1912: hande 1914; dyffuse 1955: refuse 1957; dyscorde 2015: monacorde 2016; alone 923: euerychone 924 (14 cases). *Identical suffix-rimes:* (a) *with initial consonant:*—iugement 139: auysment 140; resystence 228: sentence 229; satysfaccion 834: dysposicion 836; sadnes 1380: gladnes 1382; royally 268: sykerly 270; herytykes 678: scismatykes 679; pycture 1514: creature 1516; (b) *with initial vowel:*— varyaunce 244: ordynaunce 245; conuenyent 249: expedyent 250; precious 790: vyctoryous 791; swerers 702: morderers 704 etc. (about 140 cases of such rimes (b) and (a).

(b) *Imperfect rimes* are occasional:—am 86: man 88; strong 260: hand 262; came 785: man 787; came 862: than 864; doon 1217: com 1218; come 1336: oblyuyone 1337; came 1702; woman 1704 (7 cases of *assonance*); beste 1056: lyste 1057 (v. lyst 1297): myst 1299); neere 1616: desyre 1617 (v. desyre 1870: wyre 1872, — cf. *Schick* Intro. lxi); bedde 2038: vnderstande 2040; crysmatory 1444: sanctuary 1446; *probably imperfect:*—syt 191: yet 193 (perhaps=yit as in Chaucer); fete 566: yete 567 (cf. yet 193: syt 191); ende 1777: mynde 1778 (mynde 1923: ende 1922: spende 1920; ende 1931: mende 1932; but cf. mynde 1784: behynde 1785).

(c) *Feminine rimes* occur in the following instances:—obstacle 9: habytacle 11: tryacle 12; chases 58: places 60: manaces 61; philosophres 272: cofres 273; centre 769: entre 770; seuyn 821: heuyn 823: steuyn 824; euer 1203, 1974: neuer 1204, 1973; ?reson 1259: seson 1260; crysmatory 1444: sanctuary 1446: tary 1447; story 1513: memory 1515; fable 1686: acceptable 1687; ymages 1731: stages 1733: passages 1734; nother 1807: brother 1809; parable 1987:

fable 1988; ? compleynyd 48: constreynyd 49 (cf. herde 498: conqueryd 500=masc.); grauntyd 118, 874: hauntyd 119, 875; promysyd 482: dyspysyd 483; preuydyd 946: guydyd 948; aqueyntyd 1345: peyntyd 1347; deuydyd 1765: prouydyd 1767; ? declaryd 736: sparyd 738; ? retornyd 1119; mornyd 1120; ? excusyd 1399: dysvsyd 1400; *probably:* — requyreth 135: expyreth 137: desyreth 138 (but cf. gooth 426: wrooth 427 =masc.); sygnyfyeth 2010: applyeth 2012; chaungeth 2094: estraungeth 2096.

Doubtful cases are: — colowres 321: shoures 322 (but cf. embassatours 1016: shoures 1018); oonys 499: boonys 501: noonys 502; goddys 491: pesecoddys 493; dremes 1854: stremes 1855 (but cf. astronomers 1696: speres 1698: yeres 1699; laborers 911: freres 913); *the final e's are perhaps pronounced in these words:* — releuë (inf.) 13: sleuë (obl. sng.) 14; kepë (inf.) 107: depë (adj. pl.) 109: crepë (inf.) 110; morë 149: storë (obl. sng.) 151: sorë (adv.) 152; Saturnë 279: mornë (inf.) 280; hedë (obl. sng.) 286: leedë (obl. sng.) 287; cornë (obl. sng.) 293: hornë (obl. sng.) 294; leuë (obl. sng.) 520: foryeuë (inf.) 522: myscheuë (inf.) 523; carrë (obl. sng.) 554: marrë (inf.) 556; wydë (obl. sng.) 664: abydë (inf.) 665; hertë (obl. sng.) 1451: aduertë (inf.) 1453: stertë (inf.) 1454; foolë (obl. sng.) 1658: scoolë (obl. sng.) 1659; pylgremagë (obl. sng.) 1779: passagë (obl. sng.) 1781; holdë 1821: oldë 1823; sonnë (obl. sng.) 1896: tonnë (obl. sng.) 1897.

(d) Medial *gh* (O. E. *h*), already weak in Chaucer, has ceased to be pronounced in the cases following, and probably therefore in all cases:—about 261: fought 263: mought 264 (cf. aboute 386: route 388; mowte 760: dowte 761; abowte 1124: showte 1122: withowte 1125); ryght 489: saf condyght 490; ipocrytes 701: ryghtes 703; sodomytes 708: syghtes 710; cyrcute 757: myght 759: trypartyte 1031: lyght 1033: wyght 1034; syght 1037: wyght 1039; fyght 1112: meryt 1113; bryght 1367: whyte 1369: myght 1370 (cf. infynyte 1605: myte 1607: whyte 1608; myte 1814: appetyte 1816); myght 1801: dyspyte 1803: lyte 1804.

RIME INDEX.

A

-able 1686, 1687; 1987, 1988.
-ace 219, 221, 222; 300, 301; 316, 318; 475, 476; 538, 539; 1212, 1214; 1497; 1498; 1758, -as 1760; 1826, 1827; 1880, -as 1878, 1881, 2099, 2100. See -as.
-acle 11, 12.
-ad 345, 347, 348; 580, 581.

Rime Index.   xxiii

-ade 69, 70; 1560, 1561.
-adde 1415, 1417; 1875, 1876; 1982, 1984.
-aff 2071, 2072.
-aft 1133, 1134.
-age 1779, 1781; 1889, 1890; 1899, 1901, 1902; 1906, 1908, 1909.
-ages 1731, 1733, 1734.
-ak   366, 368, 369.
-ake 2, 4, 5; 233, 235, 236; 608, 609; 722, 724; 1014, 1015; 1052, 1054, 1055; 1220, 1222, 1223; 1388, 1390, 1391; 1409, 1411, 1412; 1420, 1421; 1457, 1459; 1812, 1813; 1905, 1907; 1947, 1949; 2043, 2044.
-ale 358, 360.
-ales 685, 686.
-all 114, 116, 117; 153, 154; 230, 231; 246, 248; 435, 437; 555, 557, 558; 776, 777; 1007, 1008; 1072, 1074; 1226, 1228; 1443, 1445; 1504, 1505; 1588, 1589; 1597, 1599; 1612, 1614, 1615; 1707, 1708; 1819, 1820; 1898, 1900.
-am   86, -an 88, 89. See -an.
-ame 132, 133; 589, 591; 713, 714; 785, -an 787; 862, -an 864; 1238, 1239; 1702, -an 1704.
-an   925, 927; 1395, 1397, 1398; 1518, 1519. See -am, -ame
-ane 2011, 2013, 2014.
-and 262, -ong 260 ; 370, 371; 1177, 1179. See -ang.
-ande 128, 130, 131; 1084, 1085; 1161, 1162; 1562, 1564; 1574, 1575; 1651, 1652; 1912, 1914; 1959, 1960.
-ape 524, 525; 1315, 1316.
-ard 601, 602.
-are 125, 126; 723, 725, 726; 807, 809, 810.
-arge 85, 87; 545, 546; 603, 605; 1632, 1634.
-arke 937, 938.
-arpe 400, 402.
-arre 554, 556.
-art 876, 878; 1940, 1942.
-ary 1446, 1447, -ory 1444.
-aryd 736, 738.
-as   274, 276; 611, 613, 614; 1065, 1067; 1339, -ase 1341, 1342; 1878, -ace 1880, 1881. See -ase, -ace.
-ase 314, 315; 461, 462; 513, 515, 516; 632, 634, 635. See -as.
-ases 58, 60, 61.
-ast 72, 74, 75; 127, 129.
-aste 1045, 1047, 1048.
-ate 27, 28; 422, 424, 425; 1483, 1484; 1546, 1547; 1639, 1641.
-ates 706, 707.
-aught 1231, 1232.
-aunce 244, 245; 335, 336; 398, 399; 407, 409; 442, 444; 659, 661; 797, 798; 835, 837, 838; 954, 956, 957; 989, 991, 992; 1094, 1096, 1097; 1147, 1148; 1374, 1376, 1377; 1430, 1432, 1433; 1450, 1452; 1507, 1509, 1510; 1598, 1600, 1601; 1660, 1662; 1714, 1715; 1835, 1837; 2003, 2005; 2060, 2062, 2063.
-aunge 1402, 1404, 1405.
-aungeth 2094, 2096.

-aunse   15, 17; 996, 998, 999.
-aunt   883, 885; 1254, 1256; 1294, 1295.
-auntyd 118, 119; 874, 875.
-ause   134, 136.
-aute   587, 588.
-ay   29, 31; 282, 284, 285; 296, 298, 299; 548, 550, 551; 666, 668; 715, 717; 727, 728; 729, 731; 743, 745; 813, 815; 958, 959; 965, 966; 979, 980; 1028, 1029; 1086, 1088; 1245, 1246; 1276, 1278, 1279; 1324, 1326; 1464, 1466; 1590, 1592; 1661, 1663, 1664; 1828, 1830; 1968, 1970.
-ayd   36, 38.
-ayde   164, -eyde 162; 207, -eyde 205.
-ayed   1998, -eyde 1996.
-ayes   692, 693.
-ayll   615, 616; 751, 753, 754; 1219, 1221; 1969, 1971, 1972.
-ayn   1567, 1568.
-ayne   1668, 1670, -eyne 1671. See -eyne.
-awe   559, 560; 1227, 1229, 1230.

E

{ -e   (gen. = -y) 121, 123, 124; 198, 200, 201; 253, 255; 271, -y 270; 457, 459, 460; 492, 494, 495; 519, 521; 552, 553; 617, 619; 650, 651; 772, 774, 775; 804, 805; 811, -ee 812; 828, 830, 831; 842, 844, 845; 919, 921, 922; 933, 935, 936; 1002, 1004; 1010, 1012, 1013; 1080, 1082, 1083; 1105, -ee 1106; 1261, 1263; 1280, 1281; 1329, 1330; 1416, 1418, 1419; 1423, 1425, 1426; 1700, 1701; 1800, 1802; 1868, 1869; 1926, 1928; 1945, 1946; 1980, 1981; 1994, 1995; 2017, 2019; ? 2038, 2040; 2057, 2058; 2067, 2069, 2070.
{ -ee   365, 367; 505, 507; 995, 997; 1136, 1138, -e 1139; 1961, -e 1963.
-eare   421, -ere 423.
-ecte   895, 896; 1847, 1848.
{ -ede 286, -eede 287; 569, 571, 572; 755, 756; 832, 833; 1000, 1001; 1035, 1036; 1129, 1131, 1132; 1360, 1362, 1363; 1378, 1379.
{ -eede 1023, 1025; 1583, 1585; 1815, 1817, 1818.
-eet   1064, -et 1063.
-eft   562, 564, 565.
{ -elde 667, 669, 670; 932, 934; 1044, 1046; 1095, 1093 -eelde.
{ -eelde 1093, -elde 1095.
{ -ele 55, 56; 1026, 1027, -eele 1024; 2068, -eele 2066.
{ -eele 1024, -ele 1026, 1027; 1637, 1638; 2066, -ele 2068.
-ell   30, 32, 33; 433, 434; 590, 592, 593; 1331, 1333; 1532, 1533.
-eme   1609, 1610.
-emes   1854, 1855.
-ence   44, 46, 47; 76, 77; 79, 81, 82; 97, 98; 174, 175; 228, 229, -ense 226; 456 458; 639, 641, 642; 645, 647; 814, 816, 817; 1135, 1137; 1163, 1165; 1436, 1438; 1490, 1491; 1611, 1613; 1863, 1865; 2001, 2002; 2025, -ens 2027, 2028; 2106, 2107. See -ens, -ense.
-ende   737, 739, 740; 1623, 1624; 1665, 1666; 1777, -ynde 1778; 1798, 1799; 1920, 1922, -ynde, 1923; 1931, 1932. See -ynde.

Rime Index.

{-ene	982, 984, 985; 1198, 1200; 1584, 1586, 1587.
{-eene	275, -ene 277, 278; 2045, 2047.
-ens	2027, 2028, -ence 2025.
-ense	226, -ence 228, 229; 653, 655, 656; 1247, 1249. See -ence.
-ent	23, 25, 26; 113, 115; 139, 140; 160, 161; 170, 172, 173; 247, 249, 250; 289, 291, 292; 415, 417, 418; 449, 451; 741, 742; 792, 794; 827, 829; 1003, 1005, 1006; 1092, -ente 1091; 1107, 1109; 1140, 1141; 1157, 1159, 1160; 1175, 1176; 1304, 1306, 1307; 1427, 1428; 1465, 1467, 1468; 1553, 1554; 1674, 1676; 1749, 1750; 1763, 1764; 1829, 1831, 1832; 1903, 1904; 2036, 2037.
-entes	839, 840; 909, 910; 918, 920.
-epe	107, 109, 110; 1255, 1257, 1258; 1296, 1298.
-ept	510, 511; 944, 945; 1682, 1684, 1685.
-er	71, 73; 163, -ere 165, -eere 166; 547, 549. See -eere.
-erde	498, -eryd 500; 625, 627, 628. See -eryd.
{-ere	50, 52; 93, 95, 96; 155, 157; 183, 185; 197, 199; 323, 325; 394, 396, 397; 423, -eare 421; 443, 445, 446; 541, 543, 544; 748, 749; 806, 808; 884, 887, -eere 886; 888, 889; 960, 962; 1128, 1130; 1233, 1235; 1541, 1543; 1556, 1558, 1559; 1602, 1603; 1626, 1628, 1629; 1742, 1743; 1933, 1935; 2004, 2006, 2007; 2029, 2030; 2081, 2083, 2084. See -eare.
{-eere	166, -ere 165; 597, 599, -ere 600; 1616, -yre 1617; 1653, -ere 1655. See -yre.
-eeres	905, -ers 907, -eres 908.
-ers	674, 676, 677; 680, 682; 681, 683, 684; 688, 690, 691; 695, 697, 698; 702, 704, 705; 907, -eeres 905, -eres 908; 911, -eres 913; 1696, -eres 1698, 1699.
-erse	405, 406.
-ert	468, 469; 503, 504; 1170, 1172; 1266, 1267; 1591, 1593, 1594; 1786, 1788; 1843, 1845, 1846.
-erte	1451, 1453, 1454.
-erue	1408, 1410.
-eryd	500, -erde 498.
-es	391, 392; 881, 882; 902, 903; 1066, 1068, 1069; 1215, -esse 1213; 1380, 1382; 1640, 1642, 1643.
-ese	232, 234; 237, 238; 1752, 1754, 1755.
-esse	8, 10; 184, 186, 187; 240, 242, 243; 254, 256, 257; 303, 305, 306; 534, 536, 537; 1059, 1061, 1062; 1213, -es 1215, 1216; 1262, 1264, 1265; 1385, 1386; 1492, 1494; 1511, 1512; 1633, 1635, 1636; 1716, 1718; 1941, 1943, 1944.
-eson	(or on) 1259, 1260.
-esshe	2080, 2082.
-est	223, 224; 342, 343; 573, 574; 820, 822; 2032, 2034, -este 2035.
-este	478, 480, 481; 1056, -yste 1057; 2035, -est 2032, 2034. See -yste.
-et	167, 168; 188, 189; 251, 252; 309, 311; 317, 319, 320; 337, 339; 384, 385; 1063, -eet 1064; 1154, 1155; 1184, 1186; 1654, -ete 1656, 1657; 1675, 1677, 1678; 1891, 1893. See -eet, -ete.
-ete	212, 214, 215; 239, 241; 344, 346; 419, 420; 527, 529, 530; 566, 567; 1030, 1032; 1287, 1288; 1332, 1334, 1335; 1656, 1657, -et 1654. See -et.
-ette	604, 606, 607; 1462, 1463.
-ettys	1695, -etys 1697. See -etys.
-etys	1697, -ettys 1695. See -ettys.
-eue	13, 14; 429, 431, 432; 520, 522, 523; 1679, 1680; 2031, 2033.

c

-euer   (or er) 1203, 1204; 1973, 1974.
-euyn   821, 823, 824.
-ew   582, 584; 961, 963, 964; 1070, 1071; 1123, -u 1121; 1364, 1365; 1373, 1375; 1506, 1508; 2046, 2048, 2049. See -u.
-ewes   699, 700.
-ewre   930, -ure 931.
-ey   156, -ay 158, 159; 378, -y 377; 623, -y 622; 873, -y 872, 870; 1188, -y 1187, 1185; 1630, -y 1631; 1728, -y 1729; 1856, 1858. See -y.
-eyde   162, -ayde 164; 205, -ayde 207, 208; 596, 598; 1996, -ayed 1998. See -ayde, -ayed.
-eyn   62, 63; 146, 147; 176, 178; 561, 563; 744, 746, 747; 1359, 1361.
-eyne   37, 39, 40; 111, 112; 610, -eygne 612; 1156, 1158; 1581, 1582; 1671, -ayne, 1670; 1808, 1810, 1811; 1966, 1967; 2085, 2086. See -ayne.
-eyngth 967, 969.
-eynt   78, 80; 258, 259; 359, 361, 362; 1644, -eynte 1645; 1793, 1795.
-eynte 1645, -eynt 1644.
-eyntyd 1345, 1347.
-eynyd 48, 49.
-ext   1502, -exte 1500.
-exte   1502, -ext 1502.

Y, I, (E).

-y   34, 35; 104, 105; 148, 150; 202, 203; 268, 270, -e 271; 281, 283; 302, 304; 330, 332; 377, -ey 378; 380, 382, 383; 401, 403, 404; 450, 452, 453; 463, 465; 485, 487, 488; 594, I 595; 622, -ey 623; 629, 630; 638, 640; 646, 648, 649; 652, 654; 657, 658; 660, 662, 663; 765, 767, 768; 800, 802, 803; 841, 843; 846, 847; 848, 850; 853, 854; 855, 857; 867, 868; 869, 871; 870, 872, -ey 873; 975, 977, 978; 1009, 1011; 1021, 1022; 1073, 1075, 1076; 1171, 1173, 1174; 1185, 1187, -ey 1188; 1189, 1190; 1289, 1291; 1346, 1348, I 1349; 1458, 1460, 1461; 1485, 1486; 1493, 1495, I 1496; 1513, 1515; 1534, 1536; 1549, 1551, 1552; 1570, 1572, 1573; 1631, -ey 1630; 1689, 1691, 1692; 1717, 1719, -uy 1720; 1729, -ey 1728; 1787, 1789, 1790; 1822, 1825, I 1824; 1840, 1841; 1989, 1991; 2039, 2041, 2042; 2064, I 2065; 2095, 2097, 2098; 2102, 2104, 2105. See -e, -ey, -uy.
-yce   825, -yse 826; 863, -yse 865, 866. See -yse.
-yde   216, 217; 288, 290; 324, 326, 327; 331, 333, 334; 349, 350; 470, 472; 624, 626; 664, 665; 716, 718, 719; 793, 795, 796; 891, 893, 894; 926, 928, 929; 940, 942, 943; 981, 983; 1283, 1285, 1286; 1499, 1501; 1525, 1526; 1555, 1557.
-ydyd   946, -uydyd 948; 1765, 1767. See -uydyd.
-yeth   2010, 2012.
-yght   373, 375, 376; 489, 490; 750, 752; 759, -ute 757; 778, 780; 972, 973; 986, 987; 993, 994; 1033, 1034, -yte 1031; 1037, 1039; 1112, -yt 1113; 1199, 1201, 1202; 1367, 1370, -yte 1369; 1381, 1383, 1384; 1392, 1393; 1471, 1473; 1476, 1477; 1801, -yte 1803, 1804; 2078, 2079. See -yt, -yte, -ute.
-yghtes, 710, -ytes 708. See -ytes.
-ygne   1224, -yne 1225; 1441, 1442. See -yne.
-yk   856, 858, 859.

Rime Index. xxvii

-ykes 678, 679.
-yll 120, 122; 575, 577; 916, 917; 1058, 1060; 1079, 1081; 1990, 1992, 1993.
-yme 953, 955.
-yn 1049, 1050; 1857, 1859, 1860.
-ynde 64, 66; 393, 395; 512, 514; 631, 633; 1343, 1344; 1387, 1389; 1542, 1544, 1545; 1647, 1649, 1650; 1756, 1757; 1778, -ende 1777; 1784, 1785; 1923, -ende 1922. See -ende.
-yne 265, 266; 372, 374; 1225, -ygne 1224; 2018, 2020, 2021.
-yng 267, 269; 1366, 1368; 1528, 1530, 1531; 1535, 1537, 1538; 1618, 1620.
-ynges 687, 689.
-ynke 2052, 2054.
-ynne 947, 949, 950; 1997, 1999, 2000.
-yre 1617, -eere 1616; 1870, 1872. See -eere.
-yreth 135, 137, 138.
-ys 106, 108; 877, 879, 880; 1310, 1312.
-yse 16, 18, 19; 225, 227; 447, 448; 568, 570; 826, -yce 825; 865, -yce 863; 1115, 1117, 1118; 1352, 1354; 1780, 1782, 1783; 1962, 1964, 1965. See -yce.
-yst 1297, 1299, 1300.
-yste 1057, -este 1056.
-ysyd 482, 483.
-yt 191, -et 193, -yte 194; 1113, -yght, 1112. See -et, -yte, -yght.
-yte 211, 213; 1031, -yght 1033, 1034; 1369, -yght 1370; 1605, 1607, 1608; 1803, -yght 1801; 1814, 1816. See -yght.
-ytes 701, 703; 708, -yghtes 710.
-yue 517, 518; 939, 941; 1849, 1851.
-yues 20, 21.

O

-o 22, 24; 41, 42; 51, 53, 54; 142, 144, 145; 169, 171; 195, 196; 218, 220; 295, 297; 471, 473, 474; 496, 497; 1210, 1211; 1248, 1250, 1251; 1322, 1323; 1353, 1355, 1356; 1527, 1529; 1539, 1540; 1563, -oo 1565, 1566.
-oo 41, -o 42; 92, 94; 1565, -o 1563.
-ood 307, 308; 1126, 1127; 1311, 1313, 1314; 1422, 1424; 1569, 1571.
-oode 540, 542; 799, 801; 1038, 1040, 1041.
-oddys 491, 493.
-oft 99, 101.
-ook 1142, 1144; 1455, 1456; 1724, 1726, 1727.
{ -oke 181, 182.
{ -ooke 1303, 1305; 1885, 1887, 1888.
-olde 387, 389, 390; 428, 430; 1766, 1768, 1769; 1821, 1823; 1934, 1936, 1937; 1983, 1985, 1986; 2059, 2061; 2073, 2075.
-oole 1394, 1396; 1658, 1659; 1952, 1953.
-ome 190, 192; 1336, -one 1337; 1406, 1407. See -one.
{ -on 43, 45; 90, 91; 636, 637; 643, 644; 834, 836; 849, 851, 852; 974, 976; 988, 990; 1103, -owne 1101; 1108, 1110, 1111; 1143, 1145, 1146; 1178, 1180, -own 1181; 1205, 1207; 1301, 1302; 1413, 1414; 1429, 1431; 1619, 1621, 1622; 1646, 1648; 1681, 1683; 1721, 1722; 1737, 1739; 1744, 1746; 1751, 1753; 1772, 1774; 1833, 1834; 1842, 1844; 1864, 1866, 1867; 1910, 1911; 1913,

xxviii   *Rime Index.*

         1915, 1916; 1919, 1921; 1975, 1977; 2008, 2009; 2022, 2023; 2053, 2055, 2056; 2101, 2003. See –eson, –own.
-oon 440, 441; 1217 –om 1218; 1667, –on 1669; 1759, 1761, 1762; 1805, 1806; 1836, 1838, –on 1839. See –om, –on.
-onde 1712, –ounde 1710; 1735, –ounde 1736. See –ounde.
-one 720, 721; 779, 781, 782; 923, 924; 1337, –ome 1336; 1745, 1747, 1748; 1839, –oon 1838. See –ome.
-ong 730, 732, 733; 1269, 1271, 1272.
-onne 1, 3; 1896, 1897.
-oonys 499, 501, 502.
-ophres 272, 273.
-orde 6, 7; 1252, 1253; 1434, 1435; 2015, 2016.
-oorde 1240, 1242.
-ore 149, 151, 152; 338, 340, 341; 771, 773; 968, 970, 971; 1308, 1309; 1472, 1474, 1475; 1604, 1606; 1794, 1797, –oore 1796; 1871, 1873, 1874; 1892, 1894, 1895.
-oore 1791, –ore 1792; 2074, 2076, 2077.
-ores 673, 675.
-orn 818, 819.
-orne 280, –urne 279; 293, 294. See –urne.
-ornyd 1119, 1120.
-ort 65, 67, 68; 204, 206; 531, 532: 671, 672.
-orte 1150, 1152, 1153; 1486, 1488, 1489.
-ory 1444, –ary 1446, 1447. See –ary.
-ose 1576, 1578.
-osse 1595, 1596.
-oost 764, 766; 783, 784; 951, 952; 1192, –ost 1194, 1195.
-oote 620, 621, –ote 618; 1350, 1351.
-othe 2092, 2093.
-ooth 426, 427; 1338, 1340.
-other 1807, 1809.
-ought 141, 143; 209, 210; 263, 264, –out 261; 412, 413; 526, 528; 786, 788, 789; 1051, 1053; 1196, 1197; 1234, 1236, 1237; 1478, 1480; 1625, 1627; 1672, 1673; 1882, 1883; 2050, 2051.
-oun 2087, 2089.
-ound 506, –ownd 508, 509; 533, 535; 1042, 1043; 1521, 1523, 1524.
-ounde 1690, –ownde 1688; 1709, 1711; 1710, –onde 1712, 1713; 1736, –onde 1735 See –onde, –ownde.
-our 464, 466, 467; 576, 578, 579; 734, 735; 1078, –owre 1077; 1100, 1102; 1206 1208, 1209; 1290, 1292, 1293; 1850, –oure 1852, 1853. See –owre.
-ours 709, 711, 712; 897, 899; 904, 906; 912, –oures 914, 915; 1016, –oures 1018; 1182, 1183; 1357, 1358; 1577, 1578, 1580.
-oures 322, –owres 321; 694, 696; 914, –ours 912; 1018, –ours 1016. See –ours, –owres.
-ous 408, 410, 411; 790, 791; 898, 900, 901.
-out 261, –ought 263, 264; 436, 438, 439; 1437, –owte 1439, 1440; 1479, 1481, 1482; 1930, –oute 1929. See –ought, –owte.
-oute 310, 312, 313; 386, 388; 758, –owte 760, 761; 1017, 1019, 1020; 1273, 1274; 1927, 1929, 1930. See –owte.

Alliteration.   xxix

-ow   762, 763; 1149, 1151; 1164, 1166, 1167; 1191, 1193; 1241, -owe 1243,
       1244; 1317, 1319; 1371, 1372; 1401, 1403; 1954, 1956; 2024, 2026.
-owe   484, 486; 1243, -ow 1241. See -ow.
-own   1181, -on 1180.
-ownd 508, -ound 506. See -ound.
-ownde 1688, -ounde 1689. See -ounde.
-owne 379, 381; 1101, -on 1103, 1104. See -on.
-owre 1077, -our 1078. See -our.
-owres 321, -oures 322. See -oures.
-owte 760, -oute 758; 1087, 1089, 1090; 1122, 1124, 1125; 1318, 1320, 1321;
       1439, -out 1437; 1861, 1862; 1924, 1925; 1948, 1950, 1951; 1976, 1978,
       1979.

U

-u   1121, -ew 1123. See -ew.
-ude   890, 892; 1703, 1705, 1706.
-ure   57, 59; 83, 84; 100, 102, 103; 363, 364; 414, 416; 454, 455; 477, 479; 860,
       861; 931, -ewre 930; 1268, 1270; 1325, 1327, 1328; 1448, 1449; 1514, 1516,
       1517; 1520, 1522; 1693, 1694; 1723, 1725; 1770, 1771; 1773, 1775, 1776;
       1877, 1879; 1884, 1886; 2088, 2090, 2091. See -ewre.
-urre 328, 329.
-urne 279, -orne 280.
-us   177, 179, 180; 1168, 1169; 1469, 1470; 1938, 1939.
-use   1917, 1918; 1955, 1957, 1958.
-ust   1098, 1099; 1275, 1277.
-usyd 1390, 1400.
-ute   757 -yght 759. See -yght.
-uy   1720, -y 1719.
-uydyd 948, -ydyd 946.

2. Alliteration is a marked feature of the verse. As is well known, the usage of combining alliteration and end-rime, which became conspicuous in western and northern England about the middle of the fourteenth century, grew in favor through the fourteenth and fifteenth centuries, reaching its highest popularity in Scotland during the second half of the fifteenth century (v. *Scottish Allit. Poems*, ed. by Amours in Scot. Text Soc.). The alliterative phrases record, clearly enough, the influence of the Old-English method of verse. In this poem alliteration occurs chiefly in formal phrases, as an ornament of the verse, rarely having any constructive significance. Lydgate followed no fixed method, though of course accent most often determines the phrase. For Chaucer's usage consult Ten Brink, *Ch. Sp.* p. 196, *et. seq.*, and *The Alliteration of Chaucer*, a thesis by Dr. C. F. McClumpha (Univ. of Minn.). I cite a few of the most notable instances:

4: *s*yttyng all *s*olytary a*l*one be*s*yde a *l*ake. 5: *m*usyng on a *m*aner how that I *m*yght *m*ake. 13: so *l*eyde I me *d*owne my *d*yssese to re*l*eue. 35: ys in a lytyll *c*orner *c*allyd Fantasy. 66: *r*oote and *r*ynde. 127: *b*oystous *b*last. 261: *f*lame of *f*yre. 270: full *s*ad and wyse he *s*emyd *s*ykerly. 303: *w*orldly *w*ysdom. 320: hyr gowne was of gawdy grene chamelet. 345: in *c*uras *c*lad. 354: *c*lad in *c*lustres. 372: *c*olour *c*rystallyne. 379: *c*opyr *c*rowne. 382: *b*eames *b*ryght. 425: *d*euyll's *d*ate. 487: *d*oole nor *d*estyny. 501: *b*oody, *b*lood and *b*oonys. 557: *w*alewyng *w*ith hys *w*awes. 556: *m*ake and *m*arre. 631: *s*lowthe so *s*lepy. 673: *b*osters, *b*raggars and *b*rybores. 675: *s*hamefull *s*hakerles, *s*oleyn *s*haueldores. 684: *m*alycious *m*urmurers. 688: *r*obbers, *r*euers, *r*auenouse *r*yfelers. 690: *m*arrers of *m*aters and *m*oney *m*akers. 806: *r*oody as a *r*oose. 848: *r*efuse of *r*ychesse. 899: *p*erpetuell *p*restes. 902: *f*ysshers of *f*owles. 907: on *p*eynfull *p*oore *p*yteous com*p*assioners. 912: *h*ooly *h*eremytes. 913: *m*onasteriall *m*onkes. 996: *c*haunger of the *c*haunse. 1166: *p*eyne *p*erpetuell. 1362: *w*ylde *w*antones *w*ede. 1603: *c*oloryd *c*rystall *c*lere. 1743: *f*eynyd *f*ables. 1886: *d*aryng as a *d*astard. 2071-2: Try out the *c*orne *c*lene from the chaff And then may ye *s*ay ye have a *s*ure *s*taff.

CHAPTER V.

THE RIME AND THE FINAL *e*.

See Paul's *Grund.* II. p. 1034, sec. 24.—The language and metre of the poem seem to be in such confusion that evidence either for or against the pronunciation of the final *e* is rarely conclusive. So far as I am able to judge from a study of the metre and of the riming words the final *e* is quite generally mute. Double forms were evidently permissible, especially in words of Old-English origin. Still the riming words show a very considerable loss of the final *e*, and a consequent change in poetic phraseology, as compared with the *Chorl and Bird* and the *Temple of Glas*, which conform much more closely to the phraseology of Chaucer. On this latter evidence I should argue for the later date of the *Assembly of Gods*. For while a skillful copyist, by the addition of monosyllabic words, might make the measure run without the *e*'s, he would not change the riming words themselves.

1. A study of the common riming words from Chaucer to Spenser will illustrate the changes in operation during the fifteenth century which affected the final *e* sound. It will be observed that the adverbial suffix –ly (O. E. *lic*), which in Chaucer[1] and contemporary works rimed only with itself, -y or the pronoun I, rimes in Lyd-

---

[1] The *Romaunt* has cases of -y and -ye rime; but the date of the MS. is late, c. 1450 (Skeat).

gate's *Assembly of Gods*, King James' *Quair* and in other poems succeeding these, with endings of Romance nouns such as company (O. F. companie, M. L. compania), melody (O. F. melodie, L. L. melodia, Gk. μελῳδία), etc., and of infinitives as testify, multiply, spy, etc. The usage of riming the ending -y and -ye became customary before the middle of the fifteenth century. Chaucer rimes regularly -yĕ with -yĕ. Thus companye rimes with maystrie, ielousye, hye, espye, envye, hostelrie, dayesye, etc.; ielousye with maystrie, folye, espye, maladye, etc. So -ly rimes regularly with itself, -y or I. Thus I rimes with properly, utterly, verraily, trewely, wikkedly, boldely, certeynly, by; utterly rimes with trewely, esely, sikerly; why rimes with casually. Chaucer has no exception to these rules.

Gower in his *Confessio Amantis* (1386–1393), Hoccleve in his *Minor Poems* (c. 1425) have Chaucer's usage very strictly. I find no instance in Lydgate's *Temple of Glas* (c. 1403) of the -y -ye rime. In the *Assembly of Gods*, however, the rule is no longer maintained. Thus company rimes with pleasauntly 380, feruently 382, melody 401, ly 404, chyualry 463, by 663, Apostasy 977, vyctory 1190, Sodechy 1549, Sophony 1551. Ey rimes with enuy 622, Pawmestry 870, deny 872, fly 1185, sodenly 1187, foly 1631, generally 1729. Hy rimes with testyfy 104, thereby 1461, certeynly 1495, I 1496, gloryosly 1572, by 1570, naturally 1691, glory 1841, magnyfy 2102, Mary 2105. Multyply rimes with indyfferency 846, deyfy 1719. Comonly rimes with Fantasy 35. Curtesy rimes with innocency 841. Memory rimes with glory 848, story 1513. Victory rimes with party 1009, glory 1789, occupy 1787. Spy rimes with pryuyly 1021, cry with sodeynly 1075 and myghtyly 1073; stody with espy 1989; occupy with testyfy 452 and deny 453.

In Lydgate and Burgh's *Secrees* (c. 1446) the latter usage obtains. The final *e* is there rarely sounded (Steele, *Intro. to Sec.* p. xx. § xvii.). Applye rimes with partye 1516, fantasye 303. Victorye rimes with pryncipally 2181, prudently 2182, hastely 2445, remedy 2448. Remedy rimes with hevyly 1735, specially 2008. Hastily rimes with denye 1846. Partye rimes with streyghtlye 2131. Mallady rimes with specially 1700; foly with discretly 2281, angry 2652; leccherye with fynally 2503 and velony 2504.

The change had already been accomplished in the *Quair* (1423) of King James I., who rimed armory with contynually, ielousye with melancholye and quhy (N. E. why), philosophye with properly, partye with I, quhy with companye, ielousye, folye, onely, I with humility, gye, supplye, etc.

In the *Pastime of Pleasure* (c. 1506), the work of Stephen Hawes, the pupil of Lydgate, and in Spenser's poems and in other sixteenth century works, the new usage is completely established. The period of transition would seem to be from about 1415 to 1450. Lydgate's own works exhibit the change, and very likely his poems can be approximately dated by reference to his treatment of this -y rime.

2. *The infinitives among the riming words* present the phenomena given in the following word list. The inflectional ending has disappeared in most cases. It is maintained somewhat in verbs of English origin but is almost completely lost in verbs of Romance origin. I use ë to indicate the conjectural pronunciation of the infinitive ending. In the table the first word in each series is the infinitive, which is followed by the words with which it rimes:

(a) *Of Teutonic Origin.*

abydë: wyde 664: tyde 718: ryde (inf.) 719: pryde (obl. sng.) 928: syde (obl. sng.) 929: gyde (inf.) 793: hyde (inf.) 894.
arysë: iustyse (obl. sng.) 18: sylogyse (inf.) 19.
astert: hert (obl. sng.) 468.
awakë: take (inf.) 1015: shake (inf.) 2044.
be: perplexyte (obl. sng.) 200: se (inf.) 201: me 255: pyte (obl. sng.) 921: vnyte (obl. sng.) 919.
beware: care (obl. sng.) 126.
blyn: syn (inf.) 1857: wyn (inf.) 1859.
borow: sorow 1166: folow (inf.) 1164.
bow: how 2026.
call: fall 1008: wall 1898.
crepë: depe (obl. pl.) 109: kepe (inf.) 107.
deelë: wele (obl. sng.) 2068.
do: so 144: to 145.
dwell: tell (inf.) 585: rebell 583.
fall: shall 231: all 246.
farë: care (obl. sng.) 809: bare 807.
feelë: yele 1026: dele (obl. sng.) 1027.
fet: banket (obl. sng.) 167: met 1154: get 1678.
fly: sodenly 1187: ey (obl. sng.) 1188.
folow: sorow 1166: borow (inf.) 1167.
forsakë: take (inf.) 1052: make (inf.) 1055.
foryetë: entrete (inf.) 241.
foryeuë: leue (obl. sng.) 520: myscheue (inf.) 523.
fulfyll: wyll (obl. sng.) 575.
fyght: myght 993.
fyndë: rynde (obl. sng.) 66: behynde 514.

The Rime and the Final e. xxxiii

gete: conterfete (inf.) 212: entrete (inf.) 214: whete 1334.
go: fro 24.
herë: fere (obl. sng.) 52 (nere 396: Omere 397): daungere (obl. sng.) 96: prysonere 93: apere 157: plesere 197: offycere (obl. sng.) 446.
hy: redely 767: ny 768.
hydë: syde (obl. sng.) 891: abyde (inf.) 893.
kepë: depe (obl. pl.) 109: crepe (inf.) 110: wepe (inf.) 1257: slepe (inf.) 1258.
lerë: geere (obl. sng.) 886: were 884.
lowte: rowte (obl. sng.) 1087: dowte 1090: abowte 1924.
ly: company 403: melody (obl. sng.) 401: Pyromancy 869.
makë: lake (obl. sng.) 4: take (inf.) 2.
markë: parke (obl. sng.) 938.
metë: shete (obl. sng.) 420.
mornë: Saturne 279.
mys: wys 879: thys 877.
nedë: spede (inf.) 571: dede (obl. sng.) 572.
ouerse: meyne (obl. sng.) 774: see (inf.) 775.
rydë: wyde 626: tyde 718: abyde (inf.) 716.
say: day 1830: deley (obl. sng.) 1858.
se: perplexyte (obl. sng.) 200: be (inf.) 198: meyne 774: ambyguyte 1012: lyberte 1013: benygnyte 1426.
shakë: awake (inf.) 2043.
slepë: wepe (inf.) 1257: kepe (inf.) 1255.
spedë: nede (inf.) 569: dede (obl. sng.) 572.
steuyn: heuyn (obl. sng.) 823: seuyn 821.
syn: wyn (inf.) 1859: blyn (inf.) 1860.
syt: yet 193: abyte 194.
takë: lake (obl. sng.) 4: make (inf.) 5: awake (inf.) 1014: forsake (inf.) 1054.
tell: dwell 32: hell (obl. sng.) 33: fell (obl. pl.) 434: rebell 583.
wepë: kepe (inf.) 1255: slepe (inf.) 1258.
wynne: ynne 949: synne 950: syn (inf.) 1857: blyn (inf.) 1860: thynne 1997: theryn 1050.
wythstandë: hande (obl. sng.) 1084.

(b) *Of Romance Origin.*

acorde: monacorde (obl. sng.) 7.
apelë: wele (obl. sng.) 56.
apperë: herbere (obl. sng.) 1935: fere (obl. sng.) 2006: here (inf.) 2004.
asaute: defaute (obl. sng.) 587.
asay: day 979: may 1278: nay 1276.
assent: content 172: iugement (obl. sng.) 170.
aualë: pale (obl. sng.) 358.
auaunce: puruyaunce 956: daunce (obl. sng.) 957.
auowë: bowe (inf.) 486.
carpe: harpe (obl. sng.) 400.
cese: dyscrese (inf.) 232: doutlese 1754: prese (obl. sng.) 1755.
chastyse: dispyse (inf.) 448.
compleyn: tweyn (obl. pl.) 146.

conclude: multitude 890.
confound: drownd 508: fownd 509.
counterfete: entrete (inf.) 214: gete (inf.) 215.
cry: sodeynly 1075: myghtyly 1073.
daunce: penaunce (obl. sng.) 1148.
deny: testify (inf.) 452: occupy (inf.) 450: Pawmestry 870: ey (obl. sng.) 873.
depart: cart (obl. sng.) 878.
depryue: lyue 518.
dereygne: cheyne (obl. sng.) 610.
deyfy: multyply 1717: guy (inf.) 1720.
dyscrese: cese (inf.) 234.
dyspyse: chastyse (inf.) 447.
dysusë: muse (inf.) 1917.
endure: mesure (obl. sng.) 102: nature (obl. sng.) 100: creature (obl. sng.) 2088: sure 2091.
enhaunse: remembraunse 998: chaunse (obl. sng.) 996.
enlumyne: discyplyne (obl. sng.) 2018: Doctryne 2021.
entrete: counterfete (inf.) 212: gete (inf.) 215: foryete 239: banket 1654: gete (obl. sng.) 1657.
escape: iape (obl. sng.) 525.
eschew: Vertew (obl. sng.) 963: sew (inf.) 964.
espy: stody (obl. sng.) 1991.
exorte: reporte 1486: sorte 1489.
fade: shade (obl. sng.) 69.
greuë: leue (obl. sng.) 429: meue (inf.) 431.
gydë: tyde 795: abyde (inf.) 796.
magnyfy: hy 2104: Mary 2105.
menteyn: peyn 746: ageyn 744.
meuë: leue (obl. sng.) 429: greue (inf.) 432: sleue (obl. sng.) 2033.
multyply: guy (inf.) 1720: deyfy (inf.) 1719.
musë: disvse (inf.) 1918.
myscheue: leue (obl. sng.) 520: foryeue (inf.) 522.
occupy: testyfy (inf.) 452: deny (inf.) 453: hy (obl. sng.) 1173: vyctory (obl. sng.) 1174
oppresse: heuynesse 10: neuerthelesse 1059: duresse (obl. sng.) 1062.
peruert: hert 1786: desert (obl. sng.) 1843: smert 1845.
promyse: wyse (obl. sng.) 225.
rebell: tell 592: well 593.
recompense: audyence (obl. sng.) 1249.
refusë: diffuse 1955: vse (inf.) 1958.
reherse: werse 405.
releuë: sleue (obl. sng.) 14.
repent: went 417: inconuenyent (obl. sng.) 415.
resorte: comforte (obl. sng.) 1152: porte (obl. sng.) 1153.
sew: Vertew (obl. sng.) 963: eschew (inf.) 961.
sylogyse: iustyse (obl. sng.) 18: aryse (inf.) 16.
tary: sanctuary 1446: crysmatory 1444.
testyfy: hy 105: occupy (inf.) 450: deny (inf.) 453.
vsë: diffuse 1955: refuse (inf.) 1957.

CHAPTER VI.

THE LANGUAGE.

A. *Vocabulary.*

The modern character of Lydgate's language has often been remarked. Warton long ago gave his judgment to the effect "that Lydgate made considerable additions to those amplifications of our language in which Chaucer, Gower and Occleve led the way; and that he is the first of our writers whose style is clothed with that perspicuity in which the English phraseology appears at this day to an English reader" (*Hist. of Eng. Poet.*, II., 270). The influence of French and Latin is more apparent in his vocabulary than in that of any other East Midland writer (v. *Dict. Natl. Biog.*, XXXIV., p. 310; Skeat *Prin. Engl. Ety.*, II., ch. viii). The *Assembly of Gods* is especially rich in words of Romance origin, and, as compared with contemporary writings, in words of recent adoption from the French. The poem is therefore especially helpful in tracing the gradual assimilation of foreign words into the language. In the Prolog to the *Canterbury Tales* in 303 words in the first 42 lines, Chaucer used 263 native English words, leaving 13 *per cent.* of foreign words. In 84 lines of the *Assembly of Gods*, of 669 words, the total number employed, 153, or nearly 23 *per cent.*, are foreign; of the 305 different words used in the same lines, 107 are of foreign origin. As Lydgate was popular long in the reign of Elizabeth, his service in naturalizing the foreign vocabulary was considerable. It will be seen that the number of obsolete words is comparatively small, the proportion of such words being less than in Chaucer or Wyclif or Pecock (Lee, *Dict. Natl. Biog.*).

B. *Grammar.*

Lydgate's grammar has been well treated by Dr. Schick in his Introduction to the *Temple of Glas* (chap. vi. p. lxiii). This MS., being of a late date, can aid but little in the construction of Lydgate's own speech. In the main, it is probable that Lydgate's phonological and inflexional system did not differ much from that of Chaucer. There was, however, in the case of Lydgate a much less certain use of inflexional endings. In the present MS. the pronunciation of many endings is purely conjectural, the metre, owing to its irregularity, being seldom conclusive. The language xxxvi   *The Language.*

is seen to be in a state of greatest confusion about the year 1450. I note below a few of the grammatical forms of this text.

I. Declension. Nouns. *In Substantives of English origin, the final ë of the sng. nom. is maintained in some cases :* tymë 137, 1751; namë 132; erthë 535. *Inorganic e occurs* in frendë 1798, 1807; wyttë 1887. *Genitives have regularly the endings* (e)s, ës, ys; whalës 1535; foës 1126; feldÿs 1451; the genitive form ladyes is found in 1178.

The dative and accusative maintain the ë in crabbë 1; ërthe 67, 1627; tymë 69; hedë 271 (: sykerly) 286, 356, 384 (perhaps hede 379); tydë 334; feldë 959; endë 1799; sonnë 1896; tonnë 1897; tylthë 1710; and others. *Plurals commonly end in* (e)s, ës, ÿs; other plurals are found, as deere 65, 68; thyng 1064; eyen 220; men 759; foon 1762; chyldren 1659.

In Substantives of Romance origin the final ë in the sng. nom. is found in only a few cases: hoostë 1124; bandë 1162; cherë 375; gownë 320. *The genitives end regularly in* (e)s, ës. *With proper names hys is sometimes used to indicate the genitive,* as Vertew hys men 1072; Vyce hys quarrell 1055. *The dative and accusative are most often without endings, though a final ë occurs in* pesë 238; charë 792; scorgë 1170; scoolë 1396, 1659. *Plurals are regularly found in* (e)s, ës, ÿs.

II. *The Adjectives are generally without case endings. The final ë appears, however, in all cases, sng. and pl.: as nom. sng.* foulë, dymmë, 313; oldë 390, 1749; *pl.* oldë 294; *in oblique cases sng.,* derkë 310; crystallynë 372; rewdë 438; foulë 648; hoolë 1172; *pl.,* sagë 389; blakë 1412.

III. *The Pronouns have the common M. E. forms;* ye *is used as singular in* 32, 95, *as plural in* 150; she *is found in* 378, se *in* 376; hit *occurs regularly;* theym *is used in* 48, 415, hem *in* 66, 126; her (their) *is used in* 47, 65, 123, 867, *and regularly. The indefinite* som, *without ending, occurs in* 865, 1196, 1198, 1199. *For relatives,* which that *and* who (rare), *are used;* by hem that lyues 20; he that 21; poetes whyche 1743; [he] who 769.

IV. *Adverbs are found with endings ë, ës or ys, ly and without endings:* sonë 36, 461, 721, 1345; whilë 181, 72; ferrë 1627; newë 562; nedÿs 21, 1372; nedës 1245; ellës 33, 1033; ellÿs 1614, 1385; eftsonës 1007.

V. *Conjugation of Verbs.* The formation of the tenses of the verbs, strong and weak, is the same as in Chaucer. *Infinitives end in ĕ*, though perhaps more often they are without endings, as fall 230, riming with shall; syt 191 riming with yet; fly 1185 riming with sodenly; bow 2024 riming with how; tell 30 riming with hell, etc. *The third person, indicative, present, has regularly the ending eth, ëth. The northern es is found in two places:* dryues 21, manaces 61 (*in pl.* lyues 20). *The past participle is without a prefix ge-, i- or y-; the strong verbs end commonly in ĕn and ĕ, the weak in yd, ĕd, t:* knowĕn 1141; beholdyn 1866; takĕn 501; takĕ 59, 267, 547, 722, 725; tane 2013; brokĕ 182; spokĕ 181; ronnĕ 1; drevĕn 1080; cropyn 1953; ouerthrow 1149 rimes with know (inf.) and 1191 with low. The form beene occurs in 2047 riming with seene, also bene 420, 1343, ben 627, byn 1798, be 115, 298, 460; bee 1136. So occur the forms goon 757, go 1396; done 48, 563, doon 84, do 195, 1248 (riming with lo), 496,; seene 545, seyne 1671.

CHAPTER VII.
THE POEM.
A. LITERARY ANALYSIS.[1]

A. *Introduction* (*stanzas 1–5*). The time: when Phœbus had nearly finished his course in the Crab. The place: I was sitting alone beside a lake. The theme: musing how I might make Reason and Sensuality to accord. The framework of the action: a dream. The director of the dream: Morpheus.

B. *The Action of the Dream: the Theme illustrated* (*6–291*). *Act I. The case of Eolus* (*6–87*). *Scene 1. At the Court of Minos in Hell* (*6–26*).—Characters at the Court: Pluto, Ruler of Hell; Minos, the Justice; Cerberus, the Constable; Diana and Neptune, plaintiffs; Eolus, the defendant; Morpheus and Lydgate, spectators. (*a*) Eolus led in by Cerberus (6). (*b*) Silence proclaimed by Pluto (7). (*c*) The complaint of Diana: Eolus had destroyed her forests with his blasts wherefore the deer were without shelter (8–11). (*d*) The complaint of Neptune: Eolus had disputed with him the jurisdiction of the sea and had caused him to turn against his natural course and to labor far out of measure, making him to ebb and flow out of his season. Moreover, Eolus had destroyed those to whom he had granted protection (12–20). (*e*) The case in judgment (21–23).

[1] I have analyzed the poem according to its dramatic divisions as if it were a Moral Play.

(*f*) The court dismissed, without action, at the invitation of Apollo to a banquet (24–27). *Scene II. At the palace of Apollo (27–87).* (*a*) Apollo sues for Diana's forgiveness of Eolus (27–34). (*b*) Neptune accepts Phebe as arbiter of his case (35). (*c*) The banquet (36–59): Apollo seats his guests at the table, Aurora and Apollo, Diana and Mars, Juno and Jupiter, Ceres and Saturn, Othea (Athena) and Cupid, Fortune and Pluto, Isis and Pan, Minerva and Neptune, Phœbus and Bacchus, Venus and Mercury. The waiters were philosophers and poets. Orpheus and Pan made music. Of dainties and meats there was a plenteous store. (*d*) Discord enters but is denied a place at the table (59–60). (*e*) Discord departs in wrath and meets with Atropos (60). (*f*) Atropos takes her part and enters the palace (61–62). (*g*) He rudely salutes the Gods (63); recites his services to them in destroying Hector, Alexander, Cæsar, etc. (64–69); charges them with assisting one whom he can not destroy (70); refuses to serve them longer (71). (*h*) The Gods in dismay swear to help Atropos and to confound this rebel. But Eolus will not help them (72–75). (*i*) Excursus: how Eolus came into the power of Pluto (76–80). (*j*) Eolus, forgiven by Neptune at the request of Phebe, promises to afflict the rebel if he be in the air (81–84). (*k*) The name of this rebel is Virtue (85–86). Pluto sends for his son Vice (87).

 Act II. The Battle between the Vices and Virtues in the field of Microcosm (88–210). Scene I. The gathering of the hosts (88–133). (*a*) Vice and his head-captains, Pride, Envy, Wrath, Covetousness, Gluttony, Lechery, Sloth (88–91); inferior captains, Sacrilege, Simony, etc., a great company (91–95); such a host of commons man never beheld — they were led by Idleness (95–102). (*b*) Virtue and his head-captains, Humility, Charity, Patience, Liberality, Abstinence, Chastity, Good-Business (103–118); inferior captains and common soldiers numbering a tenth of Vice's host (119–133). *Scene II. The preparation for the combat (134–138).* The field is Microcosm. It is entered by five highways. Conscience is judge of the battle. Freewill is Lord of the Field. (*a*) Vice and Virtue dub fourteen knights each (140–142). (*b*) They send ambassadors to Freewill (143–146). (*c*) Sensuality sows the field with wicked seeds (146–147). *Scene III. The battle (148–162).* (*a*) Virtue tarries under the Sign of the Cross and wards off the shots by the Shield of the Holy Trinity (149–150). (*b*) Virtue, abandoned by Freewill, retreats (151–154). (*c*) Other captains hold the ground and Per-

Literary Analysis. xxxix

severance brings reinforcements (155–159). (*d*) Vice is overthrown (160–162). *Scene IV. The result.* (*a*) Freewill repents (163–164). (*b*) Vice is met by Despair (165). (*c*) Prescience drives Vice and his host through the gates of Hell (166–167). (*d*) Predestination gives Virtue the palm of Victory and to all a heavenly habitation (168–170). (*e*) Some of Vice's host repent (171–174). (*f*) Freewill recompenses Virtue. Freewill is made bailiff in Microcosm under Reason. Sensuality is guided by Sadness. To Morpheus are given the five keys of the highways (178–187). (*g*) Atropos, angry at the Gods, seeks another master. He is called Death and given possession of Microcosm (188–209). (*h*) Virtue is exalted above the firmament to receive the Crown of Glory (210).

Act III. The School and Lessons of Doctrine : The Doubt Solved (211–290). The place, a garden with four pictured walls; the porter, Wit; the teachers, Doctrine, Holy Text, Gloss and Moralization; the scribe, Scripture. *Scene I.* (*a*). *The Interpretation by Doctrine of the dream and of the four " Times" pictured on the walls (211–275).* First, the imprisonment of Eolus signifies that wealth increases misrule. Every man is judged by Minos according to his wickedness. The complaint of Diana and Neptune signifies the folly of fools in seeking to bring the winds to correction. When they came to the banquet of Apollo like fools they gave up the matter to oblivion. The Gods resemble false idols. In the beginning the people slept in pagan law. The poets feigned many fables which were given places and names. Idolatry was the rule during the Time of Deviation from Adam to Moses. With Moses began the Time of Revocation which endured to the Incarnation of Christ. The New Testament opens the time of Reconciliation. The Time of Pilgrimage or War is signified by the battle between Vice and Virtue. As for Atropos his complaint signifies the constraint of friendship. Discord must needs be avenged by Death. The battle betokens the moral struggle in the soul. Microcosm is the world of man. Perseverance betokens the continuance of virtuous living. Prescience and Predestination are the rewarders of Vice and Virtue. The five keys are man's five wits. The return of man to sin is prevented by Reason and Sadness. *Scene II. The reconciliation of Reason and Sensuality: the theme completed (276–288). a.* Death, Reason and Sensuality enter. Of Death Lydgate is afraid. Reason argues that Death ought to be shunned. In this sentiment Sensuality accords. (*b*). Doctrine vanishes (289–290).

C. *The Conclusion (292-301).* (*a*). The dream broken (291-293). (*b*). Lest fault be found with me I record the vision (294-296). (*c*). The exhortation (297-301): Gentle Reader, walk alway in the path of Virtue. Fight daily against the World, the Flesh, and the Devil. Thine shall be the glory and the heavenly mansions. Let us pray that the Lord of Glory give us grace. Let us magnify his name. To you may Jesus grant eternal joy.

B. LITERARY STUDIES.

1. *The Religious Character of the Poem.*—The *Assembly of Gods* is one of Lydgate's numerous moral treatises so sounding in virtues that Bishop Alcock of Ely (b. 1430), in sermons addressed to the generation succeeding the poet, might praise it as leading to "the encrease of vertue and the oppression of vyce."[1] It is a sermon in verse, only the moral truth is "cloked," as Stephen Hawes phrases it, "with cloudy fygures." By this time Lydgate at Bury St. Edmunds must have become an excellent ecclesiastic. In the poem he freely employs the vocabulary of mediæval monasticism. The explanation by Doctrine, for instance, of the pagan deities, and indeed the whole discourse of Doctrine, is in the manner of the early theologians and schoolmen. Thus the writings of Fulgentius, the grammarian (c. 480–550), notably his *Mythologiarum (Mythologicon) Libri*, which explains the pagan names and legends, may be cited as the far source of that portion of the poem which interprets the deities, and the *Hamartigenia* and *Psychomachia* of Prudentius, the Christian hymn writer, a little earlier than Fulgentius, may be consulted for the origin of that part which contains the battle of the vices and virtues. Lydgate's immediate masters in opinion and sentiment were the compilers of the *Gesta Romanorum*.

The definite teachings of the treatise might indeed be gathered into a system.[2] The one God is thought of as a Supreme Judge, Alpha and Omega omnipotent, standing above the firmament and apportioning infinite rewards and punishments. Life is a pilgrimage, a war with the sins. Sin is the parent of all woe. Death

[1] *Sermo* on Luke viii., printed c. 1496. "Frendes I remembre dayes here before in my youthe that there was a vertuous monke of Bury called Lydgate, whiche wrote many noble histories and made many vertuous balettes to the encrease of vertue and oppression of vyce." Brydges' *Brit. Bibliog.*, iii, p. 533.

[2] That Lydgate knew his creed well is shown by *London Lackpenny*, Minor Poems, p. 106.

is the supreme object of dread. Salvation is sacramental and sacerdotal. Remedies against sin are found in the Seven Blessings of the Gospel, the Seven Virtues of God, the Ten Commandments, the Twelve Articles of the Faith, the Seven Sacraments, Veneration of the Cross and the Saints, the Doctrine of Unity and the System of Redemption in Christ. The necessity of penance is especially enjoined. The chief sacraments are Baptism and the Eucharist, the one being regarded as the sacrament of the new birth, the other as the sacrament of sanctification which maintains the new life. Of course the church is built on the stone of Peter who keeps the keys of Heaven. In all the poem there is not the least suggestion of the coming Reformation or of the work of Wyclif. A digression is made at one point to notice the error of Origen (st. 227.) And circumcision is held in derision (st. 173.). The work closes appropriately with a prayer to the Son of the Virgin Mary.

Of the artistic merits of such a treatise little can be said. The poem is simply one of the many moral poems which were so popular during the Middle Ages throughout Europe and which were calculated to gratify the almost universal taste for poetry of a serious and didactic nature. We can now consider these works hardly other than monuments of the bad taste that accompanies a low literary culture. Such writings belong however to the history of literature and without their consideration that history would be incomplete.

The *Assembly of Gods* is worthy of special attention for its complex allegory, which is one of the best of its kind. I admit at the beginning that it will furnish no pleasure to those who seek in literature for originality and imaginative power. No one today would think of echoing the praise of Lydgate's poet-friends, or of placing Lydgate's name by the side of Chaucer, though he may be fair companion for Gower and Hoccleve. That Burgh should think his master knew the muses well (*Secrees*, st. 226), that Stephen Hawes should maintain that Lydgate was the "most dulcet sprynge of famous rhethoryke" (*Pastime of Pleasure*), that Dunbar should write that Lydgate had with his "mellifluate" speech illumined the English language, and that before his coming the English Isle was "bare and desolate of rethorike or lusty fresch endyte" (*The Golden Targe*)—that this chorus of eulogy should be at all received only illustrates the imperfect literary sense of the late Middle Ages in England, that period which Taine calls appropriately, for its almost utter lack alike of the "grand style" and any high imagination, the Dark Age. Laureate Skelton, alone among these early writers, has a bit of discerning criticism of Lydgate's work in his *Phyllyp Sparrowe* (ll. 804-12):

> "It is dyffuse to fynde (difficult to understand)
> The sentence of his mynde,
> Yet wryteth he in his kynd,
> No man that can amend
> Those maters that he hath pende;
> Yet some men fynde a faute,
> And say he wryteth to haute (loftily)."

But while we cannot greatly admire a poem of this moralizing kind, it must be remembered that the work is no worse than very much of the prose and poetry of the Middle-English period, nearly all of which is ethical if not distinctly religious in character, and which might be assigned with propriety to the alcoves of the theological library. Chaucer is almost the only writer amid the multitude of preachers and satirists who obeyed his artistic rather than his moral conscience. The moral and artistic blend happily, it is true, in Langland who, although a reformer, was gifted with such Dantean earnestness and strength as to elevate his noble *Piers the Plowman* into a true and poetic allegory of the soul. Beautiful too is the poem of the Pearl in its perfect union of religious earnestness and deep and delicate poetic feeling, the lyric gem of all this period. Still on the whole it must be said that while England was ready ripe for an artistic literature in the period of the Renaissance, during the Middle Ages the secret of art was wanting. For literature with the artistic stamp we must go to the continent, especially to Italy. To Provençal poetry England presents no counterpart save perhaps the people's ballads and songs of Robin Hood. Not until the advent of the "courtly makers" of the reign of Henry VIII. was there any sign of change to an artistic literature. Religion and not Art, in short, was the "Time-spirit" of the age. So prevalent is the moral motive, indeed, that it is not surprising to find even Chaucer professing himself in his last years to be more thankful that he had translated the Consolation of Boethius and repeated Saints' Lives and religious homilies than that he had written the great works of his artistic imagination, the worldly vanities of which filled his senile mind with concern. As Mr. Lowell observes in comparing Chaucer and Dante, the main question with the former was after all the conduct of life. The conduct of life—this concern has been the characteristic English trait from Cædmon to Browning. That Lydgate's life tended to moral good if not to artistic purpose is evidenced by the prayer of Hawes in his Excusation of the *Pastime of Pleasure*, who prayed God to give him grace to compile books of "moral vertue"—

> "Of my maister Lidgate to folowe the trace,
> His noble fame for laude and renue,
> Whiche in his lyfe the slouthe did eschue;
> Makyng great bokes to be in memory,
> On whose soule I pray God have mercy."

2. *The Fear of Death and the Scorn of the World.*—It is now quite generally acknowledged that the mediæval conception of life is very accurately signified by a line in Dante's *Purgatorio* (xxxiii, 54–5) : "To those who live the life that is a race to death." It is notable that the same sentiment is repeated in almost the same words, though in broad Scotch, by William Dunbar, whose death year was just two centuries after the passing of Dante, his daily sombre line running : "Quhat is this lyfe bot ane straucht way to deid?"

These lines expressly point to what was the most characteristic feature of mediævalism, the almost universal dualism of thought. In art there was developed during the early Christian era a complete system of allegory and symbolism. A world of sense images on the one hand was set over against a universe of analogical and mystical meanings on the other, the former being strictly subordinated to the latter. This exaltation of the spiritual at the expense of the natural characterized the religious life of the whole people. As Mr. Kidd makes clear, the first fourteen centuries of our civilization were devoted to the growth and development of a stupendous system of otherworldliness. The supernatural became the object of the popular faith. And the conception of a future life simply overshadowed every consideration of the present. During the two centuries that I have noted, reckoning roughly from Dante to Dunbar, this faith in the other-world reached its culmination. Before Dante the boundaries of the dual realm had not been perfectly limned; the construction of the circles of the supernatural was the work of the poet in whom thirteen centuries of Christianity actually came to expression. After Dunbar the spirit of the Renaissance is working, introducing into this divided universe the principle of unity. It is certain that in Shakespeare unity is well nigh established. The development of the English drama away from the supernaturalism of the Miracle Play and the abstraction of the Moralities and towards a more or less consistent realism indicates the breaking-up of dualistic thought. Shakespeare having seen that men and women arrive at judgment in the world could disregard the life to come. Taking then into our view the dramatic realm of Dante, the other-world, and of Shakespeare, the present world, we discover in the centuries intervening between the life-work of these two artists the incidents of a remarkable transition in thought, the break-up of a dualistic system. In the art of the 16th century, which was more immediately the product of the Renaissance, the new principle of unity is seen to be confirmed. Naturally the tradition of religion continued longer in force. Still the Reformation church destroyed one feature of supernaturalism, the belief in Purgatory, and though it was under the necessity of maintaining the theory of Paradise and Hell, it laid greater stress than before upon the actual life of men upon the earth. It was after all a problem of the earth that Milton tried to solve — the justification of the ways of God to men.

Following the rise of the system of otherworldliness there grew in the heart of man, century by century from the founding of the church, an ever present fear, a fear that for sinful men was only increased by the joy of the martyrs, the fear of Him who was called Death, the Foeman, the invincible Archer. During the 14th and 15th centuries this dread of death was at its uttermost. On the physical side the fear at this period was heightened by the helplessness of all Europe before the ravages of the Black Plague, at the approach of which householders could only cry, "The Lord have mercy upon us." Spiritually the Day of Doom with its attendant terrors was a fully realized conception, and no man was so sure of victory that he did not tremble on the verge of the grave.

By reference to the homiletic and didactic literature of the 14th and 15th centuries in England the fear of death is found to be part and parcel of the religious feeling of the time. In the *Pricke of Conscience*, which contains the religious meditations of that strange hermit and visionary, Richard Rolle of Hampole, most of whose life was contemporary with that of Dante and who bore about with him a certain Dantean mysticism, we learn of the Unstableness of the World, of Death and why it is to be dreaded, of Purgatory, Doomsday, and the Pains of Hell. Dan Michel's *Ayenbite of Inwyt*, contemporary with Hampole's work, and illustrative likewise of the teachings of the church, takes a similar view of the present and future life. Comparing these and other typical treatises with reference to the report which they make upon death, it is seen that they accord in assigning to Death, who is invariably heralded by Dread, the execution upon all creatures of the awful sentence of doom.

It was taught, to be sure, that to good men death may be the end of evils and the beginning of every blessing. Yet the righteous could not escape from the terrors that attend death—the death that might be eternal. On the day of Doom even angels and archangels shall tremble. In a parable it was written that at the door of the house of the Spirit, Dread, the messenger of Death, should knock and demand entrance. He comes from Hell, the torments of which surpass the picturing of the imagination: in a great deep below Hell yawns, bottomless and frightful. Out of the stench and darkness rise the songs of sorrow from loathsome fiends in chains. Restless are the souls encumbered there, that are tormented by hunger and thirst, that are driven by heat and cold and bathed in burning pitch, withal feeling the turnings of the worm of conscience. Satan is there with his rake, having horns upon his head and knees, yawning with his mouth, venting fire from mouth and nostril and eyepits. This was the background of terror upon which were pictured the glories of heaven. By hopeful ones it was remembered that Christ had descended into Hell and broken the gates asunder. Gentle spirits taught that "Loue is more stranger þanne drede" (*Ay. of Inw.* p. 75) that "Love of God driveth out fear" (*Sawles Warde, O. E. Hom.* p. 259). Yet upon the foundation of fear the mediæval church was erected. The church then seemed to have been established for little else than to harass the human race.

The homiletic treatment of death and doom precedes the poetic by about a century. The characteristic utterance on these themes in English poetry is subsequent to 1400 and well along in the 16th century.[1] Yet Langland's great poem (about 1362–1393) has a content typical of the century to which it belongs. Perhaps the most striking and vigorous passage in all his Vision of the World at work is the one descriptive of the procession of Death amid the "field full of folk":

"Elde þe hore he was in þe vauntwarde,
And bare þe banere bifor deth by righte he it claymed.
Kynde come after with many kene sores,
As pokkes and pestilences and moche people shente;

[1] See Sackville's picture in the Induction to the *Mirrour for Magistrates* and Southwell's *Image of Death*, and many others of like import even in the days of the Renaissance.

> So kynde þorw corupciouns kulled ful manye.
> Deth cam dryuende after and al to doust passhed
> Kynges & knyghtes, kayseres and popes;
> Lered ne lewed he let no man stonde,
> That he hitte euene þat euere stired after.
> Many a louely lady and lemmanes of knyghtes
> Swouned and swelted for sorwe of dethes dyntes."
>
> —*P. Pl.* Pas. xx.ll. 94–104.

So in the fear of death, Dunbar, a characteristic melancholy figure of the 15th century, wrote his startling and horrible *Dance of the Sevin Deidly Synnis.* For "This fals warld," he said, "is bot transitory." When Beauty won her victory over the poet—so ran his allegory—he was consigned to the custody of Grief. Youth and loveliness, bravery and wit, all come to an end:

> "Onto the ded gois all estatis,
> Princis, prelates, and potestatis,
> Baith riche and pur of all degre;
> Timor mortis conturbat me."—*Lament.*

The poets, "the makers" themselves, for all their sweet service cannot escape the end: "I see the makers among the rest."

> "He hes done petuously devour
> The noble Chaucer, of makaris flour,
> The monk of Bery, and Gower, all thre;
> Timor mortis conturbat me."[1]—*Lament.*

At length the man that feared not Death found a place in Barclay's *Ship of Fools* (85th), the author knowing well:

> "There never was man of so greate pryde ne pompe
> Nor of such myght, youth nor man of age
> That myght gaynsay the sounde of dethes trompe.
> He makes man daunce and that without courage
> As well the state as man of lowe lynage
> His cruell cours is ay so intretable
> That mannys myght to withstand is nat able."
>
> —Barclay, *Ship of Fools,* II. p. 119.

In this manner the Fool who thought to escape Death became a prominent character in the spectacle-plays. The Fool always ended by becoming perforce Death's servant. Shakspeare refers to the action in *Measure for Measure* (Act. III. Sc. i.):

---

[1] This line occurs in one of Lydgate's poems and forms the burden of more than one of the popular songs of the day, indicating the rather "sad sincerity" of English life. And cf. Villon's ballad with the refrain: "Où sont des neiges d'antan?"

"Merely, thou art death's fool;
For him thou labour'st by thy flight to shun,
And yet runn'st toward him still."

There were many sides, of course, to mediæval life. The monks often forgot their professions of sanctity and, living for the moment for the world, incurred — rightly, no doubt — the satire of the poets and preachers. Chaucer's gay, worldling monk who "loved venerie," and the churchman who knew rimes about Robin Hood better than his prayers and could hunt a hare in the fields better than a clause in a Saints' Lives, were not, perhaps, uncommon types. Dunbar said, after all, "best to be blyth" in the face of the false world, and to his verses he often gave, like Villon, the sweetness of melancholy. Among the poems of the Percy MS. (Vol. III. 56) is one entitled *Death and Life* and thought to be late Middle-English work. It contains a gracious picture of Lady Dame Life, brighter than the sun, redder than the rose, ever laughing for love, awakening life and love in grass and tree, in bird and beast and man, as she speeds, with Comfort, Hope, Love, Courtesy, Honor, Mirth, Mercy and Disport in her train, in her conquest over Death. The sense of the piece, despite the intrusion of the "ugly fiend Dame Death," is that of gladness in the thought of life. Still the ballad shines by contrast. It was most common, it appears, to scoff at the world — that was vanity and mockery. Where there was one like Chaucer who could take a calm, sane delight in life, seeing too deeply into the nature of things to despair, there were many like Pope Innocent III. to enumerate without a gleam of hope the miseries of human conditions.[1] "þe worlde ycleped þe dane of tyeeres," expresses Dan Michel's judgment. Langland, the English Mystic, had likewise an austere and frowning face, and, having in his view the "field full of folk," burned with indignation at the worldlings there that Chaucer loved, the latter poet's sunny and sensuous tales being regarded as mortal sin. Death it was that made the world a mockery. When Graund Amoure, in Hawes' *Pastime of Pleasure*, became eager to heap up the world's riches it was Death that stood by to warn that these are valueless. So it was Death that rendered Nature unlovely. In the *Example of Virtue* Hawes brought Lusty Juventus within the glorious mansion of Dame Nature, whose perfect loveliness the youth admired; but Discretion, as was his part, led

---

[1] *De Contemptu Mundi sive de Miseria Conditionis Humanæ.*

to a place where the goddess's back was seen, which was all marred by an image of Death.

Taking now into consideration these two sentiments of mediæval life, the scorn of the world, and the fear of death, it is noteworthy that Lydgate represents most fully the religious attitude. In his youth he loved the pleasures of the world. In his *Testament*, referring to his wayward youth, he tells how he was converted:

> "When Ver is fresshest of blosmys and of flourys.
> An vnwar storm his fresshnesse may apayre.
> Who may withstande the sterne sharp shourys
> Of dethys power, wher hym list repayre?
> Thouhe the feturis fresshe, angelik and fayre,
> Shewe out in childhood, as any cristal cleer,
> Dethe can difface hem witheyne fyfteene yeere.
>
> "Which now remembryng in my latter age,
> Tyme of my childhood, as I reherse shal,
> Witheyne fifteene holdyng my passage,
> Mid of a cloistre depict vpon a wal;
> I sauhe a crucifix, whos woundys were nat smal,
> With this woord VIDE writen ther besyde,
> 'Behold my meeknesse, O child, and lefe thy pride.'"

From various sources we have the outward aspect of the monk in this "latter age" revealed. In a Shirley MS. (Addit. 16,165 Brit. Mus.) reference is made to "Lydgate the Monk clothed in blakke." Douglas, mentioning Lydgate among the poets in the Court of the Muses, witnesses that he "raid musing him allone" (*Palice of Honour*.) In the prolog to the *Story of Thebes*, written by Lydgate to complete the Canterbury Tales, he describes himself as looking pale and bloodless and wearing a cape of black — no fit companion for Chaucer's gayer pilgrims one would think. But the most perfect description is given by William Bullein in his *Dialogue against the Fever Pestilence* (Lond. 1573). Having spoken of Homer, Hesiod, Ennius and Lucan as favorites of the Muses, Bullein adds to the list of beneficiaries Gower, Skelton, Chaucer, and Lydgate. The last he thus describes: "Lamenting Lidgate, lurking emong the lilies with a bold skons, with a garland of willowes about his pate; booted he was after Sainct Benet's guise, and a black stamell robe, with a lothly monsterous hoode, hanging backwarde; his stoopyng forward, bewayling euery estate, with the spirite of prouidence forseyng the falles of wicked men, and the slipprie seates of Princes, the ebbyng and flowyng, the risyng and falling of men in auctoritie, and how vertue doth aduaunce the simple, and vice ouerthrowe the most noble of the worlde." (Bullein's *Dialogue*, E. E. T. S., p. 17.)

Of these accounts there is every justification in Lydgate's writings. The dominant themes are without question those connected with the thought of death and change. The painting at St. Paul's of the procession of Death seemed to impress his mind deeply. Beside his translation of the French verses of the Dance Macawbre more than one reference occurs in his lyrics to the "Daunce of Poules" (*Minor Poems*, p. 34, 77). Often he pictures life as a hard pilgrimage, "in which there is no stedfast abyding." He harps recurrently upon the wretchedness of human affairs—the note being taken, he affirms, from his master Chaucer! One of his favorite topics is to show the greatness of mankind and how they are brought low: "All do but show a shadow transitory."

> "Stabilnesse is founde in nothyng,
> In worldly honour who so lokithe wele;
> For dethe ne sparithe emperour ne kyng,
> Thoughe they be armed in plates made of steele;
> He castithe downe princes from fortunes wheele,
> As hir spokes rounde about goo,
> To exemplifye, who that markithe wele,
> How this world is a thurghfare ful of woo."
> *On the Wretchedness of Worldly Affairs*, M. P., p. 126.

> "Considre and see the transmutacioun,
> How the sesoun of greene lusty age,
> Force of juventus, hardy as lioun,
> Tyme of manhood, wisdom, sad corage,
> And how decrepitus turneth to dotage,
> Al cast in ballaunce, bewar, forget nothyng,
> And thu shalt fynde this lyff *a pylgrymage*,
> In which there is no stedfast abydyng."
> —*On the Mutability of Human Affairs*, p. 198.

The *Daunce of Poules* or the *Daunce Macawbre* consists of verses spoken by Death to the various persons he is leading to the grave and of their responses. All must go upon this dance, the Pope, the highest in the land, the Emperor, the Cardinal, the Empress, the King and all the lower ranks—there is none escape.

> "In this myrrour every man may fynde
> That hym behoveth to gon upon this daunce
> Who goth to forne or who schal go behynde
> Al dependeth in goddes ordynaunce.

> Wherfor eche man lowly take his chaunce.
> Deth spareth not pore ne blode ryal,
> Eche man therfor haue this in remembraunce
> Of on matere God hath forged al."

The *Assembly of Gods* is the consummate expression of Lydgate's fear of death. Death is here the central figure throughout. In the fear all accord—Lydgate, Reason and Sensuality. Very appropriately the last recorded line written by this somewhat sombre monk, line 1491 of the *Secrees of Old Philisoffres*, is of Death:

> "Deth al consumyth which may nat be denyed."

3. *The Conventional Materials.*—The *Assembly of Gods* in respect to its materials, its machinery, so to speak, is anything but original. The poet is thrown into the conventional sleep by a lake side, on the hackneyed spring morning. At once we expect the poem to be crammed full of stereotyped theology, mythology and allegory. Indeed the work as a whole is merely a mosaic of current traditions, the different parts being fitted together with more or less perfect skill. When, then, we come to estimate the literary effects of compositions of this sort, their origins and history must be taken into account. Mediæval ideas had always a definite pedigree. While modern romantic literature is most characterized by its personal element, mediæval literature may be divided rather into impersonal classes, as romances, chronicles, lays, etc. Individuality rarely appeared as an element of poetic composition. Each writer, being under no compulsion to originate or invent, simply threw what he had to say into the prevailing form. The genius of poetry, both with respect to form and materials, was conventionality.[1] An artist was held in estimation according to his skill in plagiarizing from the world's literatures. It was sufficient that he could wisely quote, that he had won a reputation for scholarship, and that the epithet "learned" be attached to him. It is characteristic of the age that Dante, after a youth spent in writing love songs, should plan a *Convito*, to be a vast encyclopædic work, so anxious was he that the title of "learned" might offset the reproach of a youth misspent in composing love sonnets. So Chaucer was called with approbation "learned" and

---

[1] This feature of mediæval literature is commonly spoken of by readers slightingly and with meagre patience. But a traditional literature is cumulative, so to speak, in its effects. Repetition is then a virtue and not a weakness. Traditions are most effective at the moment of most common use. A later age is quite incapable of giving full and due credit to conventions that have passed; it should at least exercise charity.

the "great translator." In his case, by reason of the blending in his works of his own stream of romantic fancy and feeling with this remote traditional tide, often strange anomalies of thought were produced. In fact Chaucer was differentiated from the writers of the period by his originality which worked with new results upon the materials that tradition had given him. Yet it was for his learning that he was most admired. It is not necessary to disprove the extent or accuracy of Chaucer's attainment in this respect.[1] Like other writers of the period he was learned enough to refer suggestively to matters more or less familiar to his readers, who held their own knowledge loosely, and in the manner of all middle-age erudition, without critical accuracy. A work of this period is not then to be interpreted by itself but by the class of literature to which it belongs by virtue of associated themes and *motifs*. When one first reads the opening stanzas of the *Assembly of Gods* he exclaims that it is a dream like *Piers the Plowman*, like the *Poem of the Pearl*, like the *Roman de la Rose* and the *Divina Comedia*. These poems and many more add their several contributions to one's delight. A phrase here, a thought there, the dream, the allegory, the pictured walls, the theme of death, in one way or another serve to recall pretty much the whole of mediæval literatures—just probably as the author intended. Only by thus recovering the past and setting a work in the historical current, can we understand the pleasure and profit with which a poem of this kind was read by contemporaries and by those of a later time to whom its literary traditions were familiar. We must remember that to Lydgate,[2] for a century after his death, the distinction was given of belonging with Gower and Chaucer to the great triumvirate of letters. Not alone for his "sugurit lippis and toungis aureate" was this fame acquired, though for these he seems to have been most admired by Hawes, the Scottish poets, the critic Webb, and the poet Gray; but his praise was in the mouth of his nearest disciple, Benedict Burgh, for that "ye have gadred flouris in this motli mede,"—in the literature, that is, of the past—and on this account "to yow is yeven the verray price of excellence." Of course a succeeding age, intent upon the Reformation and the New Learning, forgot the mediæval traditions, the dream, the allegory, the teachings of Doctrine, and

---

[1] Cf. Lounsbury *Studies in Chaucer*, ch. v.

[2] For the subject of Lydgate's literary fame v. Sidney Lee's summary in *Dict. of Natl. Biog.* XXXIV., p. 309-10.

Lydgate and his school were relegated to obscurity. Chaucer survives now not for his learning but because of the perrennial charm of his native genius. No one of us cares much for Boethius or Fulgentius or Prudentius, or even Dante in his doctor's robes, dead, all of them, to modern comprehension.

No one will question Lydgate's learning or the extent of his reading. He was more or less familiar with ancient and mediæval literatures, especially that written in Latin and French. His library contained much the same books that Chaucer, Gower and Langland read. He is as pedantic as they in filling his pages with the names of authors and famous men. He illustrates, as they, the influence exercised in poetry by the scholastic and encyclopædic training of the Church and School. Mr. Lee's statement on this point is sufficient:

"Lydgate mentions familiarly all the great writers of classical and mediæval antiquity. Of Greek authors he claims some aquaintance with 'grete' Homer, Euripides, Demosthenes, Plato, Aristotle and Josephus. Among Latin writers he refers constantly to Ovid, Cicero, Virgil, and his commentator Servius, Livy, Juvenal and 'noble' Persius; to 'moral' Seneca, Lucan, Statius, Aulus Gellius, Valerius Maximus, Prudentius, Lactantius, Prosper the 'dogmatic' epigrammatist, Vegetius, Boethius, Fulgentius, Alanus ab Insulis, and Guido di Colonna. Dante, Petrarch, and Boccaccio are repeatedly commended by him among Italian writers, and he was clearly acquainted with the 'Roman de la Rose,' with French fabliaux, romances, and chronicles."—*Dict. Natl. Biog.* XXXIV., p. 309.

The mosaic of the *Assembly of Gods* is made up of the following materials, all of which are traditional and common.

Introduction with the season *motif*.
The dream.
The painted walls.
The School of Doctrine.
The pagan Divinities.
The court scene and the banquet of the Gods.
The Nine Worthies and the learned men of antiquity.
The allegory.
Proverbial phrases.
The teaching of the Church.
The Seven Sins and Virtues.

The battle of Antichrist.
The Liberal Sciences.
The five Wits.
The fear of Death.
The romance of Paris and Helen.

4. *The Season Motif.*[1] The introduction of Middle-English poems by reference to the season of the year and the position of the planets seems generally to have been merely a part of the machinery of composition—a happy way of getting started. The same prelude is met with in the Provençal, French and German lyrics of the period with wearisome regularity. The May landscape especially was stereotyped into set forms that could have had but a rhetorical significance. With Chaucer and most of the Scottish poets, the nature-prelude was, one feels, something more than derivative. Chaucer, King James, Dunbar, and Douglas especially appear to draw quite directly from nature with a heartfelt feeling for the season. They write with an unction and an eye for delicate effects never exhibited in the purely conventional prelude. Chaucer's love of nature amounted almost to a passion. Whatever he touched broke into full blossom. Reading him, as Lowell says, is like brushing through the dewy grass at sunrise. Poets with Chaucer's spirit had naturally a sense for nature as a dramatic background for their compositions. Thus it was agreed that May[2] was the "mirthful month," the "quicking" season, the month of "joy and disport," the one that "among months sittith like a queen"—the time, therefore, for beginning love-poems and romantic allegories. Chaucer tells us that in the Spring he would say farewell to his books and walk out in the meadow; this was the time to compose "Seyntes Legends of Cupid." The association of the romances with the Spring was so common that there came to be a saying that "Arthur is the man of May." Where the dramatic motive was present other seasons would be employed as the occasion required. *The Pearl* occurred in the high season of August when the reapers' sickles were in the corn. Lyndesay's *Dreme* opens appropriately with a

---

[1] See McLaughlin, *Studies in Mediæval Life and Literature*, ch. i.; also Veitch, *Nature in Scottish Poetry.*

[2] There is a primitive feeling among poets that Spring is the season of delights. Keats had this sense in a large degree when he began to write *Endymion* "while the early budders are just new," hoping that no wintry season should find his work incomplete.

dreary winter's night in January. Dunbar's horrible *Dance of the Sinns* is seen in February. Sackville's *Mirrour for Magistrates*, which harks back to the Chaucer School, begins in the "wrathful winter." In one instance Chaucer opens a poem, the *Hous of Fame*, modelling his work upon Dante, with the December season. In Henryson's melancholy story of Troylus and Creseyde there is an open effort to construct a dramatic background, for the poet says in beginning :

> "*Ane doolie sesoun to ane cairfull dyte*
> *Suld correspond, and be equivalent;*
> Richt sa it wes quhen I began to write
> This tragedie, the wedder richt fervent,
> Quhen Aries, in middis of the Lent,
> Schouris of haill can fra the north descend,
> That scantlie fra the cauld I micht defend."

But there are other cases, as Langland's *Piers the Plowman*,[3] where no æsthetic value in the prelude can be determined. The last of these derivative forms, as in Skelton's *Bowge of Court*, or Fletcher's *Purple Island*, seem but rhetorical. The conventional aspect of the introduction is well displayed by Lyndesay when he begins his doleful *Monarchie* with the May morning, as if he were unable to get started in any other way, but realizing that his purpose is to describe mortal miseries, he calls a truce to his vain descriptions and turns to the matter in hand.

In the minds of some writers there may have been a thought of the planetary influences that ever streamed down from the heavens upon the earth. Astrology is known to have been an attractive theme to the mediæval poets. "It was the delight of Dante," says Dean Church, "to interweave the poetry of feeling and of the outward sense with the grandeur of order, proportion, measured magnitudes, the relation of abstract forces displayed on such a scene as the material universe." Chaucer constantly makes a literary use of astrology though personally skeptical of the pretentions of the science. This perception of the starry forces at work in the lives of men must have been present in the first of the preludes. Thus the introduction served almost the function of an invocation to the Muses. King James, indeed, invoking the Muses Nine, passes at once to consider the Spring "that full of vertu is and gude." In one of the very earliest of the poems containing the typical season

---

[1] Langland seemed to have had Mapes' Golias satire in mind when he began to write. Note Mapes' "Inter prodigia plebem innumeram."

motive, the *Apocalypse of Golias*, written toward the close of the 12th century, the astronomical allusion is prominent ·

> "A Tauro torrida lampade Cynthii
> Fundente jacula ferventis radii
> Umbrosas nemoris latebras adii,
> Explorans gratiam levis Favonii.
>
> Aestivae medio diei tempore,
> Frondosa recubans Jovis sub arbore,
> Astantis video formam Pythagorae:
> Deus scit, nescio, utrum in corpore."

May was the month of life because the planets at that season had special power of hot and moist.[1]

With Lydgate and his immediate pupils, as Hawes in the *Pastime of Pleasure*, the astronomical introduction is apparently a matter of pure literary habit. The vision of the *Temple of Glas* takes place in December, after its model the *Hous of Fame*. The opening of the *Assembly of Gods*—the only reference to nature in the work—is conventional. It is barely possible that in the monk's scholastic mind there was in the reference to the spheres the suggestion of the harmony to be achieved by Reason and Sensuality.

5. *The Vision.*[2] In the psychology of the Middle Ages the vision is perhaps the most remarkable phenomenon displayed. The records of dreams constitute in Europe and England an entire literature with features peculiar to the kind. Some of this dreamwork is in imitation of the revelations of Scripture; some works are clearly due to the hallucinations of an ascetic life; some are as plainly the results of adoration, the fruits of "contemplative life," in the exercise of which men passed from the knowledge of things of sense to knowledge of things eternal; others reveal the passion for dogmatic definition that characterized the schoolmen however mystical the theme; other forms are secular and merely a part of the higher rhetoric of poetry as then conceived and developed. After the Bible, the head sources of the mediæval visions seem to have been the "Dialogues" of St. Gregory, a compilation of many religious dreams, the *De Consolatione Philosophiæ* of Boethius, and the *Somnium Scipionis* in Cicero's treatise on The Republic. In

---

[1] For the effects of the seasons upon the lives of men see Lydgate's *Testament, The Mutability of Human Affairs*, and the *Secrees*.

[2] See Lecky's *History of European Morals*, II., pp. 116 *et seq.*, 220. For further references to the literature of the vision see Schick's Intro., p. cxviii.

general, two types of vision are distinguishable, in accordance with their monastic or worldly origin. In the visions of one class the dreamer takes into his view the circles of the supernatural, and reports as man may of the revelations accorded him either of Heaven or Hell or the intermediate states. In the other class the objects of contemplation are in the "wilderness of this world," and the dream may be but a poetical device, a kind of framework for any secular action or incident, as the experiences of a lover in the *Romaunt of the Rose*. In English literature illustration of the first type is furnished by *The Pearl*, with its view of the heavenly city; Dunbar's *Dance of the Seven Deadly Sinns*, with its vision of Hell; and Lyndesay's *Dreme*, which gives the reader sight of all the circles of the Infinite. Probably the earliest instance in England of this kind of dream is the *Apocalypse of Golias*, written in Latin by Walter Mapes (b. 1143), a work which enjoyed an extraordinary popularity during the 13th and 14th centuries. The chief examples of the second type are Langland's *Piers the Plowman*, Chaucer's several dreams, King James's *Quair*, Dunbar's *Golden Targe*, Skelton's *Bowge of Court*, etc.

The *Assembly of Gods* is in its scope a vision of the first order, though the battle takes place in Microcosm. Probably Lydgate did not have any very real sense of the other worlds, nor could he ever loose his imagination so that he really saw visions—at best he asked but for dogmatic definition as the schoolmen before him.

6. *Proverbial Phrases.* Like other writers of the period Lydgate makes a conspicuous use of conventional phrases and proverbial sayings. A considerable body of proverbs, rhetorical figures, and phrases may be gathered from his works, some of which are peculiar to his own usage and style, while others are the common property of literature. On a later page is given a list of the proverbs and phrases employed in this poem. The manner of the employment of a stock simile by writers is well illustrated by the history of the phrase "hair like gold wire" which seems to have been given currency by Lydgate. The simile first occurs in Layamon's *Brut* (ll. 7047-8), where it is employed to describe King Pir who was so wondrous fair. By Lydgate it was first used to characterize the feathers of a bird in the *Chorl and Bird*. In the *Temple of Glas* and the *Assembly of Gods* (l. 373) the reference is to Venus with her ever sunnish hair. In the *Troy-Book* it occurs no less than seven times being applied both to men and women. The larger compari-

son "hair like gold" is often found in European literature before Lydgate as in the *Roman de la Rose*, but this special phrase is Lydgate's own. From this time to the close of the sixteenth century the figure is in constant employment[1], generally descriptive of women of ideal beauty. Its force is partly spent in Shakespeare's time, for the reverence for gold hair is satirized by the saying of Benedick in *Much Ado about Nothing* (II., 3, 36): "Her hair shall be of what colour it please God." In sonnet cxxx. reference is made to Lydgate's simile in the line, "If hairs be wires, black wires grow on her head."

7. *The Painted Wall.*[2] The pictured wall was another rhetorical device common to mediæval poetry—an elastic framework into which any subject could be made to fit. It was a convenient means of extending indefinitely the scope of one's work. To such an extent was the method carried that a secondary poet like Stephen Hawes cannot mention a wall without covering it over with pictures. Instances of the usage will be found in Boccaccio's *Thesiad*, in the romance of *Guigemar* by Marie de France, Lorris's *Roman de la Rose*, Chaucer's *Boke of the Duchesse*, Lydgate's *Temple of Glas* and *Assembly of Gods*, Hawes's *Pastime of Pleasure*, Dunbar's *Dream*, Barclay's *Towre of Vertue and Honour*, etc. In the romances the stories depicted are commonly those of love. In *Guigemar*, for instance, the walls are painted with images of Venus and scenes from Ovid's Art of Love, and in the *Boke of the Duchesse* the imagery is that of the *Roman de la Rose*. In descriptions of the temples of Mars and Diana scenes of war and the hunt will appear. The siege of Troy or Thebes was a favorite theme for the walls of palaces. Scriptural scenes occur in cathedrals and cloisters. Dunbar saw on his chamber walls

"All the nobill storyis old and new,
Sen oure first father formed was of clay."

[1] For many instances of its usage see Schick's *Temple of Glas*, notes, pp. 88–90; and Kölbing, *Bevis of Hamtoun*, notes, pp. 244–5; and for a full discussion of its usage and æsthetical meaning see a paper by the present editor read before the English Club (Chicago) and reported in outline in the *University Quarterly Calendar* (May, 1895), p. 80.

[2] See Warton, *Hist. of Eng. Poetry*, II., pp. 131, 275, 402; III., p. 63; on page 402, Vol. II., is reprinted a passage from an Itinerary written in 1322 describing Westminster palace; see Longfellow's *Golden Legend* for instances of picture and play; a description of convent walls is given in *Piers the Plowman's Crede*, ll. 186, *et seq.*

While this method is an open piece of machinery when viewed as rhetoric, quite ludicrous too when as elaborate as Lydgate's arbor walls which reveal the history of the world in small, yet it should be remembered that during the Middle Ages the picture was the favorite means of conveying story and doctrine. It is a remarkable feature of mediæval art that often no positive line of division can be drawn between literature and picture or spectacular show. The paintings on royal palaces of the scenes of war, the weaving on ladies' tapestries of the incidents of romance, the picturing on cloister walls of the saints and scenes from Scripture, the depiction in public places as on the bridge at Lucerne and in the churches in France and England of such instructional processionals as the Dance of Death, the scenic representation of sacred things in liturgies, and pageants and street plays—these constituted the popular literature of the period, of far greater influence than the written page that issued from the scriptorium of the monastery. Allegory, the written picture, necessarily adopted the scenic method for which the mind was already prepared. This interplay of imagery between picture and allegory contributed much to the later establishment of an independent literature. But for the present the pictorial was the literary. Even Chaucer was not freed from the necessity of "drawing of picture."

8. *The Admixture of Pagan and Christian Traditions.*—One characteristic of the *Assembly of Gods* is the curious admixture in it of pagan and Christian traditions. The pagan deities are all ranged on the side of the Vices of Christendom. The Christian Vice is represented as the son of Pluto, who is the Lord of the Christian Hell. The ancient Fateful Atropos, who cut with shears the thread of pagan life, is transformed into Death with a lance, the dread of the Christian Church.

It was the almost universal practice of the poets of late Middle English to confound the mythology of all peoples and to mix up incongruously the pagan myths and Christian allegories, constituting in fact a veritable mythology of their own. Gower in his *Confessio Amantis*, Douglas in his *Palice of Honour*, King James in his *Quair*, and others of the allegorical school display their learning in this manner. Such usage points to the renaissance of paganism, accompanying the temporary decay of Christianity in the 14th century, and to the rise of a new mythology, and foreshadows the new learning of the next century. The results of this renaissance in Europe a century later are well exhibited by Browning in his poem, *The Bishop Orders his Tomb*, where Pans and Nymphs, symbols of Delphic wisdom and Bacchic revels, the Saviour on the Mount, St. Praxed in his glory and Moses with his tables are brought into juxtaposition on the sculptured tomb. We know too that in Italy Plato was called the second Moses and Orpheus, Empedocles, Parmenides and others were placed on a level with David and the prophets.

In some cases there seems to be more than a poetic use of the machinery of mythology — as if some profound meaning was read into the ancient myths. Always when traditional currents from different sources blend, the underlying human meanings are transferred and commonly understood. When Angelo painted in the Last Judgment an Herculean Christ he was clearly not irreverent. Dante wrote Olympus for Paradise (*Purg.* c. xxiv. l. 15). He spoke of Christ as "Sommo Giove" who was crucified for us (*Purg.* c. vi. l. 118). In canto xxix, the Grifon naturally symbolizes the Christ. In a like spirit Milton and others have spoken of Christ as the "mighty Pan," and Milton's Deity, as Lowell observes, was a Calvanistic Zeus. Even Bunyan introduces, into his *Holy War*, Cerberus, who swears by St. Mary, and the Furies, Alecto, Megaera and Tisiphone, and the incongruity of their presence there seems to have escaped his attention. Chaucer in calling one of his works the *Seintes Legend of Cupyde* must have entered into the spirit of the heathen pantheism as a real form of religion.[1]

It is not so clear that Lydgate entered very deeply into the spirit of mythology. His usage is not very consistent. In the *Assembly of Gods* Cupid is counted among the vices. But in another piece attributed to Lydgate (Fairfax MSS. xvi. Bibl. Bodl.) the rubrics of the missal are applied to the god Cupid for whose sake many were martyrs. In the *Life of Our Lady* the beauty of the Virgin Mary is compared with that of Helen, Polyxena, Lucretia, Dido, Bathsheba and Rachel. The clearest case of insight is in his *Testament* where Jesus is spoken of as

"Our Orpheus that fro captyvyte[2]
Feit Erudice to his celestial tour."

In the present instance Doctrine is under the necessity of explaining away the heathen worship.

[1] Cf. Mr. Jephson's remark, Skeat's ed. *Pr. Tale*, notes p. 136.

[2] Jesus was frequently represented in early Christian paintings in the form of Orpheus, who overcame death.

9. *The Allegorical Type.*—Middle-English literature exhibits two types of allegory : the one religious and scholastic, having its origin in the exegetical and homiletic literature of the monks and leading on to the literature of the Reformation ; the other secular and profane, embodying the spirit of romance, personifying especially the God of Love, who was the central object of the song and worship of the continental minnesinger and troubadour, leading on in its turn to the literature of the Renaissance. The two types, differing thus in origin, while often confused with respect to form, are always distinguishable in motive.

The original *Roman de la Rose* represents in one composition the double type already established on the continent. The first part, being conceived in a love of beauty and composed with the fancy and imagination actively at play, is pure poetry. Lorris, though a belated *trouvère*, was true at heart and sang as the impulse prompted him. The second part of the *Roman*, written forty years after the first by a reformer and moralist, Jean de Meung, not to be mistaken for a poet, is didactic, satirical, and metaphysical. By the aid of Lorris's personification, Meung was enabled to expound and popularize his ideas of reform, but his impersonations recall nothing so well as the entities of the schoolmen. The personifications and materials of the didactic system were adopted by the poets whose purpose was moral or satirical, by Langland, Gower, Lydgate, Lyndesay, Skelton and Barclay, and by the Moral-plays so soon as personification became necessary in the advance of the drama from scenic representation to dramatic characterization.

Upon the model of the *Roman de la Rose*, which was translated into English with amplifications of the first part and omission of much of the second part, were formed the love allegories and romances which, being all in the "May morning" style, with sunny gardens and birdies manifold, contain whatever of poetic inspiration the later Middle Ages in England possessed. The new *Romaunt of the Rose* provided the staple model for the poets of the court. It directed the composition of the *Court of Love*, and was the chief influence that entered the *Dreme*, Chaucer's *Boke of the Duchesse* and perhaps his *Hous of Fame*. To the list we may add Lydgate's *Temple of Glas*, which was modeled upon Chaucer's *Hous of Fame*, and probably Hawes's *Pastime of Pleasure*. To the same family of romance allegory belongs much of the literature of Scotland written during the 15th century, that at least of most refinement and delicacy, notably Dunbar's *Thissil and the Rois* and the *Golden Targe*, and the beautiful *Quair* by James, "the best poet who ever was a king." In the romantic vein Gawain Douglas wrote his *Palace of Honour*, a more serious style appearing in *King Hart*, which allegorizes the progress of human life. This stream of romantic allegory flows on to Spenser, forming in the *Faery Queene* the supreme type of poetic allegory. Though Spenser was an artist of the Renaissance he was yet the literary descendant of Chaucer and the mediæval romanticists, of those who were too great as artists to be ever dominated by the moralities.

As for the rest of the allegorical literature in late Middle-English the tendency is to sermonize. In the case of Langland and perhaps of Lyndesay their seriousness is of such a nature as to claim our attention as artistic. Gower might have been a romancer if he had not seen behind every tale some hidden form of Vice. John Skelton, laureate of Henry VII, the last of the school which called Chaucer master, while writing some pieces in the romantic spirit, yet is more pleased to satirize follies and vices as in his *Bowge of Court*. Characteristic of the times now that the Reformation was near at hand is the *Ship of Fools* (1508), a satirical allegory after the model of Brandt's Swabian poem, by Barclay who caught up for the purpose of satire the idea of a navy of practical vices sailing out presumably into the ocean of ruin. Erasmus in a corresponding spirit wrote his satirical *Praise of Folly*. The allegory of the Reformation culminates at length in Bunyan's Visions.

To this now primary and now secondary stream of moral and allegorical literature Lydgate's *Assembly of Gods* belongs. This is not, however, satirical or very serious concerning reform, and it strives after certain effects of the *Romaunt of the Rose*. But so far as Lydgate is concerned the romantic tide has ebbed—he is a monk with the interest of the church at heart.

10. *The Relationship between the Allegory and the Moral Play.—* The close relationship between the moral plays and the *Assembly of Gods* is clearly seen. In an earlier period[1] such poems as the *Cursor Mundi* and the contemporary miracle plays exactly corresponded, the only difference being that one was recited and the

---

[1] It is conjectured with good reasons that the demon frolics in Dante's *Inferno*, c. xxi and xxiv, were reproduced from some dramatic mystery plays of which the performances on the Ponte Carraia at Florence in 1304 are conspicuous instances (Plumptre).

other acted. The same correspondence existed later between the moral plays, which represented the natural dramatic evolution from the miracle plays, and the allegories, which exhibit a like advance in dramatic expression. This interaction between the two forms of art is important to observe. The moral play involved allegory as an essential part of its artistic apparatus. In the very earliest pageants and plays, allegorical characters, taken from both profane and sacred writings, played a more or less important part. The miracle plays required the introduction of such characters as Sin and Death, Faith, Hope and Charity. Among the first innovations were representations of Veritas, Justitia, Pax and Misericordia, as in the "Parliament of Heaven" in the English Coventry series (XI). As early as Henry VI., whose reign may be fixed upon as the epoch of the permanent adoption of the moral play (Collier, *An. of the St.*, p. 32), personification of the Sciences, Nature, Grace, Fortune, and the moral qualities was well known. The World, Flesh and Devil appeared in character in *Originale de Sancta Maria Magdalena*, a play of the time of Henry VII. The play of *Everyman*, belonging perhaps to the time of Edward IV., is one of the most perfect allegories ever given form. In the Vices and Virtues especially there was something inevitably dramatic in the very nature of contrast. So that with few exceptions the allegory of the Moral-plays is based on the contest between good and evil in the mind of man; of this character is the allegory of the *Castle of Perseverance, Min Will and Understanding, Nature, The World and the Child, Hick-Scorner, Everyman, Lusty Juventus*, etc. It is probable indeed that the one allegorical figure Vice, in his Protean character of Infidelity, Iniquity, Hypocrisy, Desire and the like, has played a more conspicuous part upon the stage than any other single dramatic personage.

Thus the familiar use of allegorical personages upon the stage contributed to the popular taste for allegorical poems. The names representing abstract qualities recalled so vividly the actual persons seen upon the stage that the mere recitation of the qualities was sufficient to body forth the form. The catalog of names in the *Assembly of Gods* is tedious enough to the modern reader, but in an age of objective dramatic presentation the names and persons were intimately associated.

The *Assembly of Gods* finds its analogue then in the contemporary Moral-plays. The poem may actually be divided into scenes and the *personæ* speak in character. Some portions, as the assembly of the gods and the gathering of the different hosts, might take the form of a masque.[1] Poem and play differ only in the method of presenting the same form of thought.

The dramatic cast of the poem might well be expected in the case of Lydgate, who seemed as well able to direct a street pageant as to write verses in a cloistre. He devised pageants for the Mercers' and Goldsmiths' Companies in honor of Wm. Estfield, who was London's mayor in 1429 and 1437 (v. *Dict. Natl. Biog.*, XXXIV, p. 306). Stowe in his *Annals of England* (p. 385) witnesses that in 1445, at the reception in London of Queen Margaret, the wife of Henry VI., several pageants were exhibited at Paul's gate with verses written by Lydgate (v. *Hist. Eng. Pageants*, ed. Howes, p. 385; *Pur le Roy*, M. P.). According to Ritson (*Bibl. Poet*, p. 79) Lydgate wrote a Disguising or Mumming before the King at Eltham. Ritson also inserts in his list of Lydgate's works "a procession of pageants from the creation." This is exceedingly doubtful, for, as Halliwell says (M. P. p. 94), Ritson only copied from Tanner, whose conjecture it was that the Coventry Series of Miracle Plays was written by Lydgate. But the *Processioun of Corpus Christi* (title given by Shirley), attributed by Ritson to Lydgate and so printed by Halliwell, while not dramatic in form, contains an enumeration and description, as if in procession, of Patriarchs and Saints from Adam to Thomas Aquinas. The *Dance of Death* and the *Pilgrimage of the World* are essentially dramatic. The dramatic element of *Bycorne and Chichevache*, which was doubtless borrowed from a French mystery play,[2] is also worthy of note. Certainly not the least excellence of the *Assembly of Gods* is its dramatic picturesqueness. It was this characteristic which Collier noted that he remarked "the story is very dramatic, and far less dull than most pieces of the kind" (*An. of the St.* p. 31).

11. *The Allegory of the Vices and Virtues.*—In considering the central allegory of the *Assembly of the Gods* the reader is brought into relation with one of the great themes of literature, the almost universal subject of war, the war that proceeds within the soul—

[1] It seems to be well established that the English masque, and the pageants, derived their popularity and meaning from the allegorical poems and plays. Dunbar's Dance of the Sins is a masque in form. The Dance of Death was a graveyard processional.

[2] See Dodsley's *Old Plays*, XII. p. 302.

how man battles through trials and temptations to heaven's gate, how he falls oft but rises again, how he wins at length the victory over Sin and Death. This is in truth the dominant allegory of man. So universal, indeed, is the treatment in the literature of Christendom of the theme of man's salvation that the collected volumes of that literature may be said to constitute a veritable Epic of Penance. For note how often in great literatures, in the works of Dante, Langland, Chaucer, Spenser, Bunyan, Goethe, Tennyson and Browning, to name the greatest, the real content of life is described in the terms of pilgrimage and battle—the life that in the Middle Age was in very fact a Crusade and a Tournament, an ascent up the Mount of Purgatory, that was in Reformation times a Pilgrim's Progress and a Holy War, that is still a "War of Sense with Soul," where the obligation never ceases to "Fight on, fare ever." The literature of this struggle, wherein not only the soul of man is involved but also the spiritual powers beyond our world, where Earth and Heaven and Hell are mingled in contest, constitutes in its entirety the most stupendous epic which the genius of man has conceived.

In some form the subject is older than Christianity. War itself is a primitive theme. The heathen myths pictured the agents of nature as engaged in warfare, the healing and harmful forces, the Light and the Darkness, the Summer and the Winter, the sun-gods and the frost-giants. In one of the earliest of historic religions, Zoroasterism, the idea of antagonism in the moral life occurs, the contest between the Prince of Light and the Prince of Darkness being figured upon the earthly sphere. On the spiritual side Plato's myth of the contending steeds is again a record of the primitive soul. Thus the necessity has been laid on man from the first of "working out the beast" and "letting the ape and tiger die." It is true that Christianity brought into greater prominence the need of warfare. "*Estote fortes in bello et pugnato cum antiquo serpente*"—thus the Scriptures exhorted the Christian convert to the fearful battle against sin. Then when paganism came in contact with Christianity the terms of war and of military society were naturally applied to the new life and to the kingdom of Heaven. Christ was King. His apostles were thegns who went forth to the wars. With the spiritual conceptions of the new gospels was mingled the mythology which dealt with the warfare of Nature. The conflict between Day and Night was transferred to Christ and Satan, to Eternal Light and Eternal Darkness.

Chivalry, gathering from paganism all that was best in war, strength, prudence, courage, knightly honor, and from Christianity an ideal of spiritual perfection, now became the established principle of society, a society that received its personal ideal in the figure of King Arthur and its social ideal in the Order of the Round Table.

While society itself was thus being organized in accordance with the ideal of militant Christianity, the severest of spiritual battles were being fought out within the cloisters of the monks. A severer morality was naturally exacted from the monks than from the ordinary Christian. It was then within the monasteries of the third and fourth centuries that the "Olympian battle with Sin" began. By Ambrose (340–397) and his pupil Augustine (354–430) the Platonic virtues called "cardinal," Wisdom, Justice, Fortitude, and Temperance, were resolved into Christian graces. To these were added the triad of theological virtues, Faith, Hope and Love. Against these seven were arrayed for the trial of the saints seven deadly sins, Pride, Avarice, Anger, Gluttony, Lust, with two others selected from Envy, Vain-glory, Tristitia or Accidia. An intense and concentrated struggle against human weakness was thus set on foot. On the basis of these sins a penitential system was devised, some form of pilgrimage up the mount of Purgatory.

By the time that Dante wrote his *Comedia* the exactions of monastic virtue were enforced upon all the children of the Church and a penitential pilgrimage enjoined. In the *Inferno* a classification of the sins is given as found in the *Summa Theologica* of St. Thomas Aquinas, which is based upon the ethical principles of Aristotle as interpreted, probably, by Averrhoes. Sin, having been triumphant, is come to punishment in Hell according to what Dante calls the law of "contrapass" [retribution] (*Inferno* xxviii, 142.). But in Purgatory sin is not allowed to develop into act but appears as an inner incitement. It is shown, therefore, not as punishment but as recreation where struggle must enter, the will for holiness being victorious.

> "And I will sing that second realm instead,
> Wherein man's spirit frees itself from stain,
> And groweth worthy Heaven's high courts to tread."
> —*Purg.* ll. 4–6.

For this purpose Dante employed the popular penitential system of the Church which brought into prominence the necessity of discipline by struggle against sin in the pilgrimage of this world. Thus the various stairs of Penitence are named after the seven monastic moralities.

When Dante is resting on the fourth terrace of Purgatory, Virgil explains to him the nature and relation to each other of the seven mortal sins. He is explaining the teachings of St. Augustine and considers sin with respect to its causes. Love is the common ground. Love perverted by selfishness and erring in its object is pride, envy and anger. Love remiss, defective in vigor, is sloth. Love excessive is avarice, gluttony and lust. (So earlier Augustine defined virtue as *amor ordinatus*, vice as *amor non ordinatus* (*Civ. D.* XV. 221). Sin is mortal because it attacks the conditions of spiritual life, preventing in society the exercise of love. Pride is the most deadly, nearest therefore to the state of hell, because it strikes directly at love and hinders to the utmost the soul's higher life.

The current ethics of the church during the thirteenth and fourteenth centuries respecting the nature of the vices is also contained in a poem entitled *Septem Peccata Mortalia*, of doubtful authorship but ascribed by some (Witte, Krafft and others) to Dante.

> "In Pride the root of every sin doth lie;
>   Hence man himself doth hold in loftier fame
> Than others, and deserving lot more high.
>
> Envy is that which makes us blush for shame,
>   With grief beholding others' happiness,
> Like him, whom we the face of God proclaim.
>
> Wrath still more woe doth on the wrathful press,
>   For its fierce mood lights up hell's fiery heat;
> Then ill deeds come, and loss of holiness.
>
> Sloth looks with hate on every action meet,
>   And to ill-doing ever turns the will,
> Is slow to work, and quick to make retreat.
>
> Then Avarice comes, through which the whole world still
>   Vexes its soul, and breaks through every law,
> And tempts with gain to every deed of ill.
>
> Both fool and wise foul Gluttony doth draw,
>   And he who pampers still his appetite,
> Shortens his life, to fill his greedy maw.
>
> And Lust that comes the seventh in order right,
>   The bonds of friendship breaks and brotherhood,
> At variance still with Truth and Reason's light."
>
> —Trans. by Plumptre, II., p. 324.

The Allegory of the Vices and Virtues.

In tracing now in literature this allegory of life we are led back to a favorite classic of the dark ages, the *Psychomachia* of Prudentius, the work of a Christian poet who flourished during the early part of the fifth century, who is best known to the modern world for his Hymns, repeated editions of which were issued during the fifteenth, sixteenth and seventeenth centuries.

The *Psychomachia*[1] (Migne, *Patrol.* Ser. L. Vol. 60), written in hexameters in ecclesiastical Latin, represents allegorically the conflict between the vices and virtues for the soul of man. The poem is an expansion of an earlier work by the same writer entitled *Hamartigenia* (Migne, *Patrol.*, Vol. 59, p. 1007) which is theological in character, an explanation of the origin of evil in refutation of the heresies of the day, notably that of Marcion, the dualist. The *Psychomachia* is an expansion of a portion of the *Hamartigenia*, where Anger, Superstition, Sadness, Strife and Luxury, war against the soul. The allegory in the later poem is carried out into great detail, being intended to represent the successive stages of Christian conflict amid the temptations of the world. A first struggle is necessary to overcome the worship of the pagan gods and to become a Christian. The next conflicts occur between Chastity and Lust, and between Patience and Wrath, resulting in victory for the virtues. Pride then attacks Humility, Righteousness, Temperance, Fasting, Shame and Simplicity. But a pit is dug for Pride by Treachery and by Hope the vice is slain. Then comes the battle between Luxury, who is driven in a chariot by Love scattering flowers, and Temperance who bears the standard of the cross. These Desires having been vanquished Avarice with her train appears and attacks the Christian under the guise of Frugality, but Almsgiving rescues the soul. The last battle is with Heresy, who is slain, and the soul is at peace.

For the popular theological confirmation of such a warfare one may turn to St. Augustine's *City of God*, the latter part of which was contemporary with the *Psychomachia* and written perhaps with the poem in mind. The 19th Book of the *City of God* reveals the discords between the heavenly and earthly cities and in the tenth chapter announcement is made of the rewards prepared for the saints: "There the virtues shall no longer be struggling against any vice or evil but shall enjoy the reward of victory, the eternal peace which no adversary shall disturb."

[1] Cf. *Hist. of Latin Lit.*, G. A. Simcox, II., p. 360.

The *Psychomachia*,[1] sanctioned by the usages and doctrines of the church, became the model for a series of poems, generally moral and didactic in motive, called variously Bataille, Debat, Tournoiement, Disputoison and Pélerinage (v. *Lit. Fr. an Moyen Âge*, par Gaston Paris, pp. 158, 159, 169, 227, 228). Among the later works of this class are the *Anticlaudianus* (12th century) by Alanus; *Débat du corps et d l'âme* (12th century); *Tournoiement d' Antéchrist* (1235) by Huon de Méri, which contains the battle between the Vices and Virtues under the leadership of Antichrist and Christ respectively; *Pélérinage de la vie humaine* (1330–5), by Guil. De Deguilville, a favorite work in England and the prototype of Bunyan's *Pilgrim's Progress;* certain of the *Bestiares* which satirize the vices of the time, as the *Renart le Nouvel* (1288), by Jacquemart Giélée, the animals of which, attacking the holy castle Maupertius, fight like the seven deadly sins with which they are for the first time mixed; episodes also found in the love poems, that series of Ars d'Amour which ended with the *Roman de la Rose*, as the battle for the rose in the *Roman* (*Lit. Fr.* G. Paris, p. 169).

Typical of these mediæval works that deal with the war of the vices and virtues is the *Anticlaudianus, sive de Officio Viri Boni et Perfecti*,[2] one of the most important books of the period, and one familiar to Lydgate and his fellow monks. It was written by Alanus de Insulis, during the second half of the 12th century, to oppose an invective of Claudian against Rufinus, the prime minister of Theodosius the Great, who was represented as the embodiment of all that is vicious, having been perverted by all the passions of hell. The poem is well summarized by Mr. Steele in his edition of Lydgate's *Secrees* (note, p. 109) whose outline is here quoted.

"Nature, perceiving its failure in bringing about perfection, decides to join in one being all the virtues and excellences possible. She therefore summons all these allegorical personages, and lays

[1] The *De Consolatione Philosophiæ* by Boethius may be mentioned as one other source of the battle *motif*. A French version of a part of this work is found in a poem called *De Fortune et de Felicite* which is said by Warton (II, p. 216) to be the source of the *Tournoyement de l'Antichrist* (c. 1228) by Huon de Meri, which contains a combat of the Vices and Virtues; this latter work was employed by Langland for the battle scene of the Antichrist at the close of *Piers the Plowman* (Skeat). Gaston Paris, however, thinks that most of these scenes of moral warfare may be referred to the *Psychomachia*.

[2] v. Migne, *Patrol.* t. 210, or *Anglo-Lat. Satir. Poets*, Roll's Series, ed. Wright. Cf. Lounsbury's *Chaucer Studies*, II, p. 348.

before them her plan. Prudence (Phronesis) and Reason remark that none of them can give to man the highest of all gifts—a soul, and that they must ask it from God. This mission is imposed on them; they at first refuse it, but Concord gets them to accept it. A car is made for them by the seven liberal arts, to which five horses representing the senses are yoked. Grammar lays the framework, Logic makes the axles of the wheels, Rhetoric adorns the frame with gems and flowers of silver, Arithmetic, Music, Geometry and Astronomy make the wheels, and Reason drives the chariot.

"They pass through the air, the clouds, the home of the evil spirits of the air, the spheres of the planets, and arrive at the firmament, when Reason faints and the senses become useless. Theology appears, and on the condition that Reason and the senses—except that of hearing—are abandoned, offers to guide Phronesis. The firmament, the empyrean heavens, the dwellings of saints, angels, and the Mother of God are next described. Here Prudence faints, but Faith revives her, and explains the mysteries of human destiny, grace, etc.

"God now orders Intelligence to frame a model of a soul such as was asked for, and making it, it is sent to Nature, who makes a body which Harmony, Music and Arithmetic fit for and join to the soul. All the allegorical divinities add a gift—even Nobility and Fortune bring theirs—which Wisdom checks and moderates.

"But Hell learning of this new creation resolves to destroy it, and Allecto unites all the vices against it. After a long battle the new man puts them all to flight, and inaugurates upon the earth the reign of Justice and Happiness."

The English books of Penance are many in number. Among the theological works in prose which treat in whole or in part the subject of the vices and virtues there are to be mentioned especially a Homily by Ælfric (Thorpe's ed. Ælfric Soc. II, p. 219), *Old English Homilies* (E. E. T. ed. Morris), the *Ancren Riwle* (Morton's ed. p. 198–204), Dan Michel's *Ayenbite of Inwyt* (Morris' ed. p. 16), *Vices and Virtues* (E. E. T. ed. Holthausen), Dan John Gaytryge's *Sermon on Shrift* and the *Mirrour of St. Edmund* (*Relig. P.* ed. Perry, p. 1, 15), a sermon by Wyclif (Works ed. by Arnold III., p. 225) and Chaucer's *Persones Tale*. Among the religious pieces in verse which treat the theme are Aldhelm's *De Octo Principalibus Vitiis* (in Latin, Migne, *Patrol.* Ser. Lat. 89, p. 282), the book of Penance added to the *Cursor Mundi* (E. E. T. pt. V., p. 1524 *et seq.*), verses in *Religious Pieces* and in *Political Religious and Love Poems* (E. E. T. ed. Furnivall, p. 215), the *Manuel of Sins*, translated from a work by Bishop Grosseteste by Robert Mannyng, tracts in the Vernon MS. (ed. Horstmann, E. E. T.) entitled *How to Live Perfectly* No. XXXII.) and *The Spur of Love* (No. XXXV.), being translations from the popular *Speculum* of Edmund Rich, in the same MS. the *Dispute Between a Good Man and the Devil* (No. XXXVII.), *The Mirrour of the Periods of Man's Life* in *Hymns to the Virgin and Christ* (E. E. T. ed. Furnivall, p. 58), and a poem by William de Shoreham entitled *De Septem Mortalibus Peccatis* (Percy Soc., Vol. 28, p. 102), etc.

These treatises set forth the common theory of ethics as taught by the Latin Church. In classification and definition of the principal vices and virtues the works generally accord. There is occasional difference in the number, in the order of mention of the cardinals and in the names and number of the "branches" which spring from the parent stems.

The English Benedictine monks, following the older continental system, enumerate eight principal vices and virtues. Ælfric (Hom. ed. Thorpe, Vol. II, p. 219) sets in opposition, on the one hand the vices gifernys (greediness), galnyss (lust), gitsung (covetousness), weamet (anger) unrotnys (discontent), asolcennys o*dd*e æmelnys (sloth or aversion), idel gylp (vain-glory), and modignys (pride); on the other hand the healing virtues gemetegung (moderation), clænnys (chastity), cystignys (bounty) gedyld (patience), gastlicer blis (ghostly joy), anrædnys (steadfastness), lufe (love) and eadmodnys (humility).

In the mediæval treatises the number of each class is regularly seven. The classification in the Parable of the Castle of Love in the *Cursor Mundi* (ll. 10040–10052) is the following: pride, envie, glotony, lust, gredines, wreth, hevynes, with the corresponding virtues, buxumnes, charite, abstinens, chastite, liberality, mekenes, and gostly gladnes. In the *Cursor Mundi's* Book of Penance the list is: pride, envy, wraþ, slauþe, couatyse, glotori and drunkenhede, lichery; and mekeness, loue, thalmodenes, gastely ioy, lele of hert, and fre of gyft, abstinence and sobirte, chastite.

The Ayenbite of Inwyt has in one place (p. 16 and 123) prede, envye, wreþe, sleauþe, icinge (avarice) couaytise, glotounye, lecherie; and for virtues the Pauline triad of beleave, hope and charite, and the cardinals of the "yealde philosofes" sleyþe (prudence) temper-

The Allegory of the Vices and Virtues. lxxi

ance, strengþe, and dom (justice); in another place (p. 159) prede, enuye, felhede (hate), slacnes, scarsnes, lecherie, glotounye and boysamnes (humility) loue, mildenes, proues, larges, chastete, sobrete.

In the *Mirrour of St. Edmund* occur pryde, envy, ire, slouth, couetyse, glotony, lechery; and wysdom, vndirstandynge, consaile, stalworthenes, cunnynge, pete, drede of Godde, four of which are said to be needful for the active life and three for the contemplative life. Dan Jon Gaytryge's sermon recounts the regular vices and for virtues, trouthe, hope and charyte, the theological virtues, and ryghtwysenes, sleghte (prudence), strenghe, and methe (temperance), the natural virtues. The Latin titles occur in *Gyf me Lysens to Lyve in Ease* (*Pol., Rel., and Love P. E. E. T.* ed. Furnivall p. 215) superbia, invidia, ira, avoryssia, accidia, gula, luxuria, with the corresponding umylitas, carytas, amor cum paciencia, vigilate et orate, elymosina, abstinaunce, chastite. In the tract *How to Live Perfectly* (Vernon MS. E. E. T. No. 32) the remedies for sin are the Seven Blessings of the Gospel and the medicine for the sins are Wisdom, Understanding, Strength, Counsel, Wit, Pity, Fear of God.

Chaucer's list in the *Persones Tale* is pride, envye, ire, accidie, avarice, glotenye, leccherie; and humilite, love, mansuetude and pacience, strengthe, misericorde and pite, abstinence, and chastite. Gower employs the same classification in his *Confessio Amantis*.

The most original treatise on the theme is perhaps Wyclif's tract on the *Seven Deadly Sins* (*Works*, ed. Arnold III, p. 119). The cardinals are the conventional ones but the condemnation of the practical sins of the clergy and people is from the Lollard point of view. The sins have this origin: "þe fende, and þo worlde, and monnis owne flesche, stiren hym to couyte ageynes God's wille. And so ich one takes at other, and þese make seven. Pride, envye, and wrath ben synnes of þo fende; wrathe, slouthe, and avarice ben synnes of þe world; avarice, and glotenye, and þo synne of lechorye ben synnes of þo flesche" (p. 121). These are thus defined: "Pride is wicked liif of a monnis hyenesse;" "Envye is unordynel wille of mon to his neghtbore;" "Wrathe is unskillful wille of vengeaunce;" Slouthe is "slouthe in God's service;" Covetise is "avarice of worldly godis;" "Glutonye falles þen to mon, when he takes mete or drink more þen profites to his soule;" "Lechorye stondis in þis þing, þat mon mysusis lymes or powers of his body, þat God haves ordeyned unto men for his kyndely gendrure" (p. 121 *et seq*).

In the more imaginative treatises various mystical and allegorical features appear. Chaucer's Parson pictures the life of God's chosen as a pathway filled with stumbling blocks. In the *Mirrour of the Periods of Man's Life* a man is tempted from birth to age. In *Gyf me Lysens to Lyve in Ease* the sins are as wounds to be healed by medicines in the form of plasters and herbs, the remedial virtues. In *Piers the Plowman* the sins are the muck with which Haukyn, the active man, has soiled his coat (Pas. xiii). Often sin is described as a tree with branches and twigs as in the *Ayenbite of Inwyt*. When personified the sins may come as warriors in armor on horse or a foot, as in the Parable of the Castle of Love in the *Cursor Mundi*, or as in Lydgate's *Assembly of Gods*, Spenser's *Faery Queene*, Fletcher's *Purple Island* and Bunyon's *Holy War*. In the moral play, *The World and the Child*, the vices are exhibited as seven kings. Chaucer in the "A B C" laments that he is chased by "theves seven." Dunbar pictures the sins as dancers down in hell. Gower assigns the vices to a lover. Langland describes the virtues as "sisters," Pride alone among the vices being personified as a woman. Dan Michel declares Pride to be the devil's own daughter. In the *Sawles Warde* the cardinal virtues are the daughters of the lord of the house. In the *Ancren Riwle* each sin is symbolized by an animal: Pride by a Lion, Envy by an Adder, Wrath by a Unicorn, Lechery by a Scorpion, Avarice by a Fox, Gluttony by a Sow, Sloth by a Bear. The *Ayenbite of Inwyt* presents most mystical features: St. John in a vision saw a beast come out of the sea having a leopard's body, a bear's feet, a lion's throat, and it had seven heads and ten horns. This beast, explains Michel, betokeneth the devil who cometh from the sea of hell; its guile is denoted by the leopard's spots, his strength by the bear's feet, his cruelty by the lion's throat. The seven heads are the seven deadly sins and the ten horns the guilts of the commandments.

Without exception these writings accord in assigning to Pride the first place among the sins. Pride, said Ælfric, is "ord and ende ælces yfeles : se geworhte englas to deoflum and ælcre synne anginn is modignys." Pride in the *Cursor Mundi* is the chief sin that fights against Love: it is said that Lucifer fell by pride, that it is fouler than any devil in hell. *The Ayenbite of Inwyt* pictures Pride as the devil's own daughter, the sin of Lucifer and the angels, the first to assail our Lord and the last to abandon Him. In *Gyf me Lysens to Lyve in Ease*, Pride is the first wound "more bytter than ever was gall." By Wyclif Pride is considered to be the chief sin, being accorded to the Fiend. Said Gower "Pride is the heaved of all sinne" (I, p. 153). Barclay, at the beginning of the period of the Reformation, wrote of Pride that it is

> "A vyce so moche abhomynable
> That it surmountyth without any fable
> All other vyces in furour and vylenes
> And of all synne is it rote and maystres."
> — *Ship of Fools*, II, p. 159.

So Pride leads the dance of the sins in hell in Dunbar's poem. It was the first to receive punishment in the *Shepheard's Kalendar*. It cast Satan and the rebel angels out from heaven in Milton's *Paradise Lost*. With Shakespeare it appears as ambition:

> "By that sin fell the angels." *Henry VIII*, III, 2, 441.

The consensus of mankind seems then to be written by Sir Thomas Browne that Pride is "the first and father sin, not only of man but of the devil; a vice whose name is comprehended in a monosyllable, but in its nature not circumscribed with a world (Works, II, p. 435).

Turning from the theological treatises on the moralities, and taking up the works of real artistic value wherein the imagination of writers was truly kindled by a perception of the poetic capacities of the theme of battle and pilgrimage, we enter a most important field, perhaps to be called, when considering the actual epical and dramatic development of the theme, the most important field in early English literature. The many chivalric Romances would be included in the survey, perhaps also the earlier *Guthlac*. With a more specific treatment is the long series beginning with Bishop Grosseteste's *Chateau d'amour*, which received several translations at the hands of later writers, continuing in the parable of the Castle of Love in the *Cursor Mundi*, the English *Bestiares*, the Moral-plays, Langland's *Piers the Plowman*, Gower's *Confessio Amantis*, perhaps the *Romaunt of the Rose*, Lydgate's *Assembly of Gods*, Hawes's *Pastime of Pleasure*, Dunbar's *Dance of the Sins*, Barclay's *Ship of Fools* and *Mirrour of Good Manners*, the anonymous *Shepheard's Kalendar*, religious pieces of the type of the *Mirrour of the Periods of Man's Life*, Spenser's *Faery Queene*, John Day's *Peregrinatio Scholastica*, Bernard's *Isle of Man*, and, last of these stirring allegories, Fletcher's *Purple Island*

f

(1633), and Bunyan's *Pilgrim's Progress* (1678) and *Holy War* (1682).

In almost the earliest teaching on the subject of sin, in Ælfric's Homily on Midlent Sunday (ed. Thorpe, II, 212) the Christian life is described as a warfare. In the homilies the word commonly used for Virtues was *mihtan* (*Old-Eng. Hom.* I, p. 105), it being explained that by God's help, if fight were keen, the devilish sins would be overcome (p. 107).[1] The *Psychomachia* of Prudentius was known to the English monks as it is referred to by Beda in his *De Ratione Metrica* as the book " quem de virtutum vitiorumque pugna heroico carmine composuit." There is an echo of its triumph in *Guthlac* where the hero meets in deadly combat with Satan and his troops of sin-smiths that roar and rage like wild beasts. In the manner of the *Psychomachia* Aldhelm wrote in Latin his *De Octo Principalibus Vitiis* (Migne, *Patrol.* Lat. Ser., 89, p. 282) arraying the opposing forces in battle form.

For this warfare man was given the gift of Power. This is a Virtue described by Dan Michel (*Ayenbite of Inwyt*, p. 169) as a tree with seven boughs which betokened the seven battles that the Christian must wage. This Christian battle is again likened by Michel to the gladiatorial fights at Rome, wherein those who desired fame must overcome all who are sent against them by the master of the field; the holy Christ is the master who suffers no one to be tried above his strength. Bishop Grosseteste, employing the chivalric idea, figures Love as a strong castle standing high on a polished rock. The castle is enclosed by four stone walls and a deep moat, and fortified with four towers and seven barbicans. A clear, all healing well springs from the central tower. Within the tower is a brilliant throne. Being interpreted, the castle is a shield to the human soul. The rock is Mary's heart. The four towers are the cardinal Virtues, Strength, Skill, Rightfulness, and Temperance. The seven barbicans are the seven virtues that receive the attacks of the deadly sins. The well is Mary's mercy. The throne is Christ. This figuration, so beautiful in its symbolism, caught the fancy of succeeding writers. The castle betokens refuge and strength and victory. As a symbol of the Virgin Mary it is employed in the *Cursor Mundi*, in the *Abbaye of Saynte Spirite* (*Relig. Pieces*, ed. Perry, E. E. T. p. 49) in a miracle play entitled *Originale de Sancta Maria Magdalena* (v. Collier, *Hist. Dr. P.* II, p. 153–6) and in Lydgate's *Life of St. Mary*.

---

[1] Virtue is also called *thewe* in Gaytryge's *Sermon*, p. 10.

In Langland's vision the tower on the toft, partly drawn from Grosseteste's *Chateau d'amour*, is the abode of Truth or God the Father (v. Prol. l. 14; Pass. v. ll. 594 *et seq*). Grace is the doorward there and seven sisters the porters of the posterns, Abstenence, Humilite, Charite, Chestite, Pacience, Pees, and Largenesse. Mercy, or the Virgin Mary, mediates between the sinful ones at the gates and Christ and the Father. The chief battle in Langland's poem is that waged against the church of Unity (Pass. xx) by Antichrist and seven giants. Sloth and Avarice lead the assault. Peace bars the gates. But the virtues sleep and Conscience is forced to become a pilgrim over the world, seeking the Plowman. In a 13th century homily, *Sawles Warde*, man is represented as a castle inhabited by Wit, his wife Will, five servants, the five senses, and four daughters, the cardinal virtues.

Among the Moral-plays the *Castle of Perseverance* well illustrates the prevailing conception. The play was performed during the reign of Henry VI., but it is thought from its completeness that it must have had predecessors of the same kind (Collier, *Hist. Dr. P.*, II. p. 200 *et seq*.). Humanum Genus has been conducted by Good Angels to the Castle of Perseverance, which is under the wardship of the Seven Virtues. The Seven Deadly Sins attack the castle but are repulsed by the Virtues, being made "blak and blo" by the beating of roses which Charity and Patience fling from the walls. "Drery Death" alone has power over Humanum Genus whose soul is at last saved by the grace of Deity.

The later development of the theme needs only to be mentioned here. The *Faery Queene* was a natural evolution of the mediæval chivalric idea. Though the theological dogmatism is abandoned mankind is yet in the wilderness of this world, beset by sins on every side. In Book II. there is set forth the struggle of the Soul against its enemies. In Mammon's Cave the World is overcome. Arthur prevails against the Devil in the person of Maleger, the captain of the vices. Guyon, in the bower of Acrasia, resists the temptations of the Flesh. The ninth canto shadows forth the struggle of the Soul within the body. Milton and Bunyan picture the redemptive system from the Protestant point of view. For the first time in Milton's *Paradise Regained* the struggle is pictured as being withdrawn within the self—this is the beginning of the modern treatment of the theme. But Bunyan writes directly in the manner of the "old fables" that dealt with "Mansoul's wars."

One of the last of these microcosmic encounters and the most ingenious and involved of all, is the *Purple Island*, published in 1633 by the poet Fletcher, who is called by Francis Quarles "the Spenser of this age." The Purple Island is Man. Its prince is Intellect. The Senses constitute a pentarchy. Cosmos captains the rout of Vices that attack the Island. The Virtues defend and conquer (v. cantos vii–viii, ix–x, xi–xii).

Considering the possibilities of Lydgate's theme it is to be regretted that he did not grapple with it more successfully. His work exhibits intelligence, some degree of imagination, but is devoid of passion and æsthetic apprehension. He marshaled numberless hosts, his design was so comprehensive as to include the upper firmament, the lowest hell, and the earth and man, yet the *Assembly of Gods* is almost the least of the poems attempting to portray the Holy War.

THE ASSEMBLY OF GODS.

By Don John Lydgate.

*Here foloweth the Interpretacion of the names of goddys & goddesses as ys rehersyd in þis tretyse folowyng as poetes wryte:

PHEBUS:	ys as moche to sey as þe Sonne.		CERES:	Goddesse of Corne.
APOLLO:	ys the same or ellys God of Lyght.		CUPIDO:	God of Loue.
			OTHEA:	Goddes of Wysdom.
MORPHEUS:	Shewer of Dremes.		FORTUNE:	þe variaunt Goddesse.
PLUTO:	God of Hell.		PAN:	God of Shepardes.
MYNOS:	Iuge of Hell.		ISYS:	Goddesse of Frute.
CERBERUS:	Porter of Hell.		NEPTUNUS:	God of the See.
EOLUS:	þe Wynde or God of þe Eyre.		MYNERUE:	Goddesse of Batayll, or of Harueyst.
DIANA:	Goddesse of Woode & Chace.			
PHEBE:	þe Mone or Goddes of Watyres.		BACHUS:	God of Wyne.
AURORA:	Goddes of þe Morow or the Spryng of the Day.		MERCURIUS:	God of Langage.
			VENUS:	Goddesse of Loue.
MARS:	God of Batayll.		DISCORDE:	Goddesse of Debate and Stryfe.
IUBYTER:	God of Wysdom.			
IUNO:	Goddesse of Rychesse.		ATTROPOS:	Dethe.
SATURNE:	God of Colde.			

I

Whan Phebus in the Crabbe had nere hys cours ronne   1
  And toward the leon his iourne gan take,
To loke on Pictagoras speere I had begonne,
  Syttyng all solytary alone besyde a lake,   4
Musyng on a maner how that I myght make
  Reason & Sensualyte in oon to acorde;
But I cowde nat bryng about that monacorde.   7

When Phebus had nearly run his course in the Crab, alone beside a lake, I was musing how I might make Reason and Sensuality to accord.

*Omitted in B. C follows the Camb. MS., closing: Here endyth the Interpretacion of the names of Goddis and Goddesses as is rehercyd in thys treatyse folowynge.

2

In heaviness I fell asleep.

For long er I myght, slepe me gan oppresse   8
  So ponderously, I cowde make noon obstacle,
In myne heede was fall suche an heuynesse,
  I was fayne to drawe to myn habytacle,   11

Morpheus enters and takes me by the sleeve,

To rowne w*ith* a pylow me semyd best tryacle,
  So leyde I me downe my dyssese to releue.
Anone came in Morpheus & toke me by the sleue. 14

3

And as I so lay half in a traunse,   15
  Twene slepyng and wakyng he bad me aryse,

bidding me arise and attend the Court of Minos.

For he seyde I must yeue attendaunse
  To the gret Court of Mynos, the iustyse.   18
Me nought auaylyd ayene hym to sylogyse;
  For hit ys oft seyde by hem that yet lyues
He must nedys go that the deuell dryues.   21

4

When I sy no bettyr but I must go   22
  I seyde I was redy at hys co*m*maundment,

I obey and go with him towards the parliament of Pluto and Minos.

Whedyr that he wold me leede to or fro.
  So vp I aroose and forthe w*ith* hym went,   25
Tyll he had me brought to the p*ar*lyament,
  Where Pluto sate and kept hys estate,
And w*ith* hym Mynos, the Iuge desperate.   28

5

But as we thedyrward went by the way,   29
  I hym besought hys name me to tell.

On the way I ask him his name. He replies, "Morpheus."

"Morpheus," he seyde, "thow me call may."
  "A syr," seyd I, "than where do ye dwell,   32
In heuen or in erthe outher elles in hell?"

"Where do you dwell?" He answers, "in Fantasy."

  "Nay," he seyde, "myñ abydyng most comonly
Ys in a lytyll corner callyd Fantasy."   35

6

Having arrived in Hell, Cerberus, the porter, brings thither Eolus in chains, charged by Neptune and Diana with traitorous action.

And as sone as he these wordys had sayd,   36
  Cerberus, the porter of hell, w*ith* hys cheyne
Brought theder Eolus in raggys euyll arayd,
  Agayn whom Neptunus and Diana dyd co*m*pleyne 39
Seying thus, "O Mynos, thow Iuge souereyne,
  Yeue thy cruell iugement ageyn thys trayto*ur* soo
That we may haue cause to preyse thy lord Pluto." 42

7

Then was there made a proclamasion, 43
  In Plutoys name commaundyd silence
Vppon the peyne of strayte correccion,
  That Diana and Neptunus myght haue audience 46
To declare her greefe of the gret offence
  To theym done by Eolus, wheron they compleynyd.
And to begyñ Diana was constreynyd. 49

Silence is proclaimed by Pluto that Neptune and Diana may declare their grievance.

Diana, first, begins to speak,

8

Whyche thus began as ye shall here 50
  Seying in thys wyse, "O thow lord Pluto,
With thy Iuge Mynos, syttyng with the in fere,
  Execute your fury vppon Eolus so 53
Accordyng to the offence that he to me hath do,
  That I haue no cause forther to apele,
Whiche yef I do shall nat be for your wele. 56

demanding from Minos the execution of fury upon Eolus,

9

"Remembre furst howe I a goddesse pure 57
  Ouer all desertys, forestes and chases,
Haue take the guydyng and vndyr my cure.
  Thys traytour Eolus, hath many of my places 60
Dystroyed with hys blastes and dayly me manaces.
  Where any wood ys he shall make hyt pleyn
Yef he to hys lyberte may resorte ayeyñ. 63

the traitor, who had destroyed her forests,

10

"The grettest trees that any man may fynde 64
  In forest to shade the deere for her comfort,
He breketh hem asondre or rendeth hem roote & rynde
  Out of the erthe—thys ys hys dysport, 67
So that the deere shall haue no resort
  Withyn short tyme to no maner shade;
Wher thorough the game ys lykly to fade. 70

breaking and uprooting the trees, wherefore the deer are without shelter.

11

"Whyche to my name a reproche syngler 71
  Shuld be for euer whyle the world last,
And to all the goddes an hygh dyspleser
  To see the game so dystroyed by hys blast; 74
Wherfore a remedy puruey in hast,
  And let hym be punysshyd aftyr hys offence.
Consyder the cryme and yeue your sentence." 77

This brings reproach to Diana and displeasure to all the gods, and requires punishment.

The Complaint against Eolus.

12

And when thus Diana had made her compleynt 78
To Mynos, the Iuge, in Plutoys p*r*esence,
Neptune next rehearses his complaint to Minos. Came forthe Neptun*us*, w*ith* vysage pale & feynt,
Desyryng of fauo*ur* to haue audyence, 81
Saying thus, "Pluto to thy magnyfycence
I shall reherse what thys creature
Eolus hath dooñ to me out of mesure. 84

13

"Thow knowest well that I haue the charge 85
Ouer all the see, and theŕof god I am,
For himself he claims jurisdiction over the sea, No shyp may sayle, keruell, boot ner barge,
Gret karyk, nor hulke w*ith* any lyuyng man, 88
But yef he haue my safe condyte than.
Who me offendeth w*ith*yn my iurysdiccion
Oweth to submyt hym to my correccion. 91

14

"But in as mekyll as hit ys now soo 92
That ye hym here haue as yo*ur* prysonere,
I shall yow shew my compleynt loo,
Wherfore I pray yow that ye woll hit here, 95
And let hym nat escape out of yo*ur* daungere,
Tyll he haue made full seethe and recompence
For hurt of my name thorough thys gret offence. 98

15

"Furst, to begynne, thys Eolus hath oft 99
Made me to retourne my course agayñ nature
but Eolus causes him to turn against his course, W*ith* hys gret blastys, when he hath be a loft,
And chargyd me to labouŕ ferre out of mesure, 102
That hit was gret merueyle how I myght endure.
The [foom] of my ṣwet, wyll hit testyfy,
That on the see bankes lythe betyn full hy. 105

16

"Secundly, where as my nature ys 106
Bothe to ebbe and flowe and so my course to kepe,
and ebb and flow out of his season. Oft of myñ entent hath he made me mys.
Where as I shuld haue fyllyd dykes depe 109
At a full watyr I might nat thedyŕ crepe
Before my seson came to retorne ayeyne,
And then went I fastyŕ than I wold certeyne. 112

In the Court of Minos.

17

"Thus he hath me dryuen ayeñ myn entent 113 *This Eolus had done to his dishonour.*
And contrary to my course naturall.
Where I shuld haue be he made me be absent
   To my gret dyshonouȓ, & in especiall 116
   Oo thyng he vsyd that worst was of all,
     For where as I my sauegard grauntyd,
     Ay in that cost he comonly hauntyd. 119

18

"Of verrey pure malyce and of sylfe wyll, 120 *Out of very malice Eolus destroyed those to whom he had granted protection,*
   Theym to dystroy in dyspyte of me
To whom I promysyd, bothe in good and yll,
   To be heȓ protectouȓ in aduersyte, 123
   That to theym shuld fall opon the see,
     And euyn sodenly, er they coude beware,
     With a sodeyn pyry, he lappyd hem in care. 126

19

"And full oft sythe with hys boystous blast, 127 *or else brought them to wreck; wherefore his name is held in dishonor.*
   Er they myght be ware he drofe hym on the sande.
And other whyle he brak top seyle and mast,
   Whyche causyd theym to perysshe eȓ they came to lande.
   Then cursyd they the tyme that euer they me fande.
     Thus among the pepyll lost ys my name
     And so by hys labour put I am to shame. 133

20

"Consydre thys mateȓ and ponder my cause; 134 *The great offense requires a grievous punishment.*
   Tendre my compleynt as rygouȓ requyreth;
Shew forthe your sentence with a breef clause.
   I may nat long tary, the tyme fast expyreth, 137
   The offence ys gret, wherfore hyt desyreth
     The more greuous peyne and hasty iugement.
     For offence dooñ wylfully woll noon aysment." 140

21

And, when the god Pluto awhyle had hym bethought, 141 *Pluto advises Minos to judge fairly between the parties.*
   He rownyd with Mynos to know what was to do.
Then he seyd opynly, "Loke thow fayle nought
   Thy sentence to yeue without favour so, 144
   Lyke as thow hast herde the causys meuyd the to;
     And so euenly dele twene these partyes tweyn,
     That nooñ of hem haue cause on the other compleyñ."

Invitation of Apollo.

22

Minos asks for further charges,

Then seyd Mynos full indyfferently, 148
    To Dyane & Neptunus, "Ys ther any more
That ye wyll declare agayñ hym opynly?"
    "Nay in dede," they seyde, "we kepe nooñ in store. 151
We haue seyde ynough to punysshe hym sore.
    Yef ye in thys matyr be nat parciall,
Remembre your name was wont to be egall." 154

23

and wishes to hear what Eolus can say for himself.

"Well then," seyd Mynos, "now let vs here 155
    What thys boystous Eolus for hymself can sey,
For here, prima facie, to vs he doth apere
    That he hath offendyd—no man can sey nay. 158
Wherfore thow Eolus, without more delay,
    Shape vs an answer to thyne accusement.
And ellys I most procede opon thy iugement." 161

24

A messenger enters from Apollo inviting the gods to a banquet and

And euyn as Eolus was onwarde to haue seyde 162
    For hys excuse, came yn a messynger
Fro god Apollo to Pluto, and hym prayde
    On hys behalfe that he without daungere 165
Wold to hym come & bryng with hym [in] feere
    Diane & Neptunus on to hys banket;
And yef they dysdeynyd hymsylf he wold hem fet. 168

25

requests the suspension of judgment upon Eolus, if Diana and Neptune should be therewith content.

Moreouer he seyde to the god, Apollo 169
    Desyryd to haue respyte of the iugement
Of Eolus, bothe of Mynos & Pluto.
    So Dyane and Neptunus were therwith content, 172
And yef they were dysposyd to assent
    That he myght come vnto hys presence,
He hit desyryd to know hys offence. 175

26

The Court is therefore dismissed.

"What sey ye herto," seyd Pluto to hem tweyn, 176
    "Wyll ye bothe assent that hit shall be thus?"
"Ye," seyde the goddesse, "for my part certeyn."
    "And I also," seyde thys Neptunus. 179
"I am well plesyd," quod thys Eolus.
    And when they had a whyle thus togedyr spoke,
Pluto commaundyd the court to be broke. 182

27

And then togedyr̃ went they in fere, 183
  Pluto & Neptun*us* ledyng the goddesse,
Whom folowyd Cerberus w*it*h hys prysonere.
  And alther last w*it*h gret heuynesse 186
  Came I & Morpheus to the forteresse
    Of the god Apollo vnto hys banket,
    Where many goddys & goddesses met. 189

Pluto, Neptune and Diana, Cerberus and Eolus, Morpheus and I, come to the palace of Apollo, where many gods and goddesses are met.

28

When Apollo sye that they were come, 190
  He was ryght glad and prayed hem to syt.
"Nay," seyd Diane, "thys ys all and some.
  Ye shall me pardone, I shall nat syt yet. 193
  I shall fyrst know why Eolus abyte
    And what execucion shall on hym be do
    For hys offence." "Well," seyd Apollo, 196

Apollo welcomes them with gladness.

Diana refuses to sit until judgment is pronounced on Eolus.

29

"Madame, ye shall haue all your̃ plesere, 197
  Syth that hit woll none other wyse be.
But furst I yow pray let me the mater̃ here,
  Why he ys brought in thys p*er*plexyte." 200
  "Well," seyde Pluto, "that shall ye sone se."
    And gan to declare euen by and by
    Bothe her compleyntes ordynatly. 203

Pluto recounts the complaints against Eolus,

30

And when Apollo had herd the report 204
  Of Pluto, in a man*er* smylyng he seyde,
"I see well, Eolus, thow hast small comfort
  Thy sylf to excuse; thow mayst be dysmayde 207
  To here so gret compleyn*tes* ayene the layde.
    That natw*it*hstandyng, yef thow can sey ought
    For thyne owne wele, sey and tary nought." 210

who is requested to give his excuses.

31

"Forsothe," seyd Eolus, "yef I had respyte, 211
  Her̃ to an answere cowde I counterfete.
But to haue her̃ grace more ys my delyte.
  Wherfore, I pray you all for me entrete, 214
  That I may, by your̃ request, her̃ good grace gete.
    And what pyne or greef ye for me prouyde,
    W*it*hout any grogyng I shall hit abyde." 217

Eolus speaks suing for the grace of Diana.

The Complaint Dismissed.

32

Apollo pleads for Eolus that the goddess show pity, on account of his great sorrow,

"Lo, good Madame," seyd god Apollo, 218
"What may he do more but sew to yo*ur* grace.
Beholde how the teares from hys eyen go.
Hit ys satysfaccion half for hys trespase. 221
Now gloryous goddesse shewe yo*ur* pyteous face
To thys poore pryson*er* at my request.
All we for you*r* honou*r* thynke thus ys best. 224

33

and assures her if she forgive Eolus and he afterwards rebel that for every tree destroyed a hundred shall grow

"And yef hit lyke yow to do in thys wyse, 225
And to foryeue hym clerely hys offense,
Oõn thyng suerly I will yow promyse,
Yef he eft rebelle and make resystence 228
Or dysobey vnto you*r* sentence,
For eu*er*y tree that he maketh fall,
Out of the erthe an hundred aryse shall. 231

34

for the protection of game.

"So that you*r* game shall nat dyscrese 232
For lak of shade, I dar vndyrtake."
"Well, sy*r* Apollo," seyde she than, "woll I cese
Of all my ranco*ur* and mery w*ith* yow make." 235
And then god Neptun*us* of hys mater spake,

Diana grants release.

Seying thus, "Apollo, though Diana hym relese,
Yet shall he su to me to haue hys pese." 238

35

"A," seyde Apollo, "ye wend I had foryete 239
Yow for my lady Diane, the goddesse.

For Neptune's case Phebe is accepted as arbiter.

Nay, thynke nat so, for I woll yow entrete
As well as hyr w*ith*out long processe. 242
Wyll ye agre that Pheb[e] yo*ur* mastresse
May haue the guydyng of yo*ur* varyaunce?"
"I shall abyde," quod he, "her ordynaunce." 245

36

Apollo prays the gods and goddesses to fall to the banquet.

"Well then," quod Apollo, "I pray you godd*es* all, 246
And goddesses eke, that be heere p*r*esent,
That ye compaygnably wyll aboorde fall."

Athena requests that due order be preserved.

"Nay then," seyde Othea, "hit ys nat conuenyent, 249
A dew ordre in eu*er*y place ys expedyent
To be had, wherfore ye may nat let
To be you*r* owne marchall at you*r* owne banket." 252

Assembly of the Gods.

37

And when Apollo sy hit wold nooñ other be, 253 *First, with Apollo, is set Aurora, wet with morning tears.*
   He callyd to hym Aurora, the goddesse,
And seyde, "Thowgh ye wepe yet shal ye before me
     Ay kepe your course & put your sylf in [presse]." 256
So he her set furst at hys owne messe,
   With her moyst clothes with teares all be spreynt.
   The medewes in May shew therof her compleynt. 259

38

Next hyr sate Mars, myghty god & strong, 260 *Next, Mars, environed with flame, an iron crown upon his head, a spear in his hand.*
   With a flame of fyre enuyround all about,
A crowne of yron on hys hede, a spere in hys hand.
   Hyt semyd by hys chere as he wold haue fought. 263
And next vnto hym, as I perceue mought, *With him is Diana, in a mantle of silk and ermine.*
   Sate the goddese Diana, in a mantell fyne
   Of blak sylke, purfylyd with poudryd hermyne, 266

39

Lyke as she had take the mantell & the ryng. 267
   And next vnto hyr, arayed royally,
Sate the good Iupyter, in hys demenyng *Jupiter sits next, sad and wise, wearing a crown of tin.*
   Full sad, and wyse he semyd sykerly. 270
A crowñ of tynne stoode on hys hede.
   And that I recorde of all philosophres
   That lytyll store of coyne kepe in her cofres. 273

40

Ioynyd to hym in syttyng next ther was 274 *With him is Juno, dressed in royal richness.*
   The goddesse Iuno, full rychely beseene
In a sercote that shone as bryght as glas,
   Of goldsmythes werke with spanglys wrought be-dene.
   Of royall rychesse wantyd she noone I wene.
   And next by her sate the god Saturne, *Saturn next,*
   That oft sythe causeth many ooñ to morne. 280

41

But he was clad me thought straungely, 281 *arrayed in frost and snow, a bloody falchion in his hand, a ring of icicles about his neck, a crown of lead on high.*
   For of frost & snow was all his aray;
In hys hand he helde a fawchon all blody.
   Hyt semyd by hys chere as he wold make a fray. 284
A bawdryk of isykles about hys nek gay
   He had, and aboue an hygh on hys hede, [leede.
   Cowchyd with hayle stonys, he weryd a crowne of

42

With him sits Ceres in a garment of sackcloth embroidered with sheaves and sickles.

And next in ordre was set by hys syde 288
 Ceres, the goddesse, in a garment
Of sak clothe made w*ith* sleues large & wyde,
 Embrowderyd w*ith* sheues & sykelys bent. 291
  Of all man*er* greynes she sealyd the patent,
   In token that she was the goddesse of corne.
   Olde poetys sey she bereth the heruest horne. 294

43

Next Cupid, dressed in gallant array with jewels, so that the palace shone. He sits embracing Ceres with one arm.

Then was there set the god Cupido, 295
 All fresshe & galaunt & costlew in aray.
W*ith* ouches & ryng*es* he was beset so
 The paleys therof shone as though hit had be day. 298
  A kerchyef of plesaunce stood ouer hys helme ay.
   The goddesse Ceres he lookyd in the face
   And w*ith* oon arme he hyr dyd enbrace. 301

44

With him is Athena, clad in purple with a pearly crown.

Next to Cupido in ordyr by and by, 302
 Of worldly wysdom̄, sate the forteresse
Callyd Othea, chyef grounde of polycy,
 Rewler of knyghthode, of Prudence the goddese. 305
  Clad all in p*ur*pur̄ was she more & lesse,
   Safe oñ her hede a crowne ther̄ stood,
   Cowchyd w*ith* perles, oryent, fyne and good. 308

45

Pluto next, environed in mist and clothed in a smoky net, smelling of fire and sulphur.

And next to her was god Pluto set, 309
 W*ith* a derke myst enuyrond all aboute,
Hys clothyng was made of a smoky net.
 Hys colo*ur* was, bothe w*ith*yn & w*ith*oute, 312
  Foule, derke & dy*m*me; hys eyen gret & stoute.
   Of fyre and sulphure all hys odo*ur* wase;
   That wo was me whyle I behelde hys fase. 315

46

Fortune sits with him; she is dressed gaudily in green.

Fortune, the goddesse, w*ith* her party face 316
 Was vnto Pluto next in ordre set.
Varyaunt she was; ay in short space
 Hyr whele was redy to turne w*ith*out let. 319
  Hyr gowne was of gawdy grene chamelet,
   Chaungeable of sondry dyu*er*se colowres,
   To the condycyons accordyng of hyr shoures. 322

Assembly of the Gods.

47
And by her sate though he vnworthy were, 323   By her is god Pan dressed
   The rewde god Pan, of shep*er*dys the gyde,   rudely, a tar-box by his
Clad in russet frese, & breched lyke a bere,   side, a sheep-crook in his
   W*ith* a gret tar box hangyng by hys syde. 326   hand,
A shepecrook in hys hand he sparyd for no pryde.   at his feet a
   And at hys feete lay a prykeryd curre.   cur.
He ratelyd in the throte as he had the murre. 329

48
Ysys, the goddesse, bare hym company. 330   Isys keeps him company in a
   For at the table next she sat by hys syde,   dress embroid-ered with
In a close kyrtyll enbrowderyd curyously,   leaves and branches.
   W*ith* braunches & leues, brood, large & wyde, 333
Grene as any gresse in the som*er*tyde.
   Of all maner frute she had the gou*er*naunce.
Of sauerys odoryferous was her sustynaunce. 336

49
Next hyr was then god Neptun*us* set. 337   Neptune sits next. Fishes
   He sauoryd lyke a fyssher—of hy*m* I spake before.   hang at his girdle. A ship
Hyt semyd by hys clothes as they had be wet. [score.   is his crest.
   Aboute hym, in hys gyrdyll stede, hyng fysshes many a
Of hys straunge aray m*er*uelyd I sore.
   A shyp w*ith* a toppe & seyle was hys crest.
Me thought he was gayly dysgysyd at that fest. 343

50
Then toke Mynerue, the goddesse, her sete 344   With him sits Minerva, clad
   Joyntly to Neptun*us*, all in curas clad,   in armor, a hammer and
Gauntlett*es* on hyr handys, & sabatouns on hyr fete.   scythe upon her head.
   She loked eu*er* about as though she had be mad. 347
An hamer and a sythe on her hede she had.
   She weryd ii bokelers, ooñ by her syde, [pryde.
That other ye wote where; thys was all her 350

51
Then came the good Bachus, and by her set hym downe,   Bacchus sits by her, clad in
   Holdyng in hys hande a cup full of wyne.   grape clusters, a cup of wine
Of grene vyne leues he weryd a ioly crowne.   in his hand. His sign is a
   He was clad in clustres of grapes good and fyne. 354   garland of yew.
A garland of yuy he chase for hys sygne;
   On hys hede he had a thredebare kendall hood;
A gymlot and a fauset ther*r*opon stood. 357

52

With him sits pale Phebe, boasting of her rule.	Next hym sate Pheb[e], with hyr colour pale. 358
	   Fat she was of face but of complexyon feynt.
	  She seyde she rewlyd Neptunus and made hym to avale,
	     And ones in the moneth with Phebus was she meynt.
	       Also ne were she Ceres were ateynt.

She wears a silver crown.	Thus she sate & tolde the myght of hyr nature, And on hyr hede she weryd a crowne of syluyr pure.

53

Mercury seats himself next, a god of golden tongue. In his hand he has a box of quicksilver.	Ioyntly to her Mercurius tooke hys see 365
	  As came to hys course—wytnesse the zodyak.
	He had a gyldyn tong, as fyll for hys degree.
	  In eloquence of langage he passyd all the pak, 368
	    For in hys talkyng no man cowde fynde lak.
	     A box with quyksyluer he had in hys hand,
	      Multyplyers know hit well in euery land. 371

54

His companion is Venus, bright of chere, dressed curiously, her hair like gold wire.	By him sate Dame Venus with colour crystallyne, 372
	  Whoos long here shone as wyre of goold bryght.
	Cryspe was her skyñ, her eyen columbyne,
	  Rauysshyd myñ hert her chere was so lyght. 375
	    Patronesse of plesaunce, be namyd well se myght.
	     A smokke was her wede, garnysshyd curyously.
	      But aboue all other she had a wanton ey. 378

55

She wears a copper crown.	On her hede she weryd a rede copyr crowne. 379 A nosegay she had made full pleasauntly.

Between Aurora and Venus Apollo sits him down. He gives light to the company. His crown is of gold.	Betwene her and Aurora, Apollo set hym downe.
	  With hys beames bryght he shone so feruently 382
	    That he therwith gladyd all the company.
	     A crowne of pure gold was on hys hede set,
	      In sygne that he was mastyr & lord of that banket.

56

Waiting at the table are poets and philosophers: Cicero, Aristotle, Ptolemy, Dorothe, Diogenes, Plato, Messala, Socrates,	Thus was the table set rownde aboute 386
	  With goddys & goddesses, as I haue yow tolde.
	Awaytyng on the boorde was a gret route
	  Of sage phylosophyrs & poetes many folde. 389
	    Ther was sad Sychero & Arystotyll olde,
	     Tholome, Dorothe, with Dyogenes,
	      Plato, Messehala, & wyse Socrates. 392

Discord and Atropos.

57

Sortes and Saphyrus wit*h* Hermes stood behynde.	393
Auycen and Aueroys with hem were in fere.	
Galyen & Ipocras, that physyk haue in mynde,	
Wit*h* helpe of Esculapion, toward hem drow͡ here.	396
Virgyle, Orace, Ouyde and Omere,	
Euclyde, and Albert yaue he͡r attendaunce,	
To do the goddys and goddesses plesaunce.	399

Sortes, Saphirus, Hermes, Avicen, Averroes, Galen, Hypocras, Esculapius, Virgil, Horace, Ovid, Homer, Euclid and Albert.

58

Whore berdyd Orpheus was there wit*h* hys harpe	400
And as a poet musykall made he melody.	
Othyr mynstrall had they none, safe Pan gan to carpe	
Of hys lewde bagpype, whyche causyd the company	403
To lawe. Yet many mo the͡r were, yef I shuld nat ly,	
Som yong, som olde, bothe bettyr and werse,	
But mo of her names can I not reherse.	406

Orpheus and Pan act as minstrels.

59

Of all man*er* deyntees the͡r was habundaunce,	407
Of metys & drynkes foyson plenteuous.	
In came Dyscord to haue made varyaunce.	
But the͡re was no rome to set hy͡r in that hous.	410
The goddys remembryd the scisme odyous	
Among the three goddesses that [s]he had wrought	
At the fest of Peleus, wherfor they thought	413

Discord enters but can gain no seat,

60

They wold nat wit*h* he͡r dele in auenture	414
Lest she theym brought to som inconuenyent.	
She, seyng thys, was wrothe out of mesure	
And in that gret wrethe out of the paleyce went,	417
Seying to hersylf that chere shuld þey repent.	
And anone wit*h* Attropos happyd she to mete,	
As he had bene a goste came in wyndyng shete.	420

thence departs in wrath, meeting on the way with Atropos,

61

She toke hym by the hande & rownyd in hys eare	421
And told hym of the banket that was so delycate,	
Howe she was resceuyd, what chere she had there,	
And howe eu*er*y god sate in hys estate. [date!"	
"Ys hit thus!" quod Attropos, "what in the deuyllys	
"Well," he seyde, "I see well howe the game gooth,	
Ones yet for you͡r sake shall I make hem wrooth."	427

62

who takes her part, and comes into the palace.

And when she had hym all togedyr tolde, 428
From her he departyd and of hyr toke hys leue,
Seying that for hyr sake hys wey take he wolde
In to the paleyce hys matyrs to meue. 431
And er he thens went he trowyd hem to greue
With suche tydynges as he shuld hem tell.
So forthe yn he went & spake wordys fell. 434

63

He looks like a madman and salutes the company rudely.

When he came in the presence of the goddes all, 435
As he had be woode he lookyd hym about.
His shete from his body down he let fall,
And on a rewde maner he salutyd all the rout, 438
With a bold voyse, carpyng wordys stout.
But he spake all holow, as hit had be oon
Had spoke in another world þat had woo begoon. 441

64

Atropos makes his charge:

He stood forthe boldly with grym countenaunce, 442
Saying in thys wyse as ye shall here,
"All ye gret goddys yeue attendaunce

He reminds the gods of his office of death-bringing

Vnto my wordys without all daungere, 445
Remembre howe ye made me your offycere
All tho with my dart fynally to chastyse
That yow dysobeyed or wold your law dyspyse. 448

65

"And for the more sewerte ye seelyd my patent, 449
Yeuyng me full power soo to occupy,
Wherto I haue enployed myn entent
And that can Dame Nature well testyfy; 452
Yef she be examynyd she woll hit nat deny.
For when she forsaketh any creature,
I am ay redy to take hym to my cure. 455

66

unto every man.

"Thus haue I dewly, with all my dilygence, 456
Executyd the offyce of olde antiquyte,
To me by yow grauntyd, by your comon sentence.
For I spared noon hygh nor low degre, 459
So that on my part no defaute hath be.
For as sone as any to me commyttyd wase
I smete hym to the hert—he had noon other grase.

Complaint of Atropos.

67

"Ector of Troy, for all hys chyualry, 463 *All have fallen:*
   Alexaunder, the grete & myghty conquero*ur*, *Hector, Alexander,*
Iulius Cesar, wi*th* all hys company, *Cæsar, David, Joshua,*
   Dauid, nor Iosue, nor worthy Artou$\bar{r}$, 466 *Arthur, Charles,*
Charles the noble, that was so gret of honou$\bar{r}$, *Judas Machabeus, Godfrey,*
   Nor Iudas Machabee for all hys trew hert,
     Nor Godfrey of Boley$\tilde{n}$ cowde me nat astert. 469

68

"Nabugodonozor, for all hys gret pryde, 470 *Nebuchadnezzar,*
   Nor the King of Egypt, cruell Pharao, *Pharao, Jason, Hercules, Cosdras*
Iason, ne Hercules, went they neu*er* so wyde, *Hannibal,*
   Cosdras, Hanyball, nor gentyll Sypio, 473 *Scipio, Cyrus and Achilles.*
Cirus, Achilles, nor many another mo,
   For feyre or foule gat of me no grace.
     But all be at the last I sesyd hem wi*th* my mace. 476

69

"Thus hav I brought eu*er*y creature 477 *All have been brought to their end except one.*
   To an ende bothe man, fysshe, foule & beste,
And eu*er*y other thyng in whom Dame Nature
   Hath any iurysdiccion, owther most or leste, 480
Except oonly oo$\tilde{n}$ in whom yo*ur* beheste
   Ys to me broke; for ye me promysyd
     That my myght of noo$\tilde{n}$ shuld haue be dyspysyd. 483

70

"Whe$\bar{r}$of the contrary, dar I well avowe, 484
   Ys trew; for oo$\tilde{n}$ there ys that wyll nat apply *This one the gods guard*
Vnto my correccion nor in no wyse bowe *contrary to their agreement.*
   To the dynt of my dart for doole nor destyny. 487
What comfort he hath, nor the cause why
   That he so rebelleth, I can nat thynke of ryght [dyght.
     But yef ye haue hym grauntyd yo*ur* aldyrs saf con-

71

"And yef ye so haue, then do ye nat as goddys, 491
   For a godd*es* wrytyng may nat reu*er*syd be. *Therefore justice is*
Yef hit shuld I wold nat yeue II pesecoddys *demanded.*
   For graunt of yo*ur* patent of offyce ne$\bar{r}$ of fee. 494
Wherfore in thys mate$\bar{r}$ do me equyte
   Accordyng to my patent, for tyll thys be do
     Ye haue no more my s*er*uyce nor my good wyll lo."

72

The gods all promise their aid in destroying the man.	And when all the godd*es* had Attropos herde,	498
	As they had be woode they brayde vp at oonys	
	And seyde they wold nat reste tyll he were conqueryd,	
	Takeñ and dystroyed, boody, blood and boonys;	501
	And that they swere gret othes for the noonys	
	Her lawe to dyspyce, that was so malapert.	
	They seyde he shuld be taught for to be so pert.	504

73

Apollo will confound him with his car.

"Well," seyde Apollo, "yef he on erthe bee,   505
Wyth my brennyng chare I shall hym confound."
"In feythe," quod Neptun*us*, "& yef he kepe the see,

Neptune will drown him.

He may be full sure he shall sone be drownd."   508
"A syr," seyd Mars, "thys haue we well fownd
That any dysobeyed owre godly p*re*cept,
We may well thynke we haue to long slept.   511

74

Mars will pursue him with thunder and lightning,

"But neu*er*thelese where I may hym fynde   512
W*ith* thundre and leyte about I shall hym chase."
"And I," quod Saturn*us*, "before and behynde

Saturn will freeze him,

W*ith* my bytter colde shall shew hy*m* hard grase."   515
"Well," seyd M*er*curius, "yef I may see hys fase,

Mercury will deprive him of speech.

For euer of hys speche I shall hym depryue;
So that hym were bettyr be dede than a lyue."   518

75

Athena suggests that the offender may be in the air, and without help of Eolus their anger is in vain; therefore she counsels that Neptune forgive his rancor.

"Ye," quod Othea, "yet may he well be   519
In the eyre where he woll & ax yow no leue,
Wherfore, my counsell ys that all we
May entrete Neptunus hys ranco*ur* to foryeue,   522
And then I dowte not Eolus wyll hym myscheue;
So may ye be sewre he shall yow nat escape,
And elles of all you*r* angre woll he make but a iape."

76

But I have forgotten to tell you how Eolus came into Pluto's power.

But for to tell yow how Eolus was brought   526
In daung*er* of Pluto yet had I foryete,
Wherfore oñ thys mater ferther wyll I nought
Procede, tyll I therof haue knowleche yow lete.   529
Hyt fell on a day the wedyr was wete

In wet weather Eolus, to revive his spirits,

And Eolus thought he wold on hys disport
Go to reioyse hys spyryt*es* and comfort.   532

77

He thought he wold see what was in the grownd, 533	entered the earth by a crevice, which was compressed by the water, shutting Eolus in.
And in a krauers forthe he gan hym dresse.	
A drowthe had the erthe late before fownd	
That causyd hit to chyne & krany more and lesse. 536	
Sodeynly by weet constreynyd by duresse	
Was the ground to close hys superfyciall face	
So strayte that to scape Eolus had no space. 539	

78

Thys seyng Eolus he styll wi*th*yn aboode, 540	He was reported to Pluto, who ordered Cerberus to take charge of the prisoner.
Sekyng where he myght haue goon out fer or nere.	
Anone he was aspyed and ooñ to Pluto roode	
And told hym how Eolus was in hys daungere. 543	
Then seyde he to Cerberus, "Fet me that prysonere	
Till I haue hym seene; let him nat go at large.	
As thow wylt answer of hym I yeue *þ*e charge." 546	

79

Thus was thys Eolus take prysoner. 547	On that day the court of Minos sat, whither Eolus was brought as I have told you,
Then happyd hit so that the same day	
Pluto had pr*e*fyxyd for a gret mater	
Mynos to syt in his roob of ray. 550	
Wherfore Cerberus tooke the next way	
And led hym to the place where the court shalbe,	
Whedyr as I tolde yow Morpheus brought me. 553	

80

So thedyr came Diana caryed in a carre, 554	and there Diana and Neptune made their complaints as I said.
To make her compleynt as I told yow all.	
And so dyd Neptun*us*, that dothe bothe make & marre,	
Walewyng w*ith* hys wawes & tomblyng as a ball. 557	
Her matyrs they meuyd fall what may befall.	
Ther was the furst syght that eu*er* I they*m* sawe,	
And yef I neu*er* do efte I rekke nat a strawe. 560	

81

Bot now to my matyr to returne ageyñ 561	To return to my matter of Atropos.
And to begynne newe where I left—	
When all the godd*es* had done her besy peyñ	
The wey to contryue how he shuld be reft 564	
Of hys lyfe, that Attropos had no cause eft	
To compleyñ, than Pheb[e] styrt vppon her fete	
And seyd, "I pray yow let me speke a worde yete: 567	Phebe wishes to speak.

2

82

She alone dares to entreat Neptune	"Othea meneth well to sey on thys wyse, 568
But all to entrete Neptun*us*, I hope, shall nat nede.
Me semeth I alone durst take that entyrpryse
E*r* I am begylyd, or elles I shall spede. 571
How say ye, Neptun*us*, shall I do thys dede?
Wyll ye you*r* rancou*r* sese at my request?"
"Madame," quod he, "reule me as ye lyketh best." 574

83

to leave all old rancor.	"Gram*er*cy," seyd she, "of yo*ur* good wyll 575
That hit pleseth yow to shew me that fauo*ur*,
Wherefore the godd*es* hygh plesure to fulfyll,
P*er*forme my desyre & leeue all olde ranco*ur*, 578
For ou*r* aldyrs wele & sauyng of our hono*ur*,
Ageyñ thys Eolus that ye long haue had."
Neptune forgives.	"Hyt ys dooñ," quoth he, "forsoth then am I glad."

84

	Seyde he, "*N*ow then, Eolus, be thow to vs trew, 582
Kepe well the ey*r*, and owre gret rebell
May we then soone eu*er* to vs subdew."
Eolus agrees to afflict the offender with his blasts.	"Yes and that," quod Eolus, "shall ye here tell 585
No where in the eyre shall he reste nor dwell.
Yef he do the*r*of, put me in defaute,
W*ith* my bytter blastys so shall I hym asaute." 588

85

Pluto asks their enemy's name.	"What," seyde the god Pluto, "what ys hys name 589
That thus p*r*esumeth ageyñ vs to rebell?"
Atropos replies that it is Virtue; whereat Pluto grants his assistance	"V*er*tew," quod Attropos, "that haue he mykyll shame,
He ys neu*er* confoundyd, thus of hym here I tell." 592
"A," seyde thys Pluto, "in dede I know hym well,
He hathe be eu*er* myn vtter enemy.
Wherfore thys mate*r* ageyñ hym take wyll I. 595

86

"For all the baytys that ye for hym haue leyde, 596
W*ith*out myñ helpe, be nat worth a peere.
For though ye all the contrary had seyde,
Yet wolde he breede ryght nygh yo*ur* althrys eere. 599
No man*er* of thyng can hym hurt nor dere
Saue oonly ooñ, a soñ of myñ bastard,
Whos name ys Vy*c*e — he kepeth my vaward. 602

87

"Wherfore, yow Cerberus, now I the dyscharge   603   *and sends Cerberus to bring Vice to make battle with Virtue.*
Of Eolus, and wyll that thow hydyr fette
My dere son Vyce, & sey that I hym charge
 That he to me come w*ith*out any lette,   606
 Armyd at all poyntes, for a day ys sette,
  That he w*it*h Vertew for all the godd*es* sake,
  In our defense must on hym batayll take."   609

88

Forthe then went Cerberus w*it*h hys fyry cheyne   610   *Cerberus leads forward Vice who comes riding on a winged serpent breathing fire.*
And brought thedyr Vyce, as he co*m*maundyd was,
Ageyñ noble V*er*tew that batayll to dereygne.
 On a glydyng s*er*pent rydyng a gret pas,   613
 Formyd lyke a dragoñ, scalyd harde as glas,
  Whos mouth flamyd feere w*ith*out fayll.
  Wyngys had hit s*er*pentyne and a long tayll.   616

89

Armyd was Vyce all in cure boyle,   617
Hard as any horñ, blakker feȓ then soot.
An vngoodly soort folowyd hym parde,   *Following him is a host of captains, Pride on a lion, Envy on a wolf,*
Of vnhappy capteyns of myschyef croppe & roote.   620
 Pryde was the furst *þ*at next hy*m* roode, God woote,
  On a roryng lyoñ; next whom came Enuy,
  Syttyng on a wolfe—he had a scorñfull ey.   623

90

Wrethe bestrode a wylde bore, and next hem gan ryde.   *Wrath on a wild-boar,*
 In hys hand he bare a blody nakyd swerde.
Next whom̃ came Couetyse, that goth so feȓ and wyde,   *Covetousness on an elephant*
 Rydyng on a olyfaunt, as he had beñ aferde.   627
Aftyr whom̃ rood Glotony, w*it*h hys fat berde,   *Gluttony on a bear,*
 Syttyng on a bere, w*it*h hys gret bely.
  And next hym on a goot folowyd Lechery.   630   *Lechery on a goat,*

91

Slowthe was so slepy he came all behynde   631   *Sloth on an ass.*
 On a dull asse, a full wery pase.
These were the capyteyns that Vyce cowde fynde
 B[e]st to set hys felde and folow on the chase.   634   *Inferior captains are: Sacrilege, Simony, etc.*
As for pety capteyns many mo the[r] wase;
 As Sacrylege, Symony, & Dyssimulacion,
  Manslaught*er*, Mordre, Theft & Extorcion,   637

92

Arrogaunce, Presumpcion, with Contumacy,	638
Contempcion, Contempt, & Inobedience,	
Malyce, Frowardnes, Gret Ielacy,	
Woodnesse, Hate, Stryfe, and Impacience,	641
Vnkyndnesse, Oppression, with Wofull Neglygence,	
Murmour, Myschyef, Falshood & Detraccion,	
Vsury, Periury, Ly, and Adulacion,	644

93

Wrong, Rauyne, Sturdy Vyolence,	645
False Iugement, with Obstynacy,	
Dysseyte, Dronkenes, and Improuydence,	
Boldnes in Yll, with Foule Rybaudy,	648
Fornycacion, Incest, and Auoutry,	
Vnshamefastnes, with Prodygalyte,	
Blaspheme, Veynglory, & Wordly Vanyte,	651

94

Ignoraunce, Diffydence, with Ipocrysy,	652
Scysme, Rancour, Debate, & Offense,	
Heresy, Errour, with Idolatry,	
New-Fangylnes, & sotyll False Pretense,	655
Inordinat Desyre of Worldly Excellense,	
Feynyd Pouert, with Apostasy,	
Disclaundyr, Skorne, & Vnkynde Ielousy,	658

95

Hoordam̃, Bawdry, False Mayntenaunce,	659
Treson, Abusion, & Pety Brybry ;	
Vsurpacion, with Horryble Vengeaunce,	
Came alther last of that company.	662
All these pety capteyns folowyd by & by,	
Shewyng theymsylf in the palyse wyde,	
And seyde they were redy that batayll to abyde.	665

96

There is a host of commons led by Idleness,

Idylnesse set the comons in aray	666
Without the paleyse on a fayre felde.	
But there was an oost for to make a fray !	
I trow suche another neuer man behelde !	669
Many was the wepyn among hem þat þey welde !	
What pepyll they were that came to that dysport	
I shall yow declare of many a sondry sort.	672

The Vices.

97
Theī were bosters, braggars, & brybores, 673 boasters, braggers, etc.
Praters, fasers, strechers, & wrythers,
Shamefull shakerles, soleyn shaueldores,
Oppressours of pepyll, and myghty crakers, 676
Meyntenours of querelles, horryble lyers,
Theues, traytours, w*it*h false herytykes,
Charmers, sorcerers, & many scismatykes, 679

98
Pryuy symonyak*es*, w*it*h false vsurers, 680
Multyplyers, coyñ wasshers & clyppers,
Wrong vsurpers, w*it*h gret extorcioners,
Bakbyters, glosers, & fayre flaterers, 683
Malycious murmurers, w*it*h grete claterers,
Tregetours, tryphelers, feyners of tales,
Lastyuyous lurdeyns, & pykers of males, 686

99
Rowners, uagaboundes, forgers of lesyng*es*, 687
Robbers, reuers, rauenouse ryfelers,
Choppers of churches, fynders of tydyng*es*,
Marrers of maters, & money makers, 690
Stalkers by nyght, w*it*h euesdroppers,
Fyghters, brawlers, brekers of lofedayes,
Getters, chyders, causers of frayes, 693

100
Tytyuyllys, tyraunt*es*, w*it*h turmentoures, 694
Cursyd apostat*es*, relygyous dyssymulers,
Closshers, carders, w*it*h comon hasardoures,
Tyburne coloppys, and pursekytters, 697
Pylary knyght*es*, double tollyng myllers,
Gay ioly tapsters, w*it*h hostelers of the stewes,
Hoores, and baudys—that many bale brewes, 700

101
Colde blasphemers, w*it*h false ipocrytes, 701
Brothelles, brokers, abhomynable swerers,
Dryuylles, dastard*es*, dyspysers of ryghtes,
Homycydes, poyseners, & comon morderers, 704
Skoldes, caytyffys, comborouse clappers,
Idolatres, enchauntours, w*it*h false renegates,
Sotyll ambidextres, & sekers of debates, 707

102

Pseudo prophetes, false sodomytes, 708
  Quelmers of chyldren, with fornycatours,
Wetewoldes that suffre syn in her syghtes,
  Auouterers, & abhominable auauntours 711
Of syn, gret clappers, & makers of clamours;
  Vnthryftys, & vnlustes came also to that game,
  With luskes, & loselles that myght nat thryue for shame.

103

These were the comons came thedyr that day 715
  Redy bowne in batayll Vertew to abyde.
Apollo, theym beholdyng, began for to say
  To the goddes & goddesses beyng there that tyde, 718
  "Me seemeth conuenyent an herowde to ryde
  To Vertew, & byd hym to batayll make hym bone,
  Hymsylf to defende, for sowght he shalbe sone. 721

Apollo wishes to send a herald to warn Virtue.

104

"And let hym nat be sodenly take 722
  All dyspurueyde or then he beware,
For then shuld our dyshonour awake
  Yef he were cowardly take in a snare." 725
  "Ee," quod Vyce, "for that haue I no care.
  I will auauntage take where I may."
  That heryng, Morpheus pryuyly stale away, 728

Vice protests.

105

And went to warne Vertew of all thys afray, 729
  And bade hym awake & make hymsylf strong,
For he was lyke to endure that day
  A gret mortall shoure, er hit were euesong, 732
  With Vyce, wherfore he bade him nat long
  Tary to sende aftyr more socour—
  Yef he dede, hit shuld turne hym to dolour. 735

But Morpheus steals away to prepare Virtue for the battle.

106

And brefely the matyr to hym he declaryd, 736
  Lyke as ye haue herde begynnyng & ende.
"Well," quoth Vertu, "he shall nat be sparyd.
  To the felde I wyll wende how hit wende. 739
  But gramercy, Morpheus, myñ owne dere frende,
  Of your trew hert & feythefull entent
  That ye in thys mater to me ward haue ment." 742

The Virtues.

107
Thys doon, Morpheous departyd away 743
  Fro Vertu to the palyce retornyng ageyñ.
Nooñ hym aspyed, that I dar well say.
  In whyche tyme Vertew dyd hys besy peyñ 746
  Pepyll to reyse hys quarell to menteyñ.
    Ymaginacion was hys messyngere—
    He went to warne pepyll bothe fer & nere. 749

Virtue makes ready, sending out his messenger, Imagination, to bid his people to come in to his help.

108
And bade hem come in all the haste they myght 750
  For to streyngthe Vertu, for, without fayll,
He seyde he shuld haue, long or hit were nyght,
  With Vyce to do a myghty strong batayll; 753
  Of vngracious gastes he bryngeth a long tayll.
    "Wherfore hit behoueth to helpe at thys nede
    And aftyr thys shall Vertu rewarde yowre mede." 756

109
When Imaginacion had gooñ hys cyrcute 757
  To Vertews frendys thus all aboute,
Withyn short tyme many men of myght
  Gaderyd to Vertew in all that they mowte. 760
  They hym comfortyd & bad hym put no dowte
    Hys vttyr enemy Vyce to ouerthrow,
    Though he with hym brought neuer so gret arow.

Virtue's host assembles.

110
And when Vertew sy the substaunce of hys oost, 764
  He prayed all the comons to the felde hem hy,
With her pety capteynys both lest & moost,
  And he with hys capteynys shuld folow redyly. 767
  For he seyde he knew well that Vyce was full ny.
    And who mygth furst of the felde recouer the centre
    Wold kepe out that other he shuld nat esyly entre. 770

They are led towards the field.

111
Then sent he forthe Baptym to the felde before, 771
  And prayed hym hertyly hit to ouerse,
That no maner trayne nor caltrop theryn wore
  To noy nor hurt hym nor hys meyne. 774
  And wheñ he thedyr came he began to see
    How Vyce hys purseuaunte, Cryme Oryginall,
    Was entryd before and had sesyd vp all. 777

Baptism is sent to spy out the ground.

Original Sin had entered before him

	112	
but fled at Baptism's approach.	But as sone as her̄of Baptym had a syght,	778
	He fled fast awey and left the felde alone.	
	And anone Babtym̄ entred wit*h* hys myght,	
	Serchyng all about where thys Cryme had gone.	781
	But the felde was clene defaute; fonde he none.	
	Then cam V*er*tew aftyr wit*h* hys gret oost,	
Virtue and his host follow.	And hys myghty capytayns, bothe leste & moost.	784
	113	
	But to enforme yow howe he thedyr̄ came,	785
	And what man*er* capyteyns he to the felde brought—	
Virtue leads, sitting in a car adorned with gold and stones, and crowned with laurel.	Hymsylfe, sekerly, was the furst man	
	Of all hys gret hoost that thedyrward sought,	788
	Syttyng in a chare that rychely was wrought,	
	Wit*h* golde & peerles & gemmes p*re*cious,	
	Crownyd wit*h* laurer̄ as lord vyctoryous.	791
	114	
Four knights guide the car. Righteousness, Prudence, Strength and Temperance.	Foure dowty knyghtys about the chare went	792
	At eu*er*y corn*er* on hit for to gyde,	
	And convey accordyng to V*er*tew hys entent.	
	At the furst corn*er* was Ryghtwysnes that tyde,	795
	Prudence at the second was set to abyde,	
	At the thryd Streyngth, the fourth kept Temp*er*aunce.	
	These the chare gydyd to V*er*tew hys plesaunce.	798
	115	
Following Virtue come seven captains each with an appropriate crest, Humility on a lamb,	Next to the chare, seuen capteyns ther̄ roode,	799
	Ychone aftyr other in ordre by and by.	
	Humylyte was the furst; a lambe he bestroode.	
	Wit*h* countenaunce demure he roode full soburly.	802
	A fawcon gentyll stood on hys helme on hy.	
Charity on a tiger,	And next aftyr hym came there Charyte	
	Rydyng on a tygre, as fyll to hys degre.	805
	116	
	Roody as a roose ay he kept hys chere.	806
	On hys helme on hygh a pellycan he bare.	
Patience on a camel,	Next whom came Pacyence, *þ*at nowhere hath no pere,	
	On a camell rydyng, as voyde of all care.	809
	A fenyx on hys helme stood. So forthe gan he fare.	
Liberality on a dromedary,	Who next hym folowyd but Lyberalyte,	
	Syttyng on a dromedary, *þ*at was bothe good & free.	

The Virtues.

117
On hys helme for hys crest he bare an ospray. 813
And next aftyr hym folowyd Abstynence, *Abstinence on a hart,*
Rydyng on an hert, hys trapure was gay,
He semyd a lorde of ryght gret excellence. 816
A popyniay was hys crest; he was of gret dyffence.
Next hym folowyd Chastyte on an unycorñ, *Chastity on a unicorn,*
Arymd at all poyn*tes* behynde and beforñ. 819

118
A turtyldoue he bare an hygh for hys crest. 820
Then came Good Besynesse, last of the seuyn, *Good Business on a vari-coloured beast.*
Rydyng on a panteř, a sondry colouryd best,
Gloryously beseene as he had come from heuyn. 823
A crane on hys hede stood, hys crest for to steuyn.
All these seuyn capteynes had standard*es* of pryce, *Each captain bears a standard with a device.*
Eche of hem acordyng aftyr hys deuyse. 826

119
Many pety capteyns aftyr these went, 827 *Many minor captains come next, True Faith, Hope, etc.*
As Trew Feythe, & Hoope, M*er*cy, Peese, & Pyte,
Ryght, Trowthe, Mekenesse, w*ith* Good Entent,
Goodness, Concorde, & Parfyte Vnyte, 830
Honest Trew Loue, w*ith* Symplycyte,
Prayer, Fastyng, Preuy Almysdede,
Ioynyd w*ith* the Artycles of the Crede, 833

120
Confession, Contrycion, and Satysfaccion, 834
W*ith* Sorow for Synne, & Gret Repentaunce,
Foryeuenes of Trespas, w*ith* Good Dysposicion,
Resystence of Wrong, P*er*formyng of Penaunce, 837
Hooly Deuocion, w*ith* Good Contynuaunce,
Preesthood theym folowyd w*ith* the Sac*ra*ment*es*,
And Sadnesse also w*ith* the Co*m*maundement*es*, 840

121
Sufferaunce in Trowble, w*ith* Innocency, 841
Clennesse, Continence, and Virginite,
Kyndnesse, Reu*er*ence, w*ith* Curtesy,
Content & Plesyd w*ith* Pyteous Pou*er*te, 844
Entendyng Well, Mynystryng Equyte
Twene ryght & wrong, Hoole Indyfferency,
And Laboryng the S*er*uyce of God to Multyply, 847

The Virtues.

122
Refuse of Rychesse & Worldly Veynglory, 848
Perfeccion, with Parfyte Contemplacion,
Relygyoñ, Profession well kept in Memory,
    Verrey Drede of God, with Holy Predycacion, 851
    Celestiall Sapience, with Goostly Inspiracion;
      Grace was the guyde of all thys gret meyny.
      Whom folowyd Konnyng with hys genalogy— 854

123
That ys to sey, Gramer, and Sophystry, 855
  Philosophy Naturall, Logyk, & Rethoryk,
Arsmetry, Geometry with Astronomy,
    Canon & Cyuyle, melodyous Musyk, 858
    Nobyll Theology, and Corporall Physyk,
      Moralizacion of Holy Scripture,
      Profounde Poetry and Drawyng of Picture— 861

124
These folowyd Konnyng & thedyr with hym came, 862
  With many ooñ moo offryng her seruyce
To Vertew at that nede; but natwithstandyng than

Virtue refuses some captains, Nigromancy, etc.
    Som he refusyd and seyde in nowyse 865
    They shuld with hym go, and, as I coude auyse,
      These were her names: fyrst, Nygromansy,
      Geomansy, Magyk, and Glotony, 868

125
Adryomancy, Ornomancy, with Pyromancy, 869
  Fysenamy also, and Pawmestry,
And all her sequelys, yef I shult nat ly.
    Yet Konnyng prayed Vertu he wold nat deny 872
    Theym for to know nor dysdeyne with hys ey
      Oñ hem to loke, wherto Vertew grauntyd.
      How [be] hit in hys werres he wold nat þey hauntyd. 875

126
who then choose Vice as their master
So had they Connyng lyghtly to depart 876
  From Vertew hys felde, and they seyng thys
By comon assent hyryd theym a cart
    And made hem be caryed toward Vyce y-wys. 879
    Fro thensforth to serue hym they wold nat mys.
      Full lothe they were to he mastyrles;
      In stede of the bettyr the worse ther they ches. 882

The Virtues.

127
But foorth to relese all the remenaunt 883 *Other minor captains with Virtue are Moderate Diet, etc.*
Of pety capteyns that with Vertu were,
Moderat Dyete, & Wysdom auenaunt,
 Euyn Wyght & Mesure, Ware of Contagious Geere, 886
 Lothe to Offende, and Louyng ay to Lere,
 Worshyp, & Profyt, with Myrthe in Manere,
 These pety capteyns with Vertew were in fere. 889

128
Comones hem folowyd a gret multitude. 890 *A great multitude of commons follows, yet numbering no one-tenth of Vice's host.*
But in [comparyson] to that other syde
I trow ther was nat, brefely to conclude,
The xth man that batayll to abyde. 893
 Yet neuerthelese, I shall nat fro yow hyde
 What maner pepyll they were & of what secte,
 As neere as my wyt therto wyll me dyrecte. 896

129
Ther were notable and famous doctours, 897 *There are famous doctors etc.*
Example yeuers of lyuyng gracyous,
Perpetuell prestes and dyscrete confessours,
Of Holy Scriptur declares fructuous, 900
 Rebukers of synne & myschefes odyous,
 Fysshers of fowles, & lovers of clennes,
 Dyspysers of veyn & worldly ryches, 903

130
Pesyble prelates, iustyciall gouernours, 904
Founders of churches, with mercyfull peeres,
Reformers of wrong of her progenitours
 On peynfull poore pyteous compassioners, 907
 Well menyng merchauntes, with trew artyfyceres,
 Vyrgyns pure, and also innocentes,
 Hooly matronys, with chaste contynentes, 910

131
Pylgryms, & palmers, with trew laborers, 911
Hooly heremytes, goddes solycitours,
Monasteriall monkes, & well dysposyd freres,
 Chanons, & nonnes, feythfull professoures, 914
 Of worldly peple trew coniugatoures,
 Louers of Cryst, confounders of yll,
 And all that to godward yeue her good wyll, 917

132

Mayntenours of ryght, verrey penytent*es*, 918
  Distroyers of errour̄, causers of Vnyte,
Trew actyf lyuers that set her entent*es*
  The dedes to p*er*forme of m*er*cy and pyte, 921
  Contemplatyf peple that desyre to be
    Solytary s*er*uaunt*es* vnto God alone,
    Rather then to habounde in rychesse eu*er*ychone. 924

133

These, w*i*th many mo then I reherse can, 925
  Were come thedyr redy that batayll to abyde,
And take such part as fyll to V*er*tew than.
  Vyce to ou*er*come they hopyd for all hys pryde, 928
  All though that he had more pepyll on hys syde,
    For the men that V*er*tu had were full sewre
    To trust on at Nede & Konnyng in armure. 931

134

The name of the field is Microcosm.

Macrocosme was the name of the felde 932
  Where thys gret batayle was set for to be.
In the myddes therof stood Conscience, & behelde

In the midst is Conscience, the judge of the combat.

  Whyche of hem shuld be brought to captyuyte. 935
  Of that nobyll tryu*m*phe iuge wold he be.
    Synderesys sate hy*m* w*ith*yn closyd as in a parke,
    W*ith* hys tables in hys hand her dedys to marke. 938

135

Five highways lead to the field.

To come in to the felde were hygh weyes fyue, 939
  Free to bothe partyes, large, broode and wyde.
Vertu wold nat tary, but hyghyd hym thydyr blyue,

Thither Virtue hastens.

  Lest he were by Vyce deceuyd at that tyde. 942
  Long out of the felde lothe he was to abyde,
    · In auentur̄ that he out of hyt were nat kept,
    For then wolde he haue thought he had to long slept.

136

In thys mene tyme whyle V*er*tu thus preuydyd 946
  For hym and hys pepyll the feld for to wynne,

Meanwhile Original Sin had reported to Vice.

He chargyd eu*er*y man by Grace to be guydyd,
  And all that eu*er* myght the felde to entre ynne. 949
  In all that seson̄ went Orygynall Synne
    To lete Vyce know how Baptym̃, w*ith* hys oost,
    Had entryd Macrocosm*e* & serchyd eu*er*y coost. 952

137

"A," seyde Vyce, " than I se well hit ys tyme   953   *Vice commands the standards to advance.*
Ba*ner*s to dysplay & standardys to auaunce.
Allmost to long haddyst thow taryed, Cryme,
To let vs haue knowlege of thys puruyaunce.   956
Yet I trow I shall lerne hem a new daunce.
Wherfore I co*m*maunde yow all w*it*h*out* delay
Toward the felde drawe, in all the haste ye may."   959

138

Then seyde the god Pluto that all men myght here,   960   *Pluto charges Vice to overthrow Virtue.*
"Vyce, I the charge, as thow wylt eschew
Ouȓ heynous indignacion, thow draw nat arere
But put the forthe boldly to oue*r*throw V*er*tew."   963   *If he fail, Atropos threatens to withdraw his service.*
"In feythe," quot*h* Attropos, "and I shall aftyr sew
For yef he escape youȓ handys thys day,
I tell yow my s*er*uyce haue ye lost for ay."   966

139

Forthe then rode Vyce w*it*h all hys hoole streyngth,   967   *Vice and his host advance.*
On hys steede se*r*pentyñ, as I tolde yow before.
The oost that hym folowyd was of a gret leyngth.
Among whom were penowns & guytornes many a score.
But as he went thederward—I shall tell yow more
Of hys pety capteyns—he made many a knyght,
For they shuld nat fle but manly w*it*h hyɱ fyght.   973

140

He dubbyd Falshood, w*it*h Dyssymulacion,   974   *As they march Vice dubs fourteen knights, Falsehood, etc*
Symony, Vsure, Wrong, and Rebawdy,
Malyce, Deceyte, Ly, w*it*h Extorcion,
Pe*r*iury, Diffidence, and Apostasy,   977
W*it*h Boldnesse in Yll to bere hem company—
These xiiii knyght*es* made Vyce that day;
To wynne theyȓ spores they seyde they wold asay.

141

In lyke wyse, Vertew dubbyd on hys syde   981   *Virtue makes a similar number, Faith, etc.*
Of hys pety capteynes other fourtene,
Whyche made her avowe w*it*h hym to abyde.
Heȓ spores wold they wynne *þ*at day, hit shuld be sene
These were her names, yef hit be as I wene:
Feythe, Hope and Me*r*cy, Trouthe, & also Ryght,
W*it*h Resystence of Wrong, a full hardy wyght,   987

142

    Confession, Contricion, with Satisfaccion,   988
     Verrey Drede of God, Performyng of Penaunce,
   Perfeccyon, Konnyng, and Good Dysposicion.
     And all knyt to Vertu they were by allyaunce. 991
     Wherfore to hym they made assewraunce,
      That felde to kepe as long as they myght
      And in hys quarell ageyñ Vyce to fyght.   994

143

The lord of Microcosm is Freewill, to whom Virtue sends three ambassadors to sue his favor.

    The Lord of Macrocosme and rewler of that fee 995
     Was callyd Frewyll, chaungeř of the chaunse,
   To whom Vertew sent embassatours three,
     Reson, Discresion, & Good Remembraunse, 998
     And prayed hym be fauorable hys honour to enhaunse,
      For but he had hys favour at that poynt of nede
      He stoode in gret doute he coude nat lyghtly spede.

144

In like wise Vice sends three.

    In lyke wyse, Vyce embassatours thre,   1002
     For hys party, vnto Frewyll sent,
   Temptacion, Foly, & Sensualyte,
     Praying hym of fauour that he wold assent 1005
     To hym, as he wolde at hys commaundment
      Haue hym, eftsones, when he lyst to call
      Oñ hym for any thyng þat aftyrward myght fall. 1008

145

Freewill gives an ambiguous answer.

    Answere yaue he nooñ to neyther party,   1009
     Saue oonly he seyde the batayle wold he se.
   To wete whyche of hem shuld haue the victory,
     Hit hyng in hys balaunce the ambyguyte. 1012
     He seyde he wold nat restrayne hys lyberte.
      When he come where sorow shuld awake,
      Then hit shuld be know what part he woll take. 1015

146

    Whan Vertew and Vyce, be heř embassatours, 1016
     Knew of thys answere, they stood in gret doute.
   Neuerthelese, they seyde they wold endure tho shoures

Vice sends forth as a spy Sensuality.

     And make an ende shortly of that they went aboute.
     So forthe came Vyce with all hys gret route.
      Eř he came at the felde he sent yet pryuyly
      Sensualyte before, in maner of a spy,   1022

147

Whyche sewe the felde wi*th* hys vnkynde seede   1023   who sows the field with wicked seed of weeds.
  That causyd Vertu aftyr mykyll woo to feele.
For therof grew nought but all oonly weede,
  Whyche made the grounde as slepyr as an yele.   1026
    He went ayene to Vyce and told hym eue*ry* dele
      How he had done, and bade hym com away   [day.
      For he had so purueyde that Vyce shuld haue the

148

Soo, as hit happyd, at the felde they mete,   1030
  Freewyll, Ve*r*tew & Vyce, as trypartyte,
Safe Ve*r*tew a lytell before the felde had gete,
  And elles hys auauntage forsothe had he full lyght   Virtue's men are encumbered by Sensuality's weeds.
    Nat for then encombryd so was neue*r* wyght
      As Ve*r*tew and hys men were wi*th* the ranke wede
      That in the felde grew of Sensualytees sede.   1036

149

But as sone as Vyce of Vertu had a syght,   1037
  He gan swage gonnes as he had be woode.   Virtue commands every man to pause under the sign of the cross.
That heryng, Ve*r*tew co*m*maundyd eue*ry* wyght
  To pauyse hym vndyr the sygne of the roode,   1040
  And bad hem nat drede but kepe styll wher they stoode.
    Hyt was but a shoure shuld soone confound, [grou*n*d.
    Wherfore he co*m*maundyd they*m* stand & kepe her

150

And when Vyce came nerer to the felde,   1044
  He callyd soore for bowes and bade hem shote faste.   They ward off the shots of Vice by the shield of the Holy Trinity.
But Ve*r*tew and hys meyny bare of wi*th* the shelde
  Of the blessyd Trynyte ay tyll shot was paste.   1047
  And when shot was dooñ, Vyce came forthe at laste,
    Purposyng the felde wi*th* assawte to wyn.   [theryn.   Vice proposes to make assault.
    But Ve*r*tew kept hit long — he myght nat entyr

151

All that tyme Frewyll & hym̄ bethought   1051
  To whyche he myght leue & what part he wold take.
At last Sensualyte had hym so fer brought   Freewill inclines to the side of Vice.
  That he seyde pleynly he Vertu wold forsake,   1054
  And in Vyce hys quarell all hys power make.
    "Y-wis," quoth Reason, "that ys nat for the beste."
    "No forse," seyde Frewyll, "I wyll do as my lyste."

152

 Vertu was full heuy, when he sy Frewyll 1058
  Take part with Vyce, but yet neuerthelesse

Virtue is compelled to retreat.
 He dyd that he myght the felde to kepe styll.
  Tyll Vyce, with Frewyll, so sore gan hym oppresse
   That he was constreynyd clerely by duresse
    A lytyll tyne abak to make abew retret.
    All thyng consyderyd hit was the best feet. 1064

153

 Furst to remembre how Vyces part was 1065
  Ten ayene ooñ strengor by lyklynes,
 And than how Frewyll was with hym allas,
  Whoo cowde deme Vertew but in heuynes; 1068
  Moreouer to thynke how that slyper gres,
   That of Sensualyte hys vnkynde seede grew
    Vndyr foote in standyng encombryd Vertew. 1071

154

 Yet natwithstandyng, Vertew hys men all 1072
  Nobully theym bare and faught myghtyly.
 Howe be hyt, the slepyr grasse made many of hem̃ fall,
  And from thense in maner depart sodeynly. 1075
  That seyng, Vyce hys oost began to showt and cry
   And seyde, "On in Pluto name! On! & all ys owre!
   For thys day shall Vyce be made a conquerour!"

155

 Thus Vertew was by myght of Vyce & Frewyll 1079
  Dreuen out of the felde—hit was the more pyte.

Baptism, Faith, Hope and others hold their ground.
 Howe be hit, yet Baptym kept hys ground styll,
  And with hym aboode Feythe, Hoope and Unyte, 1082
  And Kunnyng also, with comons a gret meyne,
   Confessyon, Contricion were redy at her hande,
   And Satysfaccion, Vyce to wythstande. 1085

156

 But all the tyme whyle Vertew was away 1086
  A myghty conflycte kept they with Vyce his rowte,
 And yet neuerthelese for all that gret affray
  Hoope stood vpryght & Feythe wold neuer lowte; 1089
  And euermore seyd Baptym̃, "Syres put no dowte
   Vertu shall retorne & haue hys entente.
   Thys felde shalbe our & elles let me be shent."

157

And whyle these pety-capteynes susteynyd thus the feelde, Virtue is
reinforced by
   With Vertew hys rerewarde came Good Perseueraunce, Perseverance
An hogy myghty hoost, & when he behelde who chides
   How Vertew hym withdrew he toke dysplesaunce, 1096 him for his retreat.
And when he to hym came he seyde, "Ye shall your chaunce
   Take as hit falleth, wherfore returne ye must.
Yet oonys for your sake with Vyce shall I iust. 1099

158

"Allas that euer ye shuld leese thus your honour, 1100 .
   And therwith also, the hygh perpetuell crowne,
Whyche ys for yow kept in the celestiall tour.
   Wherfore be ye callyd Cristes Champyon? 1103
How ys hit that ye haue no compassyon
   On Baptym, Feythe, & Hoope, Konnyng, & Vnyte,
That stant so harde be stadde & fyght as ye may see?

159

"All the tresour erthely vndyr the fyrmament, 1107
   That euer was made of goddes creacion
To rewarde theym euynly, were nat equyualent
   For her noble labour in hys afflyccion. 1110
Wherfore take vppon yow your iurysdyccion.
   Rescu yondyr knyghtes & recontynu fyght.
And elles adew your crowne for all your gret meryt."

160

With these & suche wordys, as I haue yow tolde, 1114
   By good Perseueraunce vttryd in thys wyse, Virtue returns
Vertu hym remembryd & gan to wex bolde to the struggle
   And seyd, "Yeue trew knyghtes to rescu I auyse. 1117
Let vs no lengor tary from thys entrepryse."
   Agayn to the felde so Vertew retornyd,
That causyd hem be mery þat long afore had mornyd.

161

"Avaunt baner," quoth he, "in the name of Ihesu." 1121 in the name of
   And with that hys pepyll set vp a gret showte Jesus.
And cryed with a lowde voyce, "A Vertew! A Vertew!"
   Then began Vyce hys hooste for to loke abowte, 1124
But I trowe Perseueraunce was nat long withowte
   He bathyd hys swerde in hys foes blood.
The boldyst of hem all nat oonys hym withstood.

162

They are victorious.

Constaunce hym folowyd & brought hym hys spere. 1128
 But when Perseueraunce saw Vyce oñ hys stede,
No man cowde hym let tyll he came there.
 For to byd hym ryde, I trow hit was no nede. 1131
 All Vertew hys ost prayde for hys good spede.
  Agayñ Vyce he roode with hys gret shaft
  And hym ouerthrew for all hys sotyll craft. 1134

163

Freewill comes to Conscience to repent and asks counsel;

That seyng, Frewyll came to Conscience, 1135
 And gan hym to repent that he with hym had bee,
Praying hym of counsell for hys gret offence

Conscience sends him to Humility,

That he agayñ Vertew had made hys armee, 1138
 What was best to do. "To Humylyte," [sent
  Quoth Conscience, "must þou go." So he hym̃ thedyr
  Disguysyd that he were nat knowen as he went. 1141

164

Humility to Confession;

And when he thedyr came, Humylyte hym took 1142
 A token, & bad hym go to Confessyon,

thence to Contrition,

And shew hym hys mater̃ with a peteous look.
 Whyche dooñ he hym sent to Contrycion, 1145
 And fro thensforth to Satysfaccion.

Satisfaction, and lastly to Penance.

  Thus fro poost to pylour was he made to daunce,
  And at the last he went forthe to Penaunce. 1148

165

But now for to tell yow—when Vyce was ouerthrow 1149
 A gret parte of his oost about hym gan resorte.
But he was so febyll that he cowde no man know.

Vice is carried from the field, meeting Despair who fetches his reward.

 And when they sy þat they knew no comforte, 1152
 But caryed hym awey be a pryuy porte.
  And as they hym caryed Dyspeyre with hym met;
  With Vyce hys reward he came theym for to fet. 1155

166

Alpha and Omega despatch from the heavens two goodly ladies; one named Prescience to chastise Vice and his host;

Then came ther̃ downe goodly ladyes tweyne, 1156
 From the hygh heuyn aboue the firmament,
And seyde the gret Alpha & Oo, most souereyne,
 For that nobyll tryumphe, had hem thedyr sent; 1159
 Ooñ of hem to dryue Vyce to gret torment
  With a fyrry scourge that she bare in her̃ hande.
  And so he dede dyspeyre and all his hoole bande.

167

The name of thys lady was callyd Prescience. 1163 *she pursues them through the gate of Hell.*
She neuer left Vyce, ne nooñ that wold hym folow,
Tyll they wer commyttyd by the diuine sentence
 All to peyne perpetuell and infynyte sorow. 1166
 Ryghtwysnes went to see that no man shuld hem borow.
  Thus all entretyd sharpely were they, tyll Cerberus
  Had hem beshut withyn hys gates tenebrus. 1169

168

And all the whyle that Prescience with her scorge smert
 To rewarde Vyce gan hyr thus occupy, *The other lady bears to Virtue the palm of victory.*
With all hys hoole bende, aftyr her desert,
 That other gloryous lady that came fro heuyn on hy, 1173
 Hauyng in her hande the palme of vyctory,
  Came downe to Vertu and toke hym to that present,
  Seying thus that Alpha & Oo haue hym sent. 1176

169

And as ferre as I aryght cowde vndyrstand 1177 *Her name is Predestination; she grants them a heavenly habitation.*
 That ladyes name was Predestinacion.
Vertu & hys hoost she blessyd with her hand
 And in heuen grauntyd hem habitacion, 1180
 Where to eche of hem reseruyd was a crowñ,
  She seyde, in token that they enherytours
  Of the glory were and gracious conquerours. 1183

170

Whyche dooñ, thoo ladyes ayene togedyr met 1184 *Which done, the ladies depart suddenly.*
 And toward heuyn vp they gan to [fly],
Embrasyd in armes as they had be knet
 Togedyr with a gyrdyll; but so sodenly 1187
 As they were vanysshyd saw I neuer thyng with ey.
  And anon Vertew with all hys company *Virtue and his host thank God for the victory.*
  Knelyd downñ and thankyd God of that vyctory. 1190

171

Yet had I foryete when Vyce was ouerthrow 1191 *Some of Vice's host seek Peace, beseeching mercy to plead to Virtue, or Faith, or Hope,*
 To haue tolde yow how many of Vyce hys oost
Gan to seek Peese, and darkyd downe full low,
 And besought Mercy, what so euer hys cost, 1194
 To be her mene to Vertew, elles they were but lost.
  And som in lyke wyse to Feythe & Hoope sought
  What to do, for peese they seyde they ne rought. 1197

172

or Baptism. Som also to Baptym̄ sewyd to be her mene; 1198
  Som to ooñ, som to other, as they hem gete myght.
  But all to Confession went to make hem clene. [lyght,
All must go to Confession. And as they came by Conscience he theym bad goo
  Er than olde Attropos of hem had a syght.
  For yef he so theym tooke lost they were for euer.
  He seyde Vyce to forsake ys bettyr late then neuer.

173

Some seek Circumcision who bids them go to Faith; he to Baptism and Virtue by process. Som eke for socour drew to Circumcysion, 1205
  But by hym cowde they gete but small fauour,
  For he in that company was had but in derysion.
  Neuerthelese to Feythe he bade hem go labour, 1208
  Praying theym for olde acqueyntance theym socour.
  "Well," quoth Feythe, "for hys sake, I shall do that I
  But furst for the best wey Baptym̄ go ye to. [may do

174

  "For by hym sonnest shull ye recouer grace, 1212
  Whyche shall to Vertu bryng yow by processe;
  Wherfore in any wyse looke ye make good face,
  And let no man know of your heuynes." 1215
  So they were by Baptym brought out of dystres—
Virtue commands Freewill to come near Turnyd all to Vertew; & when thys was dooñ,
  Vertu commaundyd Frewyll before hym com̄. 1218

175

and charges him for taking Vice's part. To whom thus he seyde, "I haue gret meruayll 1219
  Ye durst be so bolde Vyces part to take.
  Who bade yow do so & yaue yow that counsayll?
  Iustly vnto that ye shall me pryuy make." 1222
  Then seyde Frewyll & swemfully spake,
  Knelyng on hys kne with a chere benygne,
Freewill lays the blame "I pray yow, syr, let pyte your eares to me enclyne

176

upon Sensuality. "And I shall yow tell the verrey sothe of all, 1226
  Howe hit was, & who made me that wey drawe.
  For sothe, Sensualite, hys propre name they call."
  "A," seyde Reason, "then I know well that felawe.
  Wylde he ys & wanton, of me stant hym noon awe."
  "Ys he soo?" quod Vertu, "well he shalbe taught
  As a pleyer shuld to drawe another draught." 1232

Virtue's Judgments.

177

And with that came Sadnesse with hys sobre chere, 1233 *Sadness brings Sensuality*
Bryngyng Sensualyte, beyng full of thought, *prisoner to Virtue.*
And seyde that he had take hym prysonere. [sought.
"A welcome!" seyde Vertew, "now haue I that I
Blessyd be that good lord as thow wolde ys hit nought."
"Why art thow so wantoun & wylde," he seyde, "for shame!
Er thow go at large thow shalt be made more tame.

178

"But stande apart awhyle tyll I haue spoke a woorde 1240
With Frewyll a lytell, & then shalt thow know
What shalbe thy finaunce;" & then he seyde in boorde
Vnto Frewyll, "The bende of your bowe 1243 *Virtue requires*
Begynneth to slake, but suche as ye haue sowe
Must ye nedes reepe—ther ys noon other way.
Natwithstandyng that let see what ye can say. 1246

179

"What ys your habylyte me to recompense 1247
For the gret harme that ye to me haue do?" *recompense from Freewill.*
"Forsothe," seyd Frewyll in opyn audyense,
"But oonly Macrocosme more haue I nat lo. 1250 *Freewill agrees to deliver Microcosm*
Take that, yef hit plese yow, I wyll that hit be so.
Yef I may vndyrstand, ye be my good lorde."
"In dede," seyde Vertu, "to that wyll I acorde." 1253

180

Then made Vertu Reson hys lyeftenaunt, 1254 *which is given again to the charge of Reason and Freewill.*
And yaue hym a gret charge Macrocosme to kepe.
That dooñ, Sensualyte yelde hym recreaunt,
And began for to angre byttyrly to wepe. 1257
For he demyd sewerly hys sorow shuld nat slepe.
Then made Vertu Frewyll bayll[e] vndyr Reson,
The felde for to occupy to hys behoue that seson. 1260

181

And then seyde Vertu to Sensualyte, 1261 *Virtue orders Sensuality to forsake his fragility and be guided by Sadness.*
"Thow shalt be rewardyd for thy besynesse.
Vndyr thys fourme all fragylyte
Shalt thow forsake, bothe more & lesse, 1264
And vnder the guydyng shalt thow be of Sadnesse.
All though hit somewhat be ageyñ thy hert,
Thy iugement ys yeuyn—thow shalt hit nat astert."

182

With that Nature enters, protesting that Sensuality, her servant, should be given liberty.

And euen with that came in Dame Nature,   12
  Saying thus to Vertew, "Syr ye do me wrong
By duresse & constreynt to put thys creature,
  Gentyll Sensualyte, that hath me seruyd long,   12
    Cleerly from hys liberte, & set hym among
      Theym that loue hym nat, to be her vnderlowte,
      As hit were a castaway or a shoo clowte.   12

183

Virtue grants Sensuality freedom within Microcosm under the restraint of Sadness.

"And, parde, ye know well a rewle haue I must   12
  Withyn Macrocosme; forsoth, I sey nat nay."
Quoth Vertu, "But Sensualyte shall nat performe your l[
  Lyke as he hath do before thys, yef I may.   12
    Therfro hym restrayñ Sadnesse shall assay.
      Howe be hit, ye shall haue your hoole lyberte
      Withyn Macrocosme, as ye haue had, fre."   12

184

This done, Virtue sees Morpheus standing by,

And when Vertu had to Nature seyd thus,   12
  A lytyll tyne hys ey castyng hym besyde,
He sy in a corner standyng, Morpheus,
  That hym before warnyd of the verryly tyde.   12
    "A syres," seyd Vertu, "yet we must abyde.
      Here ys a frende of owre may nat be foryete.
      Aftyr hys desert we shall hym entrete."   12

185

and thanks him for his troth and labor.

"Morpheus," seyd Vertu, "I thanke yow hertyly   12
  For your trew hert & your gret labour,
That ye lyst to come to me soo redyly,
  When ye undyrstood the commyng of that shour.   12
    I thanke God & yow of sauyng of myñ honour.
      Wherfore thys pryuylege now to you I graunt,
      That withyn Macrocosme ye shall haue your hau[

186

He is given care of the five gates.

"And of fyue posternes the keyes shall ye kepe,   12
  Lettyng in and out at hem whom ye lyst,
As long as in Macrocosme your fadyr woll crepe.
  Blere whos ey ye woll hardyly with your myst,   12
    And kepe your werkes close there as in a chyst.
      Safe I wold desyre yow spare Pollucion,   [cio[
      For nothyng may me plese that sowneth to corrr[

187

And when he had thus seyde, þe keyes he hym tooke, 1303
   And toward hys castell with hys pepyll went,   *Virtue and his people leave for the castle.*
Byddyng Reasoñ take good heede & about looke,
   That Sensualyte by Nature were nat shent. 1306
"Kepe hym short," he seyde, "tyll hys lust be spent.
   For bettyr were a chylde to be vnbore,
   Then let hyt haue the wyll & for euer be lore." 1309

188

And when olde Attropos had seeñ & herde all thys, 1310
   How Vertew had opteynyd, astonyed as he stood,
He seyd to hymsylf, "Somwhat ther ys amys,   *Atropos again complains to the gods.*
   I trow well my patent be nat all good," 1313
And ran to the palyse as he had be wood,
   Seying to the goddes, "I see ye do but iape,
   Aftyr a worthy whew haue ye made me gape. 1316

189

"Howe a deuyll way shuld I Vertu ouerthrow, 1317
   When he dredyth nat all your hoole rowte!
How can ye make good your patent, wold I know.
   Hyt ys to impossybyll to bryng that abowte; 1320
   For stryke hym may I nat — that ys out of dowte."
"A, good Attropos," seyd god Apollo,
   "An answer conuenyent shalt thow haue herto. 1323 *Apollo answers:*

190

"The wordys of thy patent, dar I well say, 1324 *His patent is legal only within the jurisdiction of Nature. The destruction of Virtue is therefore no for him.*
   Streche to no ferther but where dame Nature
Hath iurisdiccion; there to haue thy way,
   And largesse to stryke as longeth to thy cure. 1327
   And as for Vertu he ys no creature
   Vnder the predicament conteynyd of quantyte.
   Wherfore hys destruccion longeth nat to the." 1330

191

"A haa!" seyd Attropos, "then I se well 1331
   That all ye goddes be but counterfete.
For oo God ther ys that can euery dell
   Turne as hym lyst, bothe dry & whete, 1334
   In to whos seruyce I shall assay to gete.
   And yef I may ones to hys seruyce come   *Atropos departs in wrath.*
   Your names shalbe put to oblyuyone." 1337

192

Meanwhile Residivacion, disguised like a pilgrim, makes his way to Microcosm.	Thus went Attropos fro the paleyce wrooth. 1338
	But in the mene tyme, whyle that he there was,
	Glydyng by the palyce, Resydyuacion gooth
	   Toward Macrocosme, with a peyntyd fase, 1341
	   Clad lyke a pylgrym̄, walkyng a gret pase,
	     In the forme as he had benè a man of Ynde.
	   He wende haue made Reson & Sadnesse boþe blynde.

193

He becomes acquainted with Sensuality but is ordered by Reason to depart.	With Sensualyte was he soone aqueyntyd, 1345
	   To whom̄ he declaryd hys matyr pryuyly.
	Yet he was espyed for all hys face peyntyd.
	   Then Reson hym commaundyd pyke hym thens lyghtly.
	   "For hys ease," quoth Sadnes, "so counseyll hym wyll I."
	     So was Sensualyte ay kept vndyr foote,
	   That to Resydyuacion myght he doo no boote. 1351

194

No help is found in Nature.	Then went he to Nature & askyd hyr̄ auyse, 1352
	   Hys entent to opteygne what was best to do.
	She seyde: " Euer syth Vertew of Vyce wan the pryse,
	   Reson with Sadnes hath rewlyd the fylde so, 1355
	   That I and Sensualyte may lytyll for the do.
	     For I may no more but oonly kepe my cours.
	   And yet ys Sensualyte strengor kept & wours." 1358

195

Residivacion leaves full of sorrow.	Thus heryng, Residiuacion fro thens he went ageyñ, 1359 Full of thought & sorow þat he myght nat spede. Then Reson & Sadnesse toke wede hokes tweyñ,

Then Reason and Sadness clear the ground of the seeds of Sensuality.	And all wylde wantones out of the fylde gan wede, 1362
	   With all the slyper grasse that grew of the sede
	     That Sensualyte before ther̄yn sew;
	   And for thens forthe kept hit clene for Vertew. 1365

196

New grass springs up in a marvelous manner.	Then began new gresse in the fylde to spryng, 1366
	   All vnlyke that other, of colour̄ fayre & bryght.
	But then I aspyed a meruelous thyng.
	   For the grounde of the felde gan wex hoore & whyte.
	   I cowde nat conceyue how that be myght,
	     Tyll I was enformyd & taught hit to know,
	   But where Vertew occupyeth must nedys well grow.

197

Yet in the mene tyme, whyle the fylde thus grew, 1373
 And Reson with Sadnesse therof had gouernaunce,
Many a pryuy messynger thedyr sent Vertew,
 To know yef hit were guydyd to hys plesaunce; 1376
 Now Prayer, efte Fastyng, & oftyn tyme Penaunce,
  And when he myght goo pryuyly, Almesdede,
  And bade hym to hys power helpe wher he sy nede.

Virtue sends secret messengers to Microcosm.

198

Whyle that fylde thus rewlyd Reson with Sadnes, 1380
 Mawgre Dame Nature for all her carnall myght,
Came thedyr Attropos, voyde of all gladnes,
 Wrappyd in hys shete, & axyd yef any wyght 1383
 Cowde wysshe hym the wey to the Lorde of Lyght,
  Or ellys where men myght fynd Ryghtwysnesse.
  "Forsothe," seyde Reason, ".I trow, as I gesse, 1386

Atropos draws near and asks Reason the way to the Lord of Light.

199

"At Vertu hys castell ye may soone hym fynde, 1387
 Yef ye lyst þe labour thedyr to take,
And there shall ye know, yef ye be nat blynde,
 The next wey to the Lorde of Lyght, I vndyrtake." 1390
 So thedyr went Attropos, peticion to make
  To Ryghtwysnes, praying that he myght
  Be take in to the seruyce of the Lord of Lyght. 1393

He is directed to Virtue's castle.

Atropos seeks from Righteousness to serve the Lord of Light.

200

"What," seyde Ryghtwysnes, "thow olde dotyng foole,
 Whome hast thow seruyd syth the world began
But oonly hym? Where hast thow go to scoole?
 Whether art thow double, or elles the same man 1397
 That thow were furst?" "A syr," seyde he than,
  "I pray yow hertyly holde me excusyd.
  I am olde & febyll; my wittes ar dysvsyd." 1400

He is assured by Righteousness that the Lord is his master.

201

"Well," seyde Ryghtwysnes, "for as moche as thow 1401
 Knowest nat thy mastyr, thy name shall I chaunge.
Dethe shalt thow be callyd, from hens forward now,
 Among all the pepyll thow shalt be had straunge. 1404
 But when thow begynnest to make thy chalaunge,
  Dredde shalt thow be, wher so thow become,
  And to no creature shalt thow be welcome. 1407

His name is changed to DEATH, and to no creature shall he be welcome.

202

Those whom he formerly served shall be put to oblivion.

"And as for theym whom thow dedyst serue,
    For as moche as they p*re*sume on hem to take
That hygh name of God, they shall as they deserue
        Therfore be rewardyd, I dar vndyrtake,
        Wi*th* peyñ p*er*petuell, among fend*es* blake,
            And her names shall be put to oblyuyoñ
            Among men, but hit be in derysyon."

203

"A ha!" seyde Attropos, "now begyñ I wex gladde
    That I shall thus avengyd of hem be,
Syth they so long tyme haue made me so madde."
    "Yee," quoth Ryghtwysnes, "here what I sey to the
    The Lord of Lyght sent the worde by me

Death is given a place in Microcosm.

        That in Macrocosme sesyne shalt thow take;
        Wherfore thy darte redy loke thow make."

204

And as sone as Vertu that vndyrstood,

Virtue then despatches Priesthood to the field with the sacraments.

    He seyde he was plesyd that hit shuld so be.
And euyñ forthewi*th* he *com*maundyd Presthood
    To make hym̄ redy the felde for to se.
    Soo thedyr went Presthood wi*th* benygnyte,
        Conueying thedyr the blessyd sacrament
        Of Eukaryst. But furst were theder sent

205

Previously had come thither Confession, etc.

Confession, Contricion, and Satisfaccion,
    Sorow for Synne, & gret Repentaunce,
Holy Deuocion, wi*th* Good Dysposicion —
    All these thedyr came & also Penaunce,
    As her dewte was to make puruyaunce
        Ageyñ the *com*myng of that blessyd Lorde.
        Feythe, Hoope, & Charyte therto were acorde.

206

The field is cleansed within and without, and the Lord of Light is received with fitness.

Reason wi*th* Sadnes dyd hys dylygence
    To clense the fylde wi*th*yn & wi*th*out.
And when they sy the bodyly p*re*sence
    Of that hooly Eukaryst, lowly gan they lowte.
    So was that Lord receuyd, out of dowte,
        Wi*th* all humble chere, debonayr & benygne,
        Lykly to hys plesure — hit was a gret sygne.

207

Then came to the fylde the mynystre fynall, 1443
 Called Holy Vnccion, w*i*th a crysmatory.
The v hygh weyes in especiall
 Theȓof he anoyntyd & made hit sanctuary. 1446
Whom folowyd Dethe, whych wold nat tary
 Hys feruent poweȓ there to put in vre,
As he was co*m*maundyd, grauntyng Dame Nature.

Holy Unction anoints the five highways.

Then enters Death his power to try.

208

He toke hys darte, callyd hys mortall launce, 1450
 And bent hys stroke toward the feldys herte.
That seyng, Presthoode bade Good Remembraunce
 Toward the felde turne hy*m* & aduerte. 1453
For except hy*m* all v*er*tues thense must sterte.
 And euyn w*i*th that, Dethe there sesyne took;
And then all the company clerely hit forsook. 1456

None can resist.

209

And as sone as Dethe thus had sesyn̄ take, 1457
 The colo*ur* of the felde was chaungyd sodenly,
The grasse theȓyn, seere as though hit had be bake.
 And the fyue hygh weyes were muryd opon hy, 1460
That fro thensforward noon̄ entre shuld therby.
 The posternes also were w*ith*out lette,
Bothe inward & outward, fyn fast shette. 1463

The grass becomes sere and the gates shut.

210

Whyche doon̄, sodenly Dethe vanysshyd away, 1464
 And Vertu exaltyd was aboue the firmament,
Where he toke the crowne of glory that ys ay
 Preparate by Alpha & Oo omnipoten[t]. 1467
The swete Frute of Macrocosme þedyȓ w*i*th hy*m* went.
 And on all thys mateȓ as I stood musyng thus,
Agayn fro the felde to me came Morpheus, 1470

Suddenly Death vanishes and Virtue is exalted above the firmament.

To me musing again comes Morpheus.

211

Seying thus, "What chere! howe lyketh the thys syght?
 Hast thow sene ynowgh, or wyll thow se more?"
"Nay syr," I seyde," my trouthe I þow plyght,
 Thys ys suffysyent, yef I knew wherfore 1474
Thys was to me shewyd, for theȓof the lore
 Coueyte I to haue, yef I gete myght."
"Folow me," quod he, "and haue thy delyght." 1477

I ask Morpheus the meaning of the sight.

212

I am brought to an arbor with four walls	So I hym folowyd, tyll he had me brought 1478
	To a fouresquare herber wallyd round about.
	"Loo," quoth Morpheus, "here mayst thow þat þow sought
	Fynde, yef thow wyll, I put the out of dout." 1481
	A lytyll whyle we stood styll there without,
	Tyll Wytte, chyef porter of that herber gate,
and admitted by Wit.	Requyryd by stody, let vs in therate. 1484

213

But when I came in I meruelyd gretly   1485
   Of that I behelde & herde there reporte.
For furst, in a chayar, apparaylyd royally,

It is the school of Doctrine.
   There sate Dame Doctryne, her chyldren to exorte.
And about her was many a sondry sorte;
   Som wyllyng to lerne dyuerse scyence,
   And som for to have perfyte intellygence.   1491

214

Crownyd she was lyke an Emperesse,   1492

Doctrine is crowned with three crowns— I cannot tell you all.
   With iii crownes standyng on her hede on hy.
All thyng about hyr an infynyte processe
   Were to declare, I tell yow certeynly.   1495
Neuerthelese som in mynde therof haue I,
   Whyche I shall to yow, as God wyll yeue me grace,
   As I sawe & herde, tell in short space.   1498

215

On one side sit Holy Text Glose and Moralization.
Fast by Doctryne on that ooñ syde,   1499
   As I remembre, sate Holy Texte,
That openyd hys mouthe to the pepyll wyde,
   But nat in comparysoñ to Glose that sate next.   1502
Moralyzacion with a cloke context

Scripture serves as scribe.
   Sate; & Scrypture was scrybe to theym all.
He sate ay wrytyng of that that shuld fall.   1505

216

'These were tho that I there knew—   1506
   By no maner wey of olde aqueyntaunce,
But as I before saw theym with Vertew
   Company in felde & hauyng dalyaunce.   1509
And as I thus stood half in a traunce,
   Whyle they were occupyed in her besynesse,

I look upon the walls
   Abowte the walles myn ey gan I dresse.   1512

The School of Doctrine.

217
Where I behelde the meruelous story   1513   where is portrayed a marvelous story.
  That eu*er* I yet saw in any pycture,
For on tho walles was made memory
  Singlerly of eu*er*y creature   1516
  That there had byñ, bothe forme and stature;
    Whos names reherse I wyll, as I can
    Bryng they*m* to mynde in ordre— eu*er*y man   1519

218
Furst, to begyñ, there was in portrature   1520   First on one wall in portraiture is the story of Adam and Eve, Noah, etc. (Old Testament).
  Adam; & Eue holdyng an appyll round;
Noe in a shyp; & Abraham hauyng sure
  A flynt stone in hys hand; & Isaac lay bound   1523
  On an hygh mount; Iacob slepyng sound,
    And a long laddyr stood hym besyde;
    Ioseph in a cysterne was also there that tyde.   1526

219
Next whom stood Moyses, w*ith* hys tables two;   1527
  Aaron & Vrre, hys armes supportyng;
Ely in a brennyng chare was there also.
  And Elyze stood, clad in an hermyt*es* clothyng;   1530
  Dauid w*ith* an harpe & a stooñ slyng.
    Isaye, Ieremy, and Ezechiell;
    And closyd w*ith* lyons, holy Danyell;   1533

220
Abacuc, Mychee, w*ith* Malachy;   1534
  And Ionas out of a whales body co*m*myng;
Samuell in a temple; & holy Zakary
  Besyde an awter all blody standyng;   1537
  Osee w*ith* Iudyth stoode there conspyryng
    The dethe of Oloferne; and Sal[a]*m*on also,
    A chylde w*ith* hys swerde dyuydyng in two.   1540

221
Many moo p*r*ophetys certeynly there were,   1541
  Whos names now come nat to my mynde.
Melchisedech also aspyed I there,
  Bred & wyne offryng as fyll to hys kynde.   1544
  Ioachym and Anne stood all behynde,
    Embrasyd in armes to the gyldyn gate.
    And holy Iohñ Baptyst in a desert sate.   1547

222

And now co*m*myth to my remembraunce 154
   I am avysyd I saw Sodechy,
And Amos also, w*ith* sobre countenaunce,
   Standyng w*ith* her faces toward Sophony. 155
   Neemy & Esdras bare hem company.
     The holy man Ioob as an impotent,
     Then folowyd in pycture w*ith* Thoby pacyent. 155

223

These, w*ith* many mo, on that oon syde 155
   Of that grene herber portrayed were.
"A," seyde Morpheous, "a lytyll tyme abyde.
   Turne thy face where thy bak was ere 155
   And beholde well what thou seest there."
     Than I me turnyd as he me bade,
     W*ith* hert stedefast & countenaunce sade 156

[marginal note: Upon the opposite wall I see Peter, Paul, etc. (New Testament and Church Fathers).]

224

Where I saw Petyr, with hys keyes, stande; 156
   Poule w*ith* a swerde; Iames also
W*ith* a scalop; & Thomas holdyng in hys hande
   A spere; & Phylyp aprochyd hym too. 156
   Iames, the lesse, next hem in pycture loo
     Stood, w*ith* Bartylmew, whyche was all flayñ.
     Symon & Thadee shewyd how they were slayñ. 156

225

Mathy and Barnabe, drawyng lottys, stood. 156
   Next whom was Marke, a lyon hym by
Hys booke holdyng; & Mathew, in hys mood,
   Resemblyd an Aungell w*ith* wyng*es* gloryosly. 157
   Luke had a calfe to holde hys booke on hy.
     And Iohñ w*ith* a cupp & palme in hys hande;
     An Egle bare hys booke—thus saw I hem stande.

226

Gregory and Ierome, Austyn and Ambrose, 157
   W*ith* pylyons on her hedys, stood lyke doctours.
Bernard w*ith* Anselme, and, as I suppose,
   Thomas of Alquyñ, & Domynyk, confessours, 157
   Benet, & Hew, relygyous gou*er*nours,
     Martyne, & Iohñ, w*ith* bysshops tweyne,
     Were there also, & Crysostom̄ certeyne. 158

227
Behynde all these was worshipfull Beede. 1583
  All behynde & next him stood Orygene,
Hydyng hys face, as he of hys deede
    Had hem ashamyd—ye woot what I mene; 1586
    For of errour was he nat all clene.
    And on that syde stood there, last of all,
      The nobyll prophetyssa, Sybyll men hyr̄ call. 1589

228
Let me remembre me, now I yow pray, 1590
  My brayne ys so thynne, I deme in myñ hert
Som of the felyshyp that I there say,
    In all thys whyle, have I ouerstert. 1593
    A benedycyte nooñ ere cowde I aduert
      To thynke on Andrew the Apostyll with hys crosse,
      Whom to forgete were a gret losse. 1596

229
Many ooñ moo were peyntyd on that wall, 1597
  Whos names now come nat to my remembraunce.
But these I markyd in especiall. *In the midst of the harbor sits Doctrine richly appareled.*
    And moo cowde I tell, in contynuaunce 1600
    Of tyme, but forthe to shewe yow the substaunce
      Of thys matyr, in the myddes of that herbere,
      Sate Doctryne, coloryd as any crystall clere. 1603

230
Crownyd as I tolde yow late here before, 1604
  Whos apparayll was worthe tresour̄ infynyte—
All erthely rychesse count I no more
    To that in comparyson valewyng then a myte. 1607
    Ouer her̄ heede houyd a culuer fayre & whyte,
      Oute of whos byll procedyd a gret leme *Over her head hovers a culver.*
      Downward to Doctryne, lyke a son beme. 1610

231
The wordys of Doctryne yaue gret redolence, 1611 *Her words savor sweet.*
  In swetness of sauour, to her dyscyples all.
Hyt ferre excedyd myrre and frankensence
    Or any other tre spyce or ellys gall. 1614
    And when she me aspyed, anon she gan me call. *She bids me come near.*
      And commaundyd Morpheus that he shuld bryng me neere;
      For she wolde me shew the effecte of my desyre. 1617

232

Doctrine interprets the vision.

She seyde, "I know the cause of thy commyng 1618
　　Ys to vndyrstand, be myñ enformacion,
Sensybly, the mateꝛ of Morpheus hys shewyng
　　　As he hath the ledde aboute in vysyon. 1621
　　Wheꝛfore now I apply thy naturall resoñ
　　　Vnto my wordys, &, eꝛ thow hens wende,
　　Thow shalt hit know, begynnyng & ende. 1624

233

Imprisonment of Eolus signifies that unbridled wealth increaseth misrule.

"Furst, where Eolus to Pluto was brought, 1625
　　By hys owne neglygence takyñ prysonere
Withyn the erthe; for he to ferre sought—
　　　Sygnyfyed ys nomore be that matere 1628
　　But oonly to shew the howe hit dothe apere
　　　That welthe, vnbrydelyd dayly at thyne ey,
　　Encreseth mysrewle & oft causyth foly. 1631

234

"For lyke as Eolus, beyng at hys large, 1632
　　Streytyd hym sylf thorow his owne lewdenesse—
For he wold deele where he had no charge—
　　　Ryght so wantons, by her wyldenesse, 1635
　　Oft sythe bryng hem sylf in dystresse,
　　　Because they somtyme to largely deele.
　　What may worse be suffryd than ouer mykyll weele

235

Minos judges every man according to his wickedness.

"By Mynos, the iuge of hell desperate, 1639
　　May he vndyrstand Goddes ryghtwysnes,
That to euery wyght hys peyne deputate
　　　Assygneth, acordyng to hys wykydnes. 1642
　　Wheꝛfore he ys callyd Iuge of crewelnes.
　　　And as for Diana & Neptunus compleynt,

The complaint of Diana and Neptune against Eolus signifies the folly of fools in attempting the impossible.

　　Fyguryd may be fooles reson feynte. 1645

236

"For lyke as they made heꝛ suggestion 1646
　　To haue me Eolus from course of hys kynde
Whyche was impossible to bryng to correccion,
　　　For euermore hys liberte haue wyll the wynde. 1649
　　In lyke wyse, fooles otherwhyle be blynde,
　　　Wenyng to subdew, with her ooñ hande,
　　That ys ouer mekyll for all an hoole lande. 1652

237

"But what foloweth therof that shall thow heere : 1653
   When they were come to the banket,
The gret Apollo, with hys sad chere,
   So fayre & curteysly gan theym entrete, 1656 *Apollo at his banquet causes their complaint to be forgotten.*
   That he made her beerdys on the new gete.
      Loo, what wysdom dothe to a foole—
      Wherfore ar chyldren put to scoole. 1659

238

"Oft ys hit seene, with sobre contenaunce, 1660
   That wyse men fooles ouercome ay,
Turnyng as hem lyst and all her varyaunce,
   Chaunge from ernest in to mery play. 1663
   What were they bothe amendyd that day?
      When they were dreuyn to her wyttes ende,
      Were they nat fayne to graunt to be hys frende? 1666

239

"Ryght so fooles, when they haue doon 1667
   All that they can, than be they fayne   *So fools give up their matter to oblivion.*
Yeue vp her mater to oblyuyon.
   Without rewarde they haue no more brayne. 1670
   And yet full oft hath hit be seyne,
      When they hit haue foryete and set at nought,
      That they full deere haue aftyrward hit bought. 1673

240

"And as for all tho that represent 1674 *The Gods resemble false idols.*
   To be callyd goddys at that banket,
Resemble false ydollys; but to thys entent
   Was Morpheous commaundyd thedyr the to fet, 1677
   That thow shuldest know the maner & the get
      Of the paynym lawe and of her beleue,
      How false idolatry ledeth hem by the sleue. 1680

241

"For soone vppon the worldys creacion, 1681
   When Adam & Eue had broke the precept—
Whyche clerkes call the Tyme of Deuyacion,
   The worldly pepyll in paynym law slept, 1684 *In the beginning people slept in pagan law.*
   Tyll Moyses vndyr God the tables of stone kept.
      In whyche tyme poetys feynyd many a fable
      To dyscrete reson ryght acceptable. 1687 *The poets feigned many fables*

4

242

"And to the entent that they should sownde
 To the eares of hem the more plesauntly
That they shuld reede or here, þey yaue theym a grounde
 And addyd names vnto theym naturally;
  Of whom they spake & callyd hem goddes hy,
   Som for the streyngthe & myght of her nature,
   And som for her sotyll wytty coniecture.

which were given ground and names and called gods.

243

"By nature thus as the seuyn planettys
 Haue her propre names by astronomers,
But goddys were they called by oold poetys,
 For her gret feruency of wyrkyng in her speres—
 Experyence preueth thys at all yeres.
  And for as other that goddes callyd be
  For sotyll wytte, that shall I teche the.

244

"How they by that hygh name of god came.
 In thys seyd tyme, the pepyll was so rude
That what maner creature, man or woman,
 Cowde any nouelte contryue & conclude
 For the comon wele, all the multitude
  Of the comon peple a god shuld hym call,
  Or a goddesse, aftyr hit was fall

245

"Of the same thyng that was so new founde—
 As Ceres, for she the craft of tylthe founde,
Wherby more plenteuosly corne dyd habounde,
 The pepyll her callyd thorout euery londe
 Goddesse of Corne, wenyng in her honde
  Had leyñ all power of cornys habundaunce.
  Thus wer the paynemes deceyuyd by ignoraunce.

Thus Ceres was thought to increase the product of corn and was therefore called Goddess of Corn.

246

"In lyke maner, Ìsys was callyd the Goddesse
 Of Frute, for she fyrst made hit multyply
By the meane of gryffyng: and so by processe
 The name of Pan gan to deyfy,
 For he furst founde the mene shepe to guy.
  Som tooke hit also by her condicioñ
  As Pluto, Fortune, & suche other doñ.

So Isis, Pan, etc.

247

"Thus all that poetys put vndyr couerture   1723
    Of fable the rurall pepyll hit took
Propyrly as acte, refusyng the fygure;
       Which errour som of hem neuer forsook.   1726
    Oft a false myrrour deceyueth a mannys look,
       As thow mayst dàyly proue at thyne ey.
       Thus were the paynyms deseuyd generally.   1729

248

"That seyng, the dedely enemy of mankynde,   1730
    By hys power permyssyue, entryd the ymages
Withyn the temples to make the pepyll blynde
       In her idolatry, standyng on hygh stages;   1733
    In so moche, whoo vsyd daungerous passages,
       Any maner wey by watyr or be londe,
       When hyd hys sacryfyce, hys answere redy founde.

249

"Thus duryng the Tyme of Deuyacion.   1737
    From Adam to Moyses, was idolatry
Thorow the world vsyd in comon opynyoñ.
       These were the goddys that thow there sy.   1740   *The gods at the banquet are the idols, the waiters are the poets and philosophers who feigned the fables.*
    And as for the awayters that stood hem by
       They polytyk philosophyrs & poetes were,
       Whyche feynyd the fables that I speke of here. 1743

250

"Then sesyd the Tyme of Deuyacion,   1744
    When Moyses receuyd that tables of stone,
Entryng the Tyme of Reuocacion.   *The three times. Deviation, Revocation,*
       On the Mount of Synay, stondyng alone,   1747
    God yaue hym myght ayene all hys fone.
       And then began the Olde Testament
       Whyche to the pepyll by Moyses was sent.   1750

251

"And that tyme duryd to the incarnacion   1751   *Reconciliation,*
    Of Cryst, & then began hit to sese.
For then came the Tyme of Reconsylyacion
       Of man to God—I tell the doutlese—   1754
    When the Soñ of Man put hym in prese,
       Wylfully to suffre dethe for mankynde.
       In holy scrypture thys mayst thow fynde.   1757

252

"Thys Reconsylyacion was the Tyme of Grace,   1758
  When foundyd was the churche vppoñ the feyr̃ stooñ,
And to holy Petyr the key delyu*e*ryd was
  Of heuyn; then helle dyspoyled was anooñ.   1761
Thus was mankynde delyu*e*ryd from hys fooñ.
  And then began the New Testament
    That the Crystyñ pepyll beleue in p*re*sent.   1764

253

"Whyche iii tymes, a sondry deuydyd,   1765
  are portrayed upon the walls. Mayst thow here see, yef thow lyst beholde.
The furst behynde the yn pycture ys prouydyd.
  The second of the lyft hande shewe p*r*ophet*es* olde. 1768
The iii^{de} on the ryght hande here hit ys to the tolde.
  Thus hast thow in vysyon the verrey fygure
    Of these iii tymes here shewyd in purtrayture.   1771

254

"That ys to sey, furst, of Deuyacion   1772
  From Adam to Moyses, recordyng Scripture;
Şecund, fro Moyses to the incarnacion
  Of Cryst kepeth Reuocac*i*ons cure.   1775
And as for the thryd, thow mayst be v*er*rey sure,
  Wyll dure from thens to the world*es* ende.
But now the iiii^{th} must thow haue in mynde,   1778

255

The time of Pilgrimage or of War is figured upon the fourth wall. "Whyche ys callyd p*ro*purly, the Tyme of Pylgremage 1779
  Aftyr som; & som name hit otherwyse
And call hyt the Tyme of Daungerous Passage;
  And som Tyme of Werre, that fully hyt dyspyse.   1782
But what so hit be namyd, I woll the auyse—
  Remembre hit well and prynte hit in thy mynde,
Wher̃of the fygure mayst thow me behynde.   1785

256

This is signified by the battle between Vice and Virtue. "And elles remembre thysylf in thyñ hert,   1786
  Howe Vyce & V*er*tu dayly they*m* occupy,
In man*er*, ooñ of hem hym to˚ p*er*u̇ert,
  Another, to bryng hym to endeles glory.   1789
Thus they contynu fyght for the victory.
  Hyt ys no nede her̃of to tell the moore,
For in thys short vysyoñ thow hast seen hit before.

Doctrine's Interpretation.

257

"And as for Attropos greuous compleynt   1793
  Vnto the goddes betokeneth nomore
But oonly to shewe the how frendely constreynt
  On a stedfast hert weyeth full soore.   1796
  Good wyll requyreth good wyll ayene therfore.
    Dyscorde to Dethe hathe ay byn a frende,
    For Dyscorde bryngeth many to her ende.   1799

The complaint of Atropos signifies the constraint of friendship—Discord and Death.

258

"Wherfore Dethe thought he wolde avengyd be   1800
  On hys frendes quarell yef that he myght,
For her gret vnkyndnes, in so moche as she
  Was among hem all had so in despyte   1803
  And at that banket made of so lyte;
    Whyche causyd hym among hem to cast in a boon,
    That found theym gnawyng ynough euerychoon. 1806

259

"Thus oft ys seen oo frende for a nother   1807
  Wyll say & do & somtyme matyrs feyne;
And also kynnysmen, a cosyn, or a brother,
  Woll for hys aly, er he haue cause, compleyne.   1810
  And where that he loueth do hys besy peyne,
    Hys frendes matyr as hys owne to take,
    Whyche oft sythe causeth mochyll sorow awake. 1813

The alliance of friends often causes sorrow.

260

"Be hyt ryght or wrong, he changeth nat a myte-   1814
  As toward that poynt he taketh lytell heede.
So that he may haue hys froward appetyte
  Performyd, he careth nat howe hys soule speede, 1817
  Of God or deuyll have suche lytyll dreede.
    Howe be hyt, oon ther ys þat Lorde ys of all,
    Whyche to euery wyght at last rewarde shall. 1820

261

"And as for the batayll betwene Vyce & Vertew holde,
  So pleynly appereth to the inwardly,
To make exposicion therof, new or olde,
  Were but superfluyte—therfore refuse hit I. 1824
  In man shall thow fynde that werre kept dayly,
    Lyke as thow hast seen hit fowtyn before thy face;
    The pyctur me behynde shewyth hit in lytyll space.

The battle of Vice and Virtue signifies the moral struggle in the human soul.

Doctrine's Interpretation.

262

Microcosm is the world of man.

"And as for Macrocosme, hit ys no more to say 1828
  But the lesse worlde, to the comon entent
Whyche applyed ys to mañ both nyght and day—
    So ys man the felde to whyche all were sent 1831
    Oñ both partyes; & they that thedyr went
      Sygnyfy nomore but aftyr the condicioñ
      Of eue*r*y mans opynyoñ. 1834

263

Perseverance betokens the continuance of virtuous living.

"And as for the nobyll knyght P*er*seueraunce, 1835
    Whyche gate the felde when hit was almost gooñ,
Betokeneth nomore but the contynuaunce
    Of ve*r*tuous lyuyng tyll dethe hath oue*r*gooñ. 1838

Whoso perseveres is rewarded with a crown.

Who so wyll doo, rewardyd ys anoñ,
    As Vertu was w*ith* the crowne on hy,
    Whyche ys nomore but eue*r*lastyng glory. 1841

264

Prescience and Predestination are the rewarders of vice and virtue.

"And as for Prescience and Predestinacion, 1842
    That eche of hem rewardyd aftyr hys desert,
Is to vndyrstond nomore but dampnacion
    To vycyous pepyll ys the ve*r*rey scourge smert 1845
    Rewarde; for they fro V*er*tu wolde pe*r*uert.
    And endelese ioy ys to hem that be electe
    Rewardyd & to all that folow the same secte. 1848

265

The five keys are man's five wits.

"And as for the keyes of the posterns fyue, 1849
    Whyche were to Morpheus rewardyd for hys labo*ur*,
Sygnyfy nat ellys but whyle man ys on lyue
    Hys v inwarde wytt*es* shalbe eue*r*y houre 1852
    In hys slepe occupyed, in hele and in langoure,
      W*ith* fantasyes, tryfyls, illusions & dremes,
      Whyche poetys call Morpheus stremes. 1855

266

Residivacion signifies the return of man to sin.

"And as for Resydiuacion ys nomore to sey 1856
    But aftyr̃ confessioñ turnyng ayene to syn,
Whyche to eue*r*y man retorneth sauns deley
    To vycyous lyuyng ageyñ hym to wyn. 1859
    Whyle any man lyueth wyll hit neue*r* blyn,

Reason and Sadness prevent such conclusion.

      That cursyd conclusion for to bryng abowte,
      But Resoñ w*ith* Sadnes kepe hit styll owte. 1862

Doctrine's Interpretation.

267
"Here hast thow pr*o*purly the v*er*rey sentence   1863
  Herde now declaryd of thys vysyoñ.
The pycture also yeueth clere intellygence,
    The̱rof beholdyn w*ith* good discresyoñ.   1866
    Loke well aboute & take consyderasioñ,
      As I haue declaryd, whether hit so be."
      "A syr," quoth Morpheus, "what tolde I the! 1869

268
"Hast thow nat now thyne hert*es* desyre?   1870
  Loke on yoñ wall yonder before."
And all that tyme stood I in a wyre
    Whyche way furst myñ hert wold yeue more   1873
    To looke; in a stody stood I therfore.
      Neu*er*thelese at last, as Morpheus me badde,
      I lokyd forward w*ith* countenaunce sadde,   1876

269
Where I behelde in portrayture   1877   *All things as described are portrayed upon the wall.*
  The man*er* of the felde, euyñ as hit was
Shewyd me before; & eu*er*y creature
    Oñ boothe sydes beyng drawyn in small space   1880
    So curyously, in so lytell a compace,
      In all thys world was neu*er* thyng wrought;
      It were impossyble in erthe to be thought.   1883

270
And when I had long beholde that pycture—   1884
  "What," quoth Morpheous, "how long shalt thow looke,
Daryng as a dastard, oñ yoñ portrayture?
    Come of for shame; thy wytte stant a crooke."   1887
    I heryng that myñ hert to me tooke,   *I look to the fourth wall,*
      Towarde the iiii[th] wall turnyng my vysage,   *where are poets and*
      Where I sawe poetys & phylosophyrs sage,   1890   *philosophers.*

271
Many ooñ mo then at the banket   1891
  Seruyd the godd*es*, as I seyde before.
Soṁ were made standyng, & som in chayer*es* set,
    Som lookyng oñ book*es*, as they had stodyed sore, 1894
    Som drawyng almenak*es*, & in he̱r hand*es* bore
      Astyrlabes, takyng the altytude of the sonne—
      Among whoṁ Dyogenes sate in a tonne.   1897

272

And as I was lokyng on that fourthe wall, 1898
  Of Dyogenes beholdyng the ymage,
Sodeynly Doctryne began me to call,
  And bad me turne toward hyr my vysage. 1901
  And so then I dyd w*it*h humble corage.   [thentent
    "What thynkest thow," she sayde, "hast thow nat
    Yet of these foure wallys—what they rep*re*sent? 1904

273

Doctrine explains the pictures of the Times.

"The pycture on the fyrst, that standeth at my bake, 1905
  Sheweth the the p*re*sent Tyme of Pylgremage,
Of whyche before I vnto the spake,
  Whyche ys the Tyme of Daungerus Passage. 1908
  The secund, dyrectly ageyñ my vysage,
    The Tyme expresseth of Deuyacion,
    Whyle paynym̃ lawe had the domynacion. 1911

274

"The thryd wall, standyng on my lyft hande, 1912
  The Tyme rep*re*senteth of Reuocacion.
And the fourth, standyng on my ryght hande,
  Dete*r*myneth the Tyme of Reconsylyacion. 1915
  Thys ys the effect of thy vysion.
    Wherfore the nedyth nomore thef̃on to muse—
    Hit were but veyñ thy witt*es* to dysvse. 1918

275

Spend well the Time of Reconciliation.

"But duryng the Tyme of Reconsiliacion 1919
  Thy Tyme of Pylgremage looke well thow spende
And then woll gracious Predestinacion
  Bryng the to glory at thy last ende." 1922
  And euyn with that cam to my mynde

This reminds me of my former doubt.

  My furst conclusion that I was abowte
    To haue drevyñ, er̃ slepe made me to lowte— 1925

276

I pray Doctrine to reconcile Reason and Sensuality.

That ys to sey, howe Sensualyte 1926
  W*it*h Reason to acorde myght be brought aboute.
Whyche causyd me to knele downe on my kne
  And beseke Doctryne dete*r*myne that doute. 1929
  "Oo Lord God!" seyde Doctryne, "canst thow nat w*it*h
    Me that conclusioñ bryng to an ende?   [oute
    Ferre ys fro the wytte & ferther good mende." 1932

277

And euen wi*th* that Dethe gan appere,   1933   Death enters;
  Shewyng hymsylf as though that he wolde
Hys darte haue occupyed wi*th*yn that herbere.
    But the͂r was noõn for hym, yong nor olde,   1936
    Saue oonly I, Doctryne hym tolde,
      And when I herde hyr wi*th* hy*m* comon thus,
      I me wi*th*drew behynde Morpheus,   1939

278

Dredyng full soore lest he wi*th* hys dart,   1940   of whom I am afraid.
  Thorow Doctrynes word*es*, any entresse
In me wolde haue had or claymed any part—
    Whyche shuld haue causyd me gret heuynesse.   1943
    Wi*th*yn whyche tyme & short processe,
      Came theder Reason & Sensualyte.
      "A," quoth Doctryne, "ryght welcome be ye.   1946   Reason and Sensuality come thither.

279

"Hyt ys nat long syth we of yow spake.   1947
  Ye must, er ye go, dete*r*myne a dowte."
And euyn̄ wi*th* that she the mate͂r brake
    To they*m* and tolde hit eu*ery* where abowte.   1950
    I wold haue be thens, yef I had mowte.
      For feere I lookyd as blak as a coole.   I am more afraid.
      I wold haue cropyn in a mouse hoole.   1953

280

"What!" quoth Doctryne, "where ys he now,   1954
  That meuyd thys mater straunge & diffuse?
He ys a coward—I make myn̄ avow.
    He hydeth hys hede, hys mocion to refuse."   1957
    "Blame hym nat," quoth Reson, "alwey that to vse   Reason excuses my fear, since Death is to be shunned.
      When he seeth Dethe so neere at hys hande.
      Yet ys hys part hym to wythstande.   1960

281

"Or, at the leste way, ellys fro hym flee   1961   With which sentiment Sensuality accords.
  As long as he may—who dothe otherwyse
As an ydiote." Quoth Sensualyte,
    'Who dredyth nat Dethe wyse men hym dyspyse."
    "What!" seyde Doctryne, "how long hathe thys gyse
      Beholdyn & vsyd thus atwyx yow tweyne?
      Yee were nat wont to acorde certeyne."   1967

282

"Yes," quoth Reson, "in thys poynt, alway   1968
    To euery man haue we yeuen our counsayll
Dethe for to flee as long as they may.
    All though we otherwyse haue done our trauayll 1971
    Yche other to represse, yet withoute fayll
        In that poynt oonly dyscordyd we neuer.
        Thus condescendyd theryñ be we for euer." 1974

283

"A! A!" seyde Doctryne, "then ys the conclusion   1975
    Clerely determynyd of the gret dowte
This solves my question.   That here was meuyd"—& halfe in derysion
    She me then callyd & bade me loke owte.   1978
"Come forthe," she seyde, "and feere nat thys rowte."
Death, Reason, and Sensuality vanish.   And euen with that, Reson and Sensualyte
    And Dethe fro thens were vanysshyd all thre. 1981

284

Then lokyd I forthe as Doctryne me badde.   1982
    When Dethe was gooñ, me thought I was bolde
To shew my sylf, but yet was I sadde.
    Me thought my dowte was nat as I wolde,   1985
The matter is not wholly clear.   Clerely and opynly declaryd & tolde.
        Hit sownyd to me as a parable,
        Derke as a myste, or a feynyd fable.   1988

285

And Doctryne my conceyte gan espy.   1989
    "Wherfore," seyde she, "standyst thow so styll?
Whereyn ys thy thought? Art thow in stody
    Of thy question? Hast thow nat thy fyll   1992
To the declaryd? Tell me thy wyll.
    Herdest thow nat Reson & Sensualyte
        Declare thy dowte here before the?"   1995

286

"Forsothe," quoth I, "I herde what they seyde.   1996
    But neuerthelese my wyt ys so thynne,
And also of Dethe I was so afrayed,
    That hit ys oute where hyt went ynne.   1999
    And so that matyr can I nat wynne
        Without your helpe & benyuolence
        Therof to expresse the verray sentence." 2002

Accord of Reason and Sensuality.

287
"Well," quoth Doctryne "then yeue attendaunce   2003   *Doctrine interprets my vision.*
  Vnto my wordes, & thow shalt here
Opynly declaryd the concordaunce
    Atwene Sensualyte & Reson in fere.   2006
    Yef thow take hede, hit clerely dothe apere
      How they were knette in ooñ opynyon.
      Bothe agayñ Dethe helde contradyccyon.   2009

288
"Whyche concordaunce nomore sygnyfyeth   2010
  To pleyne vndyrstandyng, but in eue*r*y mane
Bothe Sensualyte & Reson applyeth   *In one point Reason and Sensuality*
    Rather Dethe to fle then w*ith* hit to be tane.   2013   *accord—in the fear of Death.*
    Loo in that poynt accorde they holly thane.
      And in all other they clerely dyscorde.
      Thus ys trewly set thy doutfull monacorde."   2016

289
I, heryng that, knelyd on my kne   2017
  An thankyd her lowly for hyr dyscyplyne,
That she vouchesafe, of hyr benygnyte,
    Of tho gret dowtys me to enlumyne.   2020
    Well was she worthy to be called Doctryne,
      Yef hit had be nomore but for the solucion
      Of my demaunde and of thys straunge vysyon.   2023

290
And as I w*ith* myne heede began for to bow,   2024
  As me well ought to do hyr reue*r*ence,   *Doctrine suddenly vanishes.*
She thens departyd — I cannat tell how.
    But w*ith*yn a moment gooñ was she thens.   2027
    Then seyde Morpheus, "Let vs go hens.
      What shuld we heere tary lengere?
      Hast thow nat herde a gene*r*all answere   2030

291
To all thy matyrs that thow lyst to meue?   2031
  My tyme draweth nere that I must rest."
And euyn therw*ith* he tooke me by the sleue
    And seyde, "Goo we hens, for that hold I best.   2034
    As good ys ynowgh as a gret feste.   *Morpheus leads me back*
      Thow hast seeñ ynowgh; hold the content."
      And euyn w*ith* that forthe w*ith* hym I went,   2037

292

<small>to my bed</small>   Tyll he hade me brought agene to my bedde,   2038
     Where he me founde, and then pryuyly
He stale awey. I cowde nat vndyrstande
<small>and secretly steals away.</small>   Where he became, but sodenly   2041
     As he came, he went—I tell yow veryly.
<small>Then I awake</small>   Whyche dooñ, fro slepe I gan to awake.
     My body all in swet began for to shake   2044

293

<small>in great dread.</small> For drede of the syght that I had seene,   2045
     Wenyng to me all had be trew
Actuelly dooñ where I had beene,
     The batayll holde twene Vyce & V*er*tew.   2048
     But when I sy hit, hit was but a whew,
     A dreme, a fantasy, & a thyng of nought.
<small>It is all a dream.</small>   To study theron I had nomore thought.   2051

294

Tyll at the last I gan me bethynke   2052
     For what cause shewyd was thys vysyon.
I knew nat; wherfore I toke pen & ynke
     And paper to make therof mencion   2055
<small>Lest fault be found in me, I write down what I have seen.</small>   In wrytyng, takyng consideracion
     That no defaute were founde in me,
     Wheron accusyd I ought for to be   2058

295

For slowthe, that I had left hit vntolde—   2059
     Nowthyr by mowthe nor in reme*m*braunce
Put hit in wrytyng; wher thorow manyfolde
     Weyes of accusacion myght turne me to greuaunce.   2062
     All thys I saw as I lay in a traunce,
     But whedyr hit was w*th* myne ey bodyly
     Or nat in certayñ, God knoweth and nat I.   2065

296

That to dyscerne I purpose nat to deele.   2066
     So large by my wyll hit longeth nat to me.
Were hit dreme or vysioñ, for your owñ wele,
     All that shall hit rede, here rad, or se,   2069
     Take therof the best & let the worst be—
<small>Take from my writing the best and leave the chaff.</small>   Try out the corne clene from the chaff
     And then may ye say ye have a sure staff   2072

Exhortation to Virtue.

297
To stande by at nede, yef ye woll hit holde   2073
  And walke by the way of Vertu hys loore.
But alwey beware, be ye yong or olde,
  That your frewyll ay to Vertu moore   2076   *Walk the way of Virtue.*
    Apply than to Vyce, the eysyer may be boore
    The burdyn of the fylde, that ye dayly fyght
    Agayñ your iii enemyes, for all her gret myght. 2079   *Fight against your enemies,*

298
That ys to sey, the Deuyll & the Flesshe   2080   *the Devil, the Flesh, and the World.*
  And also the Worlde, with hys glosyng chere,
Whyche oñ yow looketh euer newe & fresshe—
  But he ys nat as he doth apere.   2083
    Lok ye kepe yow ay out of hys daungere.
    And so the vyctory shall ye obteyne,
    Vyce fro yow exylyd & Vertew in yow reyne. 2086   *Let Virtue in you reign.*

299
And then shall ye haue the triumphall guerdouñ   2087   *Thine be the glory and the celestial mansion.*
  That God reserueth to euery creature
Aboue in hys celestiall mansiouñ,
  Joy and blys infinite, eternally to endure.   2090
    Wherof we say we wold fayñ be sure.
    But the wey thedyrward to holde be we lothe,
    That oft sythe causeth the good Lorde to be wrothe.

300
And by oure desert oure habitacion chaungeth   2094
  Fro ioy to peyne & woo perpetuelly,
From hys gloryous syght thus he vs estraungeth,
  For our vycyous lyuyng, thorough owre owne foly. 2097
    Wherfore let vs pray to that Lord of Glory,
    Whyle we in erthe bee, that he wyll yeue vs grace,   *Let us pray the Lord of Glory to give us grace.*
    So vs here to guyde that we may haue a place, 2100

301
Accordyng to oure regeneracion,   2101
  With heuynly spyrytes, hys name to magnyfy   *Let us magnify His name.*
Whyche downe descendyd for our redempcion,
  Offryng hym sylf on the crosse to hys fadyr on hy. 2104
    Now benygne Ihesu, that borñ was of Mary,
    All that to thys vysion haue yovyn her audyence,   *Jesus, grant eternal joy to the readers of my book.*
    Graunt eternall ioy aftyr thy last sentence.   2107
        Amen.

NOTES.

In the notes and introduction references are made to the following editions:

Lydgate's Minor Poems, including Pur le Roy, Chorle and Bird, and Testament, Halliwell, Percy Soc.
Æsop, Sauerstein (Anglia, IX).
Temple of Glas, Schick, E. E. T. Soc.
Dance of Macabre, *MS.* Bodl. 686.
Falls of Princes, Pynson's print, Brit. Mus.
Story of Thebes, Speght's Chaucer, Lond. 1598.
Secrees of Old Philisoffres, Steele, E. E. T. Soc.
Chaucer's Works, Skeat, one vol. (Macmillan); also the Aldine.
Langland's Piers the Plowman, Skeat, E. E. T. Soc. Text B.
Gower's Confessio Amantis, Pauli, 3 vols.
Mapes's Latin Works, Wright, Camden Soc.
Michel's Ayenbite of Inwyt, Morris.
Rolle of Hampole's Pricke of Conscience, Morris.
Ancren Riwle, Morton.
Wyclif's Works, Arnold, 3 vols.
Chronicle of Robert of Brunne (Anglia, IX).
Hawes's Pastime of Pleasure, Percy Soc.
Douglas's Works, Small, 4 vols.
Dunbar's Works, Small, Scot. Text. Soc.
Lyndesay's Works, E. E. T. Soc.
King James's Quair, Skeat, Scot. T. Soc.
Skelton's Works, Dyce.
Barclay's Ship of Fools, Jamieson, 2 vols.
Spenser's Works, Morris, one vol. (Macmillan).
Other works, as specially indicated.

P. 1, l. 1. The time is near the middle of July. Lydgate has a similar opening in *A Poem against Self-Love* (M. P., p. 156):

"Toward the eende of froosty Ianuarye,
Whan watry Phebus had his purpoose take
For a sesoun to soiourne in Aquarye
And Capricorn hadde uttirly forsake,
Toward Aurora a-morwe as I gan wake. . . . ."

Cf. the imitation by Hawes in the *Pastime of Pleasure*:

"When Phebus entred was in Geminy,
Shynyng above in his fayre golden spere,
And horned Dyane then but one degree
In the Crabbe had entred fayre and cleare;
When that Aurora did well appeare
In the depured ayre and cruddy firmament,
Forth then I walked without impediment."

The prototype is found in Mapes' poem "*Apocalypsis Goliae Episcopi*," which contains also a reference to Pythagoras as the teacher to the Greeks of the seven Arts of the Schools. P. is there represented as having the signs of

the Arts on different portions of the body. Astrology, the highest form of knowledge, is marked prominently on the forehead. (Works, Camden Soc., ed., Wright.)
Hawes, in his *Past. of Pleas.*, p. 105, affirms that
"Thus God hym selfe is chief astronomyer."

l. 2. *gan*. This usage is maintained to the present. See Browning's *Easter Day:*
"Which gan suspire."
Used as auxiliary in l. 624.

l. 3. *Pictagoras speere*. The spelling "Pictagoras" occurs in the *Rom. of the Rose* (l. 5649) for the French "Pythagoras" (l. 5007). Chaucer has "Pictagoras" in the *Bk. of the Duch.* (l. 1167). Lydgate uses "Pictagoras" in Min. P. (p. 84, 87). The philosopher was known in England for his science of number. Cf. Lydgate's *Pur le Roy* (M. P., p. 11):
"And Arsmetryk, be castyng of nombrary,
Chees Pyktegoras for her parte."
Chaucer notes he "the firste finder was of the art (of music)"—*Bk. of the Duch*, l. 1168.
The sphere is according to his mathematics the most perfect figure; it is the circle of the heavens. It was used to symbolize the Soul, the Microcosm, implying final harmony in "the Diapason closing full in man." Other figures were the triangle, the least perfect figure, symbolizing the body, and the quadrate, in the perfect proportion of 7 to 9, embracing all the powers of man. Cf. Spenser, *Faery Queene*, Bk. II., c. 9, st. 22:
"The frame thereof seemd partly circulare,
And part triangulare, O worke divine, ...
And twixt them both a quadrate was the base,
Proportiond equally by seven and nine;
Nine was the circle set in heavens place;
All which compacted made a goodly Diapase."
The ninth or cosmological sphere represented harmony, to which end, according to the philosophy, opposing elements were united. The Pythagorean sphere thus taught the poet the lesson he was seeking of concord.

P. 2, l. 9. *obstacle, habytacle, tryacle*. Other sets of rimes occur thus: obstacle, spectacle, myracle, tryacle (*Test.*, Min. P. p. 236); triacle, obstacle (*Æsop*, Fab. 4, ll. 148–50); obstacle, myracle (*Secr.*, ll. 120–22); obstacle, oracle (*Secr.*, ll. 624–26); obstacle, miracle (Chau. *Fr. Tale*, ll. 571–72); miracle, triacle (Chau. *Man of L. Tale*, ll. 379–81), etc.

l. 11. *habytacle*. Cf. Chau. *Ho. of Fame*, l. 1194:
"Weren sondry habitacles;"
Lydgate, *Min. P.* p. 140:
"Whan th'olygoost made his habitacle;"
Hawes, *Past. of Pleas.*, p. 218:
"First God made heaven is propre habitacle," etc.

l. 12. *rowne*. Commonly in M. E. a distinction is made between rowne (to mutter) and whisper. Here=to commune.

l. 12. *tryacle*. Theriaca was the name given to a medicine compounded by a Roman physician Andromachus. For the history of the word see Morley, *Lib. of Engl. Lit.*, p. 21. Lydgate uses the term frequently; thus "Gostly tryacle", Min. P. p. 98;
"Ther is no venome so parlious in sharpnes
Os whan it hathe of treacle a lyknes—" *Ch. and Bd.*, Min. P. p. 186;
"Ageyne verray poyson ordeyned is triacle—" *Æsop*, Fab. 4, l. 148;
"The name of Ihesu! swettest of namys alle!
Geyn goostly venyms, holsomest tryacle—" *Test.*, M. P. p. 236.
It is found in Chaucer, *Man of L. Tale*, l. 381:
"Crist, which that is to every harm triacle;"

and in *Piers Pl.* Pas. 2, l. 146:
> "Love is triacle of hevene."

Cf. Beau. and Fl., *Sea Voyage* (Dyce, viii., p. 360):
> "This may be treacle
> Sent to preserve me after a long fast."

The figurative use is very common.

l. 14. *Morpheus.* These dreamers almost invariably have guides. Boethius was directed by Philosophy, Dante by Virgil and Beatrice, Mapes by Pythagoras, King James by Good Hope, etc.; Morpheus as a shewer of fancies appears again in Higgin's *Mirrour for Magistrates* (1576).

l. 18. *Mynos the iustyse.* Minos is first seen as Judge of the lower world in the Odyssey. Virgil followed Homer (*Aen.* 6, 431). Dante selected him as the typical judge in the Inferno (c. v.) in the second circle of which he abides and examines sins at the entrance.

l. 19. *sylogyse.* A general term. Cf. Hawes, *Past. of Pleas*, p. 32:
> "Agaynst your fables wyll often solisgyse."

l. 21. *he must nedys go, etc.* The proverb occurs again in Skelton's *Garl. of Laur.*, l. 1434:
> "Nedes must he rin that the devyll dryvith."

Greene uses it in *The Carde of Fancie*, ed. Grosart, p. 79, l. 4. Hazlitt in his *Proverbs* quotes an instance from *Triall of Treasure* (1567).

l. 34. *abydyng.* Used as a noun. Cf. *Æsop*, Fab. 6, ll. 122-23:
> "Yonder on that other side
> Is myn abidyng."

Cf. guydyng, l. 59.

l. 35. *Fantasy.* For the dwelling place of Morpheus see Chaucer's *H. of Fame*, Invoc.; *Bk. of the Duch.*. l. 153; Spenser, *Faery Queene*, Bk. I., c. 1, st. 39; Ariosto, *Orl. Fur.*, xiv., 92; Ovid, *Met.*, xi., 592. Gower describes the Cave of Sleep in *Confes. Am.*, II., pp. 102-3. Cf. "The House of Sleep," Cook, Mod. L. Notes, V., p. 10.

l. 37. *Cerberus.* The constable is a somewhat new role for Cerberus, whom Dante describes as a demon, a cruel and monstrous beast tearing and flaying and rending the spirits in Hell (*Infer.*, c. 6). As opposing Christ he appears in Lydgate's *Test*, p. 236:
> "Ihesu
> Took out of helle soulys many a peyre,
> Mawgre Cerberus and al his cruelte."

He is called "chief porter of hell" in *Story of Thebes*, fol. 375. He was known to Bunyan as the Porter of Hell, serving also as one of the captains of Diabolus in the Holy War.

P. 3, l. 45. *strayte correccion.* Cf. *Æsop*, Fab., 4, l. 36:
> "Straitly requyreng the iuge in this matiere;"

Secrees, ll. 762-3:
> "Twen moche and lyte a mene to devise
> Of to mekyl and streight coveitise;"

idem, l. 799:
> "But he that is streyght in his kepyng."

l. 52. *in fere*=in company, together; O. E. *ge-fera*, a companion; M. E. *in fera* is a corruption of *yfera* which is restored in Spenser; and cf. Tennyson, *Conf. of Sens. Mind*:
> "And in the flocks
> The lamb rejoiceth in the year,
> And raceth freely with his fere."

Chaucer has yfere in *Leg. of G. W.*, Pr., l. 263. Douglas uses yfeir.

l. 58. *chases.* Technically a chase is a private open hunting ground to which game resorts, differing from a "forest" in being open and private. Cf. Cheviot Chase or Chevy Chase.

l. 59. *cure.* Cf. Chaucer, *Ho. of Fame*, l. 464:
"For Iupiter took of him cure."

l. 65. *comfort.* This word has a variety of meanings in M. E. Cf. Glossary.

l. 66. *roote and rynde*=wholly. Cf. l. 620, "croppe and roote." See Gower, *Conf. Aman.* I, p. 152:
"Of flour and gras and roote and rinde."

l. 69. *maner.* For this use of maner see Chaucer, *Compleynte unto Pite*, l. 24:
"What maner man dar now holde up his heed?"
The Compl. of Mars, l. 116:
"For she ne fond ne saw no maner wight."
See l. 5:
"Musyng on a maner,"
l. 1735:
"Any maner wey."
Cf. *Secrees*, l. 7:
"To euery maneer wyght;"
idem, l. 741:
"In no maner wyse."

l. 71. *syngler.* Cf. *Secrees*, l. 332:
"For my moost vertuous and singuleer counfort;"
idem, l. 1128:
"To his noblesse and his singuler glorye."

P. 4, l. 87. *kervell.* Cf. Kersey's Dict.: "Caravel or carvel, a kind of light round ship with a square Poop, rigg'd and fitted out like a Galley, holding about six score or seven score Tun." Columbus's ships were called "caravels." The vessel which Douglas saw in his vision (*Pal. of H.*) that was driven upon the sands was called the "Carwell of the State of Grace."

l. 88. *karyk*=cark, a large ship. Cf. Chaucer, *Som. Tale*, Pr., l. 24:
"Brodder than of a carrik is the sayl" (the first use of word in Engl.). The "Universal Ship" that carried Barclay's fools is called a "carake"; and see *Ship of Fools*, II., p. 220:
"That all the shyppes ne galeys vnto Spayne
Nor myghty carakes cannot them well contayne."
Cf. Beaumont and Fletcher, *Two Nob. Kins.:*
"Then would I make
A carrack of a cockle-shell."

l. 90. *who.* Note the use of who as relative. See l. 769.

l. 96. *daungere.* The M. L. *damnum* signified (1) a fine (2) the territory over which a lord ruled (3) the enclosed field of a proprietor (4) power to exact a penalty. In M. E. danger meant in general simply power or jurisdiction. Cf. *Æsop*, Fab. 5, l. 39:
"Thow were in my daungere."
See l. 543=territory or jurisdiction. It had also the modern meaning of danger as in the *Secrees*, l. 1103:
"Avoydyng al daungeer."
See Wedgwood for the history of the word.

l. 97. *seethe* = satisfaction. Cf. *Digby Myst.*, N. Shak. Soc., p. 143, l. 121-3:
"Wysdom that was god and man right,
Made a full seth to the fader of hevyn
By the dredfull deth to hym was dight."

l. 101. *a loft.* Cf. *Temp. of Glas*, l. 41 :
"Now lowe and eft aloft ;"
idem, l. 645 :
"I am set on loft ;"
Secrees, l. 1244 :
"Planetys a-lofte."

l. 104. *foom.* This was often used of sweat as in Chaucer, *Ch. Yeo. Tale*, Pr., l. 12 :
"He was of fome (from sweat) al flekked as a pye."

l. 105. *betyn.* Cf. Lydgate, Min. P., p. 168 :
"Abydithe so longe til he be betyn doune."

P. 5, l. 116. *in especiall.* A very common phrase in Lydgate. Cf. *Secrees*, ll. 536, 653, 1041, 1088, etc. I find a modern use of the phrase in Poe's *Phil. of Composition:*
"It is this latter, in especial, etc."

l. 119. *cost.* Frequently used for neighboring country. Cf. *Piers Plow.*, Pas. ii., l. 85 (B) :
"The counte of coueitise and alle the costes aboute."

l. 126. *pyry.* Cf. Ir. piorra, a blast of wind. This is an earlier instance than that given in the Cent. Dict. Cf. Hawes, *Past. of Pleas.* p. 53 :
"In the stormy pery."
lappyd = wrapped. Cf. Rob. of B. *Chron.* l. 1149 :
"And bylapped hem on ylk a side ;"
Ode by Rich. Barnfield, l. 24 :
"All thy friends are lapt in lead ;"
Breton, *Arb. of Am. Delights* (1593):
"Sing lullaby and lap it warm."
Browning uses it in *Strafford*, Act V, 2, l. 332:
"lapped round with horror."

l. 127. *boystous.* This is the form of the word in Chaucer. Cf. *Mann. Tale*, l. 107 :
"I am a boistous man ;"
Morte Arthure, Th. MS., l. 615 :
"Thos bustous churlles."
The *Story of Thebes* has "boistouslie" (fol. 370).
Boisterous is found by Shakespeare's time.

l. 140. *auysment.* Cf. Chaucer, *Parl. of F.*, ll. 554–55 :
"The water-foules han her hedes leyd
Togeder, and of short avysement ;"
Troy. and Cris., II, l. 343 :
"Avysement is good bifore the nede."

P. 6, l. 154. *egall* = equall. Cf. Lydgate, *Secrees*, l. 386 :
"Ye wer of lyff egal with hooly seyntes ;"
Min. P. p. 210 :
"So egally ther doomys to avaunce."
Paregall occurs often in Skelton. Unperegall is found in Marston, *Dutch Courtezan*, IV, v.

l. 157. *prima facie.* The date of the first instance of the Engl. usage of this phrase given in the Stanford Dict. (Latin in Engl.) is 1646. Cf. Chaucer in *Troil. and Cris.* III, l. 918 :
"This accident so pitous was to here
And eek so lyk a sooth, at pryme face."

l. 162. *onwarde.* Skeat says this did not appear before Sir Th. More (Dict.).

Notes. 67

l. 163. *messynger.* Formed from the Fr. *message.* When was the *n* introduced? Gower has messagere in *Conf. Am.*, III, p. 249. Lydgate in *Story of Thebes* uses messengers (fol. 372) and messagere (fol. 380, 386), Chaucer has both messager and messanger (see Glossary of Ch.).

l. 167. *banket.* In the fourteenth century the cloth or cushion covering a bank or bench on which dessert was served was called a "banker"; a feast came to be called a "banket" (*Mem. of Lond.*, ed. Riley, I, p. 179 and p. 44).

P. 7, l. 191. *ryght glad.* Right used in this manner is generally considered to be an Americanism (Southern) but this usage, like the American "I guess," is good Middle English.

l. 192. *all and some* = the long and short of it (Skeat). This is one of the most common phrases in L. M. E. Cf. Chaucer, *Fr. Tale*, l. 878:
  "This al and som, there is no more to seyn;"
Parl. of F., l. 650:
  "This al and som, that I wolde speke and seye," etc., etc.
Rom. of the Rose, l. 740:
  "So faire they weren alle and some;"
Gower, *Conf. Am.*, II, p. 379:
  "There ben the lordes all and some;"
Lydgate, *Temp. of Glas*, l. 1037:
  "This is al and some, the fine of my request," etc.
Cf. Spenser, *Faerie Queen*, III, xii, 30.
I remember to have seen the phrase used by Swinburne. Browning has in *Ring and Book*:
  "So do I see, pronounce on all and some."

l. 202. *by and by* = one after the other, separately. See l. 302. Chaucer has in *Rv. Tale*, l. 223:
  "Right in the same chambre, by and by;"
Rom. of the Rose, l. 4581:
  "These were his wordis by and by."

l. 217. *grogyng.* The most common word of its class in Lydgate's vocabulary, commonly spelled grucchyng.
Min. P. p. 67:
  "Nat grucchyng, but mery like thi degre;"
idem, p. 83:
  "List thank God voyde al grucchyng;"
Æsop, Fab. 2, l. 161:
  "Nor grucche in pouerte."
Often in *Temp. of Glas* (see ll. 187, 424, 853, 879, 1266) and *Secrees* (ll. 113, 775, 778, 780).
Piers the Plow., Pr., l. 153:
  "And gif we grucche of his gamen."
In Chaucer's *Pers. Tale* grucching is declared a species of Envy.
Cf. Mary Wilkin's *Pembroke*, Ch. 12:
  "I don't begrutch it to her."

P. 8, l. 232. *dyscrese.* From L.L. *discrescere*. Gower has discreseth (*Conf. Am.* II, p. 189).

l. 233. *I dar vndyrtake.* A common formula; Chaucer has it in the *Ml. Tale*, l. 355. Cf. Prol. l. 288:
  "And he nas nat right fat, I undertake."

l. 243. Neptune's *mastresse.* Cf. Chaucer, *Fr. Tale*, ll. 319-20:
  "Though Neptunus have deite in the see,
  Yet emperesse aboven him is she (Lucina)."

68   *Notes.*

l. 249. *Othea.* I have retained the spelling in the text, though I am confident that Athena is the right reading.

l. 252. *marchall.* It was the office of the marshal of a feast to set the guests in order of rank.

P. 9, l. 253. *The Gods.* The delineation of the pagan deities in the manner of pictorial art is perhaps the best thing done in the poem. For models of these images he had, perchance, the work of Albricus Philosophus, entitled *De Deorum Imaginibus,* containing sketches of the heathen gods (Van Staveren es *Auctores Mythog. Lat.*); also, of course, the work of Fulgentius (Introd. p. xl); or for that he would not need to go much farther than Gower's *Conf. Aman.* Bk. IV. In l. 294 he refers to "olde poetys" for his authority. There is a minor assembly of gods in Lydgate's *Æsop* where judgment is given concerning the marriage of Phebus. See also The Assembly in Dunbar's *Golden Targe.*

l. 256. *presse.* The MS. preef is changed to presse because of the riming word messe.

l. 258. *be spreynt.* Cf. Chaucer, *Compl.,* l. 10:
    "To Pite ran I, al bespreynt with teres;"
"dew-besprent" occurs in *Comus,* l. 541. Browne notes that besprent is Spenserian.

l. 260. *Mars myghty god and strong.* A translation of the more common epithet of Mars, "armypotent"— borrowed from Virgil (*Æn.* IX, 717). Cf. Boccaccio, *Teseide,* VII. 32.

l. 262. *yron* and the other metals. The association of the different metals with the planets is attributed to Geber (see Thomson, *Hist. of Chem.,* I, 117). The temple of Mars built by Theseus (*Knight's Tale*) was all of steel. In Chaucer's *Ho. of Fame* (ll.1446–8) it is said that "Yren Martes metal is:"
    "And the leed, withouten faile,
    Is, lo, the metal of Saturne."
The Chanouns Yeman explains the seven "bodies" (*Ch. Y. Tale,* ll. 273–6):
    "Sol gold is, and Luna silver we threpe;
    Mars yren, Mercurie quicksilver we clepe;
    Saturnus leed, and Iubiter is tin,
    And Venus coper, by my fader kin."
Gower gives the complete list in *Conf. Am.,* Bk. 4, II, p. 84:
    "The gold is titled to the sonne;
    The mone of silver hath his part;
    And iron, that stond upon Mart;
    The leed after Satorne groweth;
    And Iupiter the brass bestoweth;
    The copper set is to Venus,
    And to his part Mercurius
    Hath the quick-silver."
Note the description by Hawes of the monster of the seven metals whose head and face were gold, the neck silver, the breast and heart steel, the forelegs brass, the back copper, the hindlegs tin, the tail lead (*Past. of Pleas.* p. 192).

l. 266. *poudryd.* A term in heraldry for sprinkled.

l. 267. *take the mantell and the ryng.* This saying refers to the assumption by a widow of a ring and a "widow's mantel," probably of black silk, as evidence of a vow of perpetual widowhood. See Lydgate, *Dance of Mac.*:
    "Chastely receyved the mantel and the rynge;"
Min. P., p. 34:
    "She wol perhappous maken hir avowe
    That she wol take the mantle and the ryng."

P. 9, l. 269. *demenyng.* Cf. the *Secrees,* l. 1082:
"Sad of his cheer, in his demenyng stable;"
Temp. of Glas, l. 750:
"Hir sad demening."

l. 270. Words like sad, wise and end are dissyllabic in Chaucer, sad | de, wys | e, end | e.

l. 272. *philosophres: cofres.* A stock rime from Chaucer; cf. *Cant. Tales* Pr. l. 297–8:
"And albe that he was a philosophre
Yet hadde he but litel gold in cofre;"
see also *Man of L. Tale,* ll. 25–6; *Fr. Tale,* ll. 843–4; *Ch. Y. Tale,* ll. 283–4; *Dr. of Ph. Tale,* Pr. l. 5–6; *Leg. of G. W.,* Pr. ll. 380–1; Gower uses it in *Conf. Am.,* II., p. 197 and III., p. 163; Lydgate employs it again in *Æsop,* ll. 1–3, in *Secrees,* ll. 34–5, 435–7, 540–2. Chaucer rimes philosophre again with profre (*Sec. N. Tale,* ll. 489–90; *Ch. Y. Tale,* ll. 111–12).

l. 275. *rychely beseene.* Cf. Skelton, *Garl. of Laur.,* ll. 482–3:
"Wherein was set of Fame the noble Quene,
All other transcendynge, most rychely besene;"
Temp. of Glas, l. 1167:
"Ai fressh and welbesein."

l. 280. *morne: Saturne.* Cf. *Temp. of Glas,* ll. 480–1, *mourne: turne,* 858–9, *mourne: refourme.*

P. 10, l. 296. *fresshe*=gorgeous, gay. Cf. Skelton, *Garl. of Lau.,* l. 39:
"Garnysshed fresshe after my fantasy."

l. 306. *purpur.* The M. E. spelling. Cf. Chaucer, *Leg. of G. W.,* I., l. 75:
"With al her purpre sayle."

l. 308. *perles oryent.* Cf. Chaucer, *Leg. of G. W.,* Pr., l. 221:
"For of oo perle, fyne, oriental;"
see the *Flow. and Leaf,* line 148:
"As greate pearles, round and oriente;"
Skelton, *Garl. of Lau.,* l. 485:
"Fret all with orient perlys of garnete;"
Lydgate's *Æsop.,* l. 26:
"Perlis white, cliere, and oriental;"
John Day's Works (ed. Bullen, p. 37): "And as jewels, so the stones be orient, artfully cut and orderlie sett."

l. 314. *sulphure.* Cf. Chaucer, *Ho. of Fame,* ll. 1507–11:
"And next him on a piler stood,
Of sulfre . . . .
Dan Claudian . . . .
That bar up al the fame of helle,
Of Pluto, and of Proserpyne."

l. 316. *Fortune the goddesse.* This is that Fortune that was known to the Middle Ages. Boethius gave her form and figure in the second book of *De Cons. Phil.* Dante places her in the Fourth Circle of Hell (c. vii), saying that for the splendors of the world there was ordained a general mistress and guide who should ever and anon transfer the vain goods from race to race, and from one blood to another beyond the resistance of human wit (Norton). This is the import of Cavalcante's fine Song of Fortune, beginning,
"Lo! I am she who makes the wheel to turn;
Lo! I am she who gives and takes away."
She is shewn in full form with her wheel in the *Roman de la Rose* (2d part, ll. 4863–8492). The English *Romaunt* speaks of "The froward Fortune and contraire" (l. 5414). Chaucer describes her as going upright and yet halting, as looking fair and yet foul (*Bk. of the Duch.,* ll. 642–5):

Notes.

> "She is th' envyous charite
> That is ay fals, and semeth wele
> So turneth she her false whele
> Aboute, for it is no-thing stable."

Lydgate says in the Min. P., p. 122:
> "Fortune shewithe ay, by chaungyng hir see,
> How this world is a thurghefare ful of woo."

For a later description of Fortune and her wheel see King James' *Quair*, st. 158–172. Fluellen said to Pistol (*K. Hen. V.*, Act III., Sc. 6): "Fortune is painted blind with a muffler afore her eyes, to signify to you that Fortune is blind; and she is painted also with a wheel, to signify to you, which is the moral of it, that she is turning and inconstant, and mutability, and variation; and her foot, look you, is fixed upon a spherical stone, which rolls and rolls." Note the painting of Fortune and her wheel by E. Burne-Jones. The mediæval Fortune was pictured by Raphael on the walls of the Vatican.

l. 316. *party face*. Cf. *Court of Love*, ll. 1191–2:
> "Dissemble stode not ferre from hym in trouth,
> With party mantill, party hode and hose."

The *Temp. of Glas*, l. 1155, has the formula "in parti or in al."

l. 320. *gawdy grene chamelet*. Chamelet was a cloth made of camel's hair and silk. Cf. Chaucer, *Knights Tale*, l. 1221:
> "In gaude greene hir statue clothed was (Diana)."

l. 322. *shoures*. Figuratively=distribution, bestowment. See another usage in l. 732=assault of battle.

P. 11, l. 325. *russet*. Russet was a name given to a coarse woolen cloth, reddish brown in color and commonly worn by shepherds; "clad in russet" was proverbial for homeliness. See Skeat's note in *Piers Plow.*, p. 208. The color is taken from the cloth. Cf. Shaks. *Hamlet*, Act I., i. 166:
> "The morn in russet mantle clad."

Frese=frieze, a coarse woolen cloth.

l. 326. *tar box*. Every shepherd carried a box containing tar, which was used to annoint the sores in sheep. Cf. *Chest. Pl.*, p. 120:
> "Heare is tarre in a potte
> To heale from the rotte."

Skeat cites a carol in a Balliol MS., 354 (notes to *Piers Plow.*, p. 195):
> "The sheperd upon a hille he satt,
> he had on hym his tabard and his hat,
> hys tarbox, hys pype, and hys flagat."

See Percy's *Reliq.*, II., p. 256:
> "And least his tarbox should offend, he left it at the folde."

l. 329. *the murre*=a cold with hoarseness. Cf. Skelton, *Magnyf.*, l. 2287:
> "And I gyve hym the cowghe, the murre, and the pose" (pose=rheum in the head).

l. 330. *Isys the goddesse*. Lydgate, in his *Fall of Princes*, describes again a number of the Divinities. Of Isis he says:
> "She was right wise above other creatures,
> Secrete of cunnynge, wele experte in science,
> She taught first letters and figures
> To Egipciens by pleyn experience,
> Yave theym cunnynge and intelligence
> To till the londe, taught the labourerys
> To sowe their greyne and multiplie by yeres."

l. 340. *in hys gyrdyll stede*=in place of his girdle. But cf. Stubbes' *Anat. of Abuses* where gyrdlestead, used as a noun, signifies waist (I., p. 60).

Notes.

l. 343. *dysgysyd* = decked out in strange guise. Cf. Lang., *Piers Plow.*, Pr., l. 24:
"And some putten hem to pruyde . . . . comen *disgised*."
Cf. *Secrees*, l. 1170:
"As the sonne shewith in his guyse."

l. 344. *Mynerue*. Minerva as Pallas appears in Lydgate's *Temp. of Glas*, "with her cristal sheld" (see Schick's notes, p. 87).

l. 350. *that other ye wote where*, i. e., on her breast.

l. 356. *kendall*. Probably the "Kendal Green," formerly manufactured by the Flemish weavers who had established themselves in Kendall in the 14th century.

P. 12, l. 361. *meynt* = joined, p.p. of mingen. Cf. *Temp. of Glas*, l. 276:
"That Rose and lileis togedir were so meint;"
Spenser, *F. Q.* III. xi. 36:
"When she with Mars was meynt in joyfulnesse."

l. 362. *ne wer she*. A common M. E. idiom. Cf. *Piers Plow.*, Pr., l. 199:
"Nere (ne were) that cat of that courte that can yow ouerlepe;"
idem, Pas iii., l. 134:
"Shireues of shires were shent gif she nere;"
idem, Pr., l. 82:
"Gif thei nere;"
Chaucer, *Man of L. Tale*, l. 34:
"Nere (ne were) that a marchaunt, goon is many a yere;"
Lydgate in *Daunce of Poules:*
"Also ne were it myn entent."
See Glossary of Chaucer's Works under "nere."

l. 365. *Mercurius*. Mercury, as god of eloquence, appears in *Temp. of Glas*, ll. 130-32, and in Hawes' *Past. of Pleas.*, p. 34. Lydgate speaks of him in *Falls of Princes* as "Right fresshe, ryght lusty and full of hardyness." See Schick's notes, pp. 80-1. Cf. *Secrees*, l. 1207:
"In Rethoryk helpith Mercuryvs."

l. 365. *see* = seat. Cf. O. F. *se;* used in the sense of seat or throne in *Faery Queene*, iv., 10, 30.

l. 368. *passyd* = surpassed, excelled. Cf. *Flow. and Leaf*, l. 168:
"That of beautie she past hem everichone."

l. 371. *multyplyers*. For the "cursed craft" of multiplying, its materials and processes, see the Prolog to the Chanouns Yeman's Tale and Gower's *Conf. Am.*, II., p. 84. The "spirits" employed were quicksilver, armoniac, sulphur and arsenic. The multipliers, along with coin washers and clippers, are classed among the vices (l. 681).

l. 373. *whoos long here shone as wyre of goold bryght*, i. e., as the fine glittering threads of goldsmiths' work. A favorite and tell-tale simile of Lydgate's. See Schick, *Temp. of Glas*, notes, p. 88-90; Kölbing, *Sir B. of Hamtoun*, notes, pp. 244-5; also the introduction to this text, p. lvi.

l. 374. *cryspe* = fresh or firm. Most often crisp meant curled, as when describing hair (cf. Chaucer, *Knights Tale*, l. 1307) or rippled, as Milton's "crisped shades" (*Comus*, l. 984). Leigh Hunt has the present use in "It (laurel) has been plucked nine months, and yet looks as hale and crisp as if it would last ninety years." Cf. Browning, *Ring and Book:*
"The first crisp youth that tempts a jaded taste."

l. 374. *columbyne* = either dove-like or in color like the columbine. In Lydgate's *Pur le Roy* (Min. P., p. 8) the word is used in the first sense:
"Most columbyne of chere and of lokyng."

Chaucer (in *March. Tale*, l. 897) has,
"Come forth now with thin eyghen columbine."
Venus is always, of course, associated with doves and roses. Cf. the *Knights Tale*, ll. 1102-4:
"And on her heed, ful semely for to see,
A rose garland ful swete and wel smellyng,
And aboven hire heed dowves flikeryng."
Cf. any mediæval or modern painting of Venus when represented as the "patronesse of plesaunce."

l. 383. *gladyd* = made glad. For this transitive use of glad cf. Chaucer, *Bk. of the Duch*, l. 702:
"May gladde me of my distresse;"
Ho. of Fame, l. 962:
"And gladded me ay more and more;"
Piers Plow., Pas. vi., l. 121:
"Shal no greyne that groweth glade yow at nede;"
Temp. of Glas, l. 1211:
"Hertes to glade itroubled with derkness;"
Browning, *Ring and Book*, p. 57:
"What else shall glad our gaze."
Cf. Wyclif *Magnificat:* "My spiryt hath gladed in God myn helthe."
Lydgate also uses, l. 532, "reioyse" (= make glad) which came to take the place of glad in this sense.

l. 389. *phylosophyrs and poetes.* Lydgate follows Dante in placing the pagan philosophers and poets in Hell. See *Inferno*, c. iv. Dante mentions among the ancient teachers Socrates, Plato, Democritus, Diogenes, Anaxagoras, Thales, Empedocles, Heraclitus, Zeno, Dioscorides, Orpheus, Tully, Linus, Seneca, Euclid, Ptolemy, Hippocrates, Avicenna, Galen, and Averrhoes, and of course, Virgil, Homer, Horace, Ovid and Lucan. These were in the First Circle, which contained the spirits of those who lived virtuously but without Christianity. This is such a list as Hawes gives of those who have achieved fame, and also Douglas of those who inhabit the Palace of Honor.

P. 13, l. 397. *Orace, Ouyde and Omere.* This is the common spelling of these names. Cf. Chaucer, *Ho. of Fame* ll. 1466, 1477, 1487. Omerus is found in *Secrees* l. 378, etc. Euclyte occurs in Min. P. p. 88.

l. 400. *Orpheus.* He is mentioned also in *Temp. of Glas* (l. 1308), playing upon a harp.

l. 402. *carpe.* Commonly meaning to talk, the term is sometimes found applied to music, as here. Often in Lydgate in the sense of talk. Cf. *Chorl and Bird*, Min. P., p. 191:
"It ware but foly withe the more to carpe";
Secrees, l. 708:
"To whoos counsayl in Arrabye folk carpe," etc.
See *carpyng*, l. 439.

l. 404. *to lawe.* Cf. Chaucer, *Cant. Tales*, Pr. l. 474, "lawghe;" *Piers Plow.*, iv, l. 153, "lawghyng;" and *Secrees*, l. 2535:
"Man which lawheth with wyl and herte."

l. 408. *foyson.* Cf. Chaucer, *Ml. Tale*, Pr., l. 57:
"So that he fynde Goddes foyson there";
Lydgate, *Chorl and Bird*, Min. P., p. 184:
"And of alle deyntes plente and foisoun;"
Secrees, l. 1644:
"Or drynk old wyn in greet foysoun."
It is used in *The Tempest*, II. 1.

l. 413. *the fest of Peleus.* The story is that Discord (Eris), being excluded from the feast of Peleus and Thetis, threw among the company a golden apple inscribed "To the fairest." Then arose the dispute between Here, Aphrodite and Athena, wherein Paris was involved as judge of the fairest. The prize fell to Aphrodite, who gave to Paris Helen, whence rose the Trojan war. This was one of the most famous of the mediæval tales of romance. The strife of the goddesses is recorded in Gower's *Conf. Am.* Bk. V. The story is referred to in *Temp. of Glas*, ll. 461-67. Robert of Bruune gives a full account of the rape of Helen and the causes thereto in his *Chron.* ll. 459 *et seq.*

l. 425. *what in the deuylls date.* The meaning of this exclamation is indicated by a passage in Skelton's *Speke, Parrot*, ll. 437-38 :
"Ryn God, rynne Devyll ! yet the date of ower Lord
And the date of the Devyll dothe shrewlye accord."
The Marriage charter of Lady Mede in *Piers Plow.* (Pass. ii) is sealed "in the date of the devil," as other documents are written in the date of the Lord. Cf Skelton, *Bowge of Court*, ll. 375 and 455 :
"Lete theym go, lowse theym, in the deuylles date " ;
Magnificence ll. 2198 and 954 :
"What neded that, in the dyuyls date ! "

l. 426. *howe the game gooth.* Cf. *Rom. of the Rose*, l. 5030 :
"But how that evere the game go."

P. 14, l. 441. *woo begoon.* The opposite phrase is "well begon" as in *Roman of the Rose*, l. 693.

l. 447. *my dart.* In mediæval imagery Death is most often represented as a skeleton figure hurling against all men a spear or a dart. Cf. *Mirrour of the Per. of Man's Life:*
"Now schaketh he his spere to smite me " ;
Court of Love, l. 294 :
"Though Deth therefore me thirlith with his spere " ;
Occleve, *De Reg. Prin.* (ed. Wright, p. 76) :
"Death might have stayed his dart for a time."
See text l. 1935.
The identification of Atropos (here a male figure) with Death is one of the curious features of the poem. Cf *Temp. of Glas*, l. 782-3 :
"Right so shall I, til Antropos me sleithe
For wele or wo, hir faithful man be found."
Atropos is one of the fates in *Story of Thebes*, fol. 374.
Cf. Bullein, *A Dialogue against the Fev. Pest.* (E. E. T, p. 114) :
"Me thinke I doe see the fearful horseman lighted in the valley with a marvelous fearful saying, *En adsum vobis mors vltima linia rerum, etc.* Oh, where shall we hide vs from him ? He casteth forthe his III dartes, and taketh them vp again . . . . . it is merciless Death most fearful," etc.

ll. 449 *et. seq. Death's patent.* It was one of the favorite subjects of contemplation how death brought every man to an end, however exalted his estate. It was customary to refer to the "Nine Worthies"[1] by way of illustration; these were Joshua, Gideon, Samson, David, Judas Maccabaeus, Alexander, Julius Cæsar, Charles the Great, and Godfrey of Boulogne. When it was desirous to prove that the world was false and vain, the question would be asked, Where now is Solomon, Samson, Absalom, Jonathan, Cæsar, Dives,

---

[1] The Nine Worthies furnished stock illustrations to a late date. They are constantly referred to by the dramatists as by Beaumont and Fletcher in *Thierry* and *Theodoret* (Dyce ed. I, p. 143), *Laws of Candy* (V, p. 331), *The Double Marriage* (VI, p. 387), *The Prophetess* (VIII, p. 266). They appear on the stage in character in Middleton's *The World Lost at Tennis* (Bullen ed. VII, p. 165), where they are described by Pallas as they dance in the masque. They were favorite subjects for tapestry (Weber) as appears in Beau. and Fl. *Doub. Mar.* (Dyce ed. VI, p. 387) :
"Thou woven Worthy in a piece of arras,
Fit only to enjoy a wall."

Tully, or Aristotle (see *Hymns to the Virgin*, E. E. T., p. 86—c. 1400). Chaucer's list of those who have been brought low is given in the *Monk's Tale;* they are Lucifer, Adam, Sampson, Ercules, Nabugodonosore, Balthazar, Zenobia, Petro (of Spayne), Petro (of Cipres), Barnabo, Hugilin, Nero, Oliphern, Antiochius, Alisaunder, Julius Cesar and Cresus. Hawes enumerates these whom Fame holds in remembrance: Hector, Josue, Judas Machabeus, Davyd, Alexander, Julius Sesar, Arthur, Charles and Godfrey (*Past. of Pleas.*) To illustrate the theme that all stand in change like a midsummer rose, Lydgate cites elsewhere David, Salamon, Jonathas, Julius, Pirrus of Ynd, Alexander, Nabigodonosor, Sadociopall, Tullius, Crisostomus, Omerus, Senec, and many knights (Min. P., p. 22; see also p. 122). Cf. the tone of the Roxbury Ballad *Farewell to the World:*
"For worldlie pleasure is but vanitie;
  None can redeeme this life from death, I see;
  Nor Cresus' wealth, nor Alexander's fame,
  Nor Sampson's strength, that could Death's fury tame." Rox. B. II, p. 25.
In that most doleful of poems Wiggleworth's *Vanity of Vanities* the motive is repeated in a new land:
"If Beauty could the Beautiful defend
  From Death's dominion, then fair Absalom
  Had not been brought to such a shameful end;
  But fair and foul unto the Grave must come.

  If Wealth or Scepters could Immortal make,
  Then wealthy Croesus, wherefore art thou dead?
  If Warlike-force which makes the World to quake,
  Then why is Julius Caesar perished?

  Where are the Scipio's Thunderbolts of War?
  Renowned Pompey, Caesar's Enemy?
  Stout Hannibal, Rome's Terror known so far?
  Great Alexander, what's become of thee?
  —Libr. Amer. Lit. II, p. 17.
See also Lydgate's *Dance of Macawbre* and *Story of Thebes*, fol. 387; Barclay's *Ship of Fools*, I, p. 264; *Love's Labor's Lost*, VI, 130; V, Sc. 1. l. 130; Southwell's *Image of Death*, etc. Petrarch's *Triumph of Death* may also be compared.

P. 15, l. 470. *Nabúgodónozór*. This is the pronunciation in Chaucer. The spelling *Nabuchodonosor* occurs in the Vulgate (Dan. I., iv); this is the usage of Gower (v. *Conf. Am.* Bk. I, near end), and Chaucer (*Monk's Tale*, l. 155; *Ho. of F.* l. 515), and Langland (*Piers Plow.* Pas. vii, l. 153).

l. 471, *Pharao* is the spelling of the Vulgate; Chaucer has Pharo (*Ho. of F.* l. 516) but Pharao in *Bk. of the Duch.* l. 282.

l. 490. *aldyrs*. The final s must be a scribal error; but cf. ll. 579, 599.

l. 492. Cf. Chaucer, *Knights Tale*, ll. 445–8:
"O cruel goddes, that governe
This world with byndyng of youre word eterne
And wryten in the table of athamaunt
Your parlement and your eterne graunt."

l. 493. *pesecoddys*. This is the form employed by Lydgate in Min. P. p. 105, *Secrees* l. 1374, and by Langland in *Piers Plow.* Pas. vi, l. 294, xiii (C), l. 221, and by Skelton *Why come*, etc., l. 108. The *Secrees* has
"Benys rype and pesecoddys grene."

P. 16, l. 499. *brayde*=started up. Cf. *Æsop*, Fab. 2. l. 90:
"Til sodainly al abrayde";
Temp of Glas, l. 1054:
"Til at the last of routhe she did abraide";

Secrees, l. 308 :
"Till I abrayde in purpoos to resorte."
See "braid," N. E. Dict.

l. 501. *boody, blood and boonys.* "Blood and bone" is a common formula in the Metrical Romances.

l. 503. *malapert.* Cf. Lydgate. Min. P., p. 23 :
"Clatering pyes . . . .
Most malapert there verdit to purpose " ;
idem p. 166 :
"Maleapert of chiere and of visage" (said of a jay).

l. 513. *leyte.* The other texts read "leytenynge"—which is, of course, meant.

l. 530. *hyt fell on a day.* Lydgate has this formula in Min. P., p. 74 : "It fil on a tyme."

l. 530. *wedyr.* Weddir is still the folk pronunciation in portions of Scotland. Cf. Barbour's *Bruce* III., l. 387:
"Till wyntir weddir war away."

P. 17, l. 534. *dresse*=direct. See l. 1512 : "Myn ey gan I dresse." Cf. Chaucer, *Ml. Tale*, l. 282 :
"And to the chambre dore he gan him dresse ;"
Gentl., l. 3 :
"Must folowe his trace and alle his wittes dresse."

l. 550. *ray.* Ray means properly a ray, streak, stripe ; but was commonly used to designate a striped cloth (Skeat). See Lyd., *Lond. Lackpenny*, "a long gown of *raye.*" The plural is found in *P. Pl.* Pas. v, l. 211, "Among the riche rayes." Barclay (*Ship of Fools*, I, p. 35) refers to honest ray=striped cloth. See *Mem. of Lond.* ed. Riley. I. p. 109 for definition= "one piece of striped cloth." Cf. Peele, *Edward I.*, Sc. 6, l. 22 :
"My milk-white steed treading on cloth of ray."

l. 561. Cf. Chaucer, *Man of L. Tale* l. 483:
"But tourne ayein I wil to my mateere;"
Lydgate Min. P. p. 140 :
"But to resorte ageyn to my mateere."

l. 562. And tó | begýn | ne néw | e whére | I léft. Few lines run as smoothly as this. The final *e* comes naturally into use.

l. 563. *besy peyn.* The phrases "besy peyn" and "besy cure" are very common in Lydgate and Chaucer. See Lydgate's Min. P., p. 87 ; *Æsop*, Fab. 2, l. 55, Fab. 6, l. 136 ; *Secrees*, l. 738, 1012; Chaucer, *Parl. of F.* l. 369; *Compl.* l. 2, 119, etc. This text has it again in l. 746. Spenser uses the phrase as in *Faerie Queene* V. xii. 26.

P. 18, l. 597. *nat worth a peere.* The writers of the period had a variety of expressions signifying worthlessness. See l. 493, not give 2 pesecoddes; l. 560, rekke nat a strawe ; l. 1607, then a myte. Cf. *Mort. d'Art.* XV., cap. vi (ed. Southey, II. p. 254) :
"Vayne glory of the world, the whiche is not worth a pere."
Chaucer has "Not worth a myte" in *Knights Tale*, l. 700, *Somp. Tale*, l. 253, *Sec. N. Tale*, l. 511, *Ch. Yem. Tale*, Pr. l. 80 ; "Not worth a flye" in *Parl. of F.*, l. 501; "Not worth a bene" in *Merch. Tale*. In the *Rom. of the Rose* are "Not worth a croked brere," l. 6191 ; and "Not worth an hen," l. 6856. In *Piers Plow.* is "She counteth nought a russhe," Pas. iii, l. 141. Gower uses "Not worth a kerse," *Conf. Am.* I, p. 334, and "Not worth a stre," I, p. 364. Skelton has "Set not a nut shell," *Col. Cl.* l. 1227. Cf. Dunbar, *Fre. Hon. and Nob.* l. 42 :
"Set not by this warld a chirry."
Douglas says (Works II, p. 116, l. 19) : "I compt it neuir a myte."

l. 600. *dere*=injure. Cf. *Rom. of the Rose*, l. 4336:
"May falle a weder that shal it dere."

l. 601. *a son of myne*. With what an imperfect imagination Lydgate grasps the symbolism of his poem may be gathered by comparing this mere reference of Vice as the bastard son of Pluto with the mighty passage in Milton's *Par. Lost* (Bk. X) which describes the relationship of Satan and Sin and Death. Then I have misgivings for having attempted to revive this Lydgate; one then realizes the force of Prof. Lounsbury's remark in his *Studies in Chaucer* that it is unfortunate that the dead past cannot bury not only its dead but its bores.

l. 602. *vaward*=reduction of vantward. Cf. Shakes. *Hen. V*, iv, 3:
"I beg
My lord, most humbly on my knee
The leading of the vaward."
This form is found as late as Drayton's *Agincourt*, Ode XII:
"The eager vaward."

P. 19, ll. 610 *et seq.* the battle. Bunyan's *Holy War* offers many parallels to the conduct of this battle. Thus we are told that the Father appointed his Son to captain the forces of Good, that Emanuel chose five captains to accompany him, captains Credence, Good-hope, Charity, Innocent, and Patience, each with a standardbearer and holy escutcheon to advance ten thousand men. Emanuel rode at their head in a chariot. The army of Diabolus had set over it other captains: Diabolus the King, Incredulity, the Lord-general, the seven chief captains Beelzebub, Lucifer, Legion, Appollyon, Python, Cerberus and Belial, and minor captains Rage, Fury, Damnation, Insatiable, Brimstone, Torment, No-ease, Sepulchre and Past-Hope. This army, uncountable in number, set out from Hell-gate Hill and came by a straight course toward Mansoul, whose five gates (the five senses) they attack with varying fortune though with ultimate defeat. The general question of Bunyan's sources and models has not been fully considered. While it is apparent that he drew almost wholly from the Bible and his own conscience, yet his work must have been in part determined by the traditional accounts of Mansoul's Wars.

l. 612. *dereygne*=set in order, prepare. Cf. Chaucer, *Knights Tale*, l. 773:
"Bothe suffisient and mete to darreyne."
Cf. Spenser, *F. Q.* IV. iv. 26:
"Unable he new battell to darraine."

l. 617. *Vyce, etc.* It is possible to form from the drawings, Moral Plays and literature of the period a very accurate picture of the different vices as objectified in human symbol. If Lydgate is wanting here in descriptiveness it is probably because the work of delineation had been done before him and nothing more was needed beyond mere mention. Langland in *Piers the Plowman* (Pas. v) is especially realistic and dramatic:
"Now awaketh Wratthe with two whyte eyen,
And nyuelynge with the nose and his nekke hangynge;"
"Thanne come Sleuthe al bislabered, with two slymy eighen;"
"Eche a worde that he (envy) warpe was of an addres tonge,
Of chydynge and of chalangynge was his chief lyflode,
With bakbitynge and bismer and beryng of fals witnesse."
See especially Covetousness quoted below (l. 626).
In such character the Vices were kept constantly before the people in play and pageant, which practice was continued until late as witnessed by Richard Tarlton's play of the Seven Deadly Sins, in which Lydgate himself is presented as moving the scenes (cf. Collier, *Hist. Dr. P.* III, p. 394), and by such a remark as that made by Dick Bowyer in *Tryall of Chevalry* (c. 1605, Old Plays, ed. Bullen, III): "If I had a pageant to present of the seven deadly sinnes, he should play Slouth." So long as these characters remained

before the people Lydgate's description was sufficient. I make this note because everywhere the relation between the pictorial, scenic and literary art of the period must be emphasized.
For the subjective conception see Chaucer's *Pers. Tale* and Gower's *Conf. Am.* etc. For a later characterization see Day's *Tractates* (c. 1600) ed. Bullen.

l. 617. *cure boyle.* This is one of many expressions relating to tournament which were introduced into literature, in this case from the French, during the Middle Ages. It means literally "boiled leather." It seems that the knights wore under their coat of mail a garment made either of silk and then called "wafenhemd" or of leather and called "curie." The latter garment was worn in France. It was made of strong leather made pliable by boiling. Chaucer in *Tale of Sir Th.* l. 164 uses the phrase, "His jambeaux were of quirboily," the term being interpreted as "tanned leather." Prof. Skeat (notes to *Pr. T.* p. 166) gives references to Marco Polo (ed. Yule, II, 49) where the men of Carajan are said to wear "armes cuiraces de cuir bouille;" also to Froissart (V. IV, cap. 19) who says the Saracens covered their targes with "cuir bouille." The term occurs in Barbour's *Bruce* XII l. 21–2:
"And on his basnet hye he bar
Ane hat off qwyrbolle ay–quhar."
In *Recuyell of the Hist. of Troye* "armed well with quyer boullye" translates the Fr. "armez de moult beaux habillemens courroyez."
See Cutts, *Scenes and Char. of M. A.*, p. 344.

l. 620. *croppe and roote.* Lydgate makes a very frequent use of this formula. See *Temp. of Glas*, l. 455:
"Humble and benygne, of trouth crop and rote."
See Schick's references in notes to *Temp. of Glas*, p. 98. Chaucer has it in *Troyl. and Crys.*, II., l. 348:
"And ye, that be of beaute crop and roote."
It occurs in Dunbar, *The Flyting*, l. 73:
"Thow crop and rute of traitouris tressonable."
It is an expression still common in Scotland (W. Gregor). Dunbar has also "crop and grayne" (*The Warldis Instab.*, l. 99). Lydgate in Min. P. uses "roote and grounde" (p. 123), "gynnyng and roote" (p. 125), "gynnyng and ground" (238), and in this poem "roote and rynde" (l. 66). Caine in *The Manxman* (ch. xxii.) has "neck and crop" and Meredith the same phrase in *The Ordeal of Rich. Feverel.*

l. 621. *Pryde.* Pride is put the first as the master sin; by that sin fell the angels:
"For Lucifer with hem that felle
Bar Pride with him in to helle"—Gow., *Conf. Am.*, I., p. 153.
He appears again as General of the Army of Sin in Day's *Tractates* (Tract. 7, ed., Bullen, p. 55). See Introd. p. lxxii.

l. 622. *Pryde on a lyon, etc.* In the symbolism of the Middle Ages animals were used as signs of vices and virtues. The custom was started by the theologians, notably Jerome. In certain of the early *Bestiares*, as the *Renart le Nouvel* (1288) the animals were first associated with the Moralities. Dante in entering the dark wood was confronted by a leopard, a lion and a wolf, typical of certain sins. In the *Ancren Riwle* the symbolism is well established. In the processional described in the *Faerie Queene* (I., iv.) Idleness is seen riding upon an ass, Gluttony on a swine, Lechery on a goat, Avarice on a camel, Envy on a wolf and Wrath upon a lion. Bunyan makes some use of this traditional symbolism in the lions that guarded the palace Beautiful.

l. 622. *Enuy.* Envy is personified in the *Temp. of Glas*, l. 147; cf. also *Rom. of the Rose*, l. 248; *Court of Love*, l. 1254, etc. For the portrait of Envy see Spenser, *F. Q.*, V., xii., 29–32.

l. 626. *Couetyse.* A fine description of Covetousness is drawn by Langland in *Piers Plow.* Pas. v., ll. 188–94 :
"And thanne cam Coueytise . . . .
So hungriliche and holwe, sire Hervy hym loked,
He was bitelbrowed and baberlipped also,
With two blered eyghen as a blynde hagge ;
And as a letheren purs lolled his chekes,
Wel sydder than his chyn thei chiueled for elde ;
And as a bondman of his bacoun his berde was bidraueled."
This Vice is often mounted upon a horse that he may speed more quickly, as in *Evil Times of Ed., II.* (Polit. Songs, p. 326) :
"Coveytise upon his hors he wole be sone there
And bringe the bishop silver, and rounen in his ere."
Covetise is personified in the *Temp. of Glas*, l. 244. The fifth book of Gower's *Conf. Am.* is devoted to Avarice.

l. 627. *olyfaunt.* This is the spelling of Maundeville and Skelton. "Oliphantes" is found in Lyndesay's *Monarche*, l. 2295.

l. 631. *Slowthe.* Sloth is personified in *Temp. of Glas*, l. 244. See *Rom. of the Rose*, ll. 531, 593, 1273, etc. ; *Faery Queene*, I., iv, 18, etc.

l. 636. *Symony.* Note the feeling of Langland in this matter, *Piers Plow.*, Pas. ii., ll. 62–3, 86 :
"Ac Symonye and cyuile and sisoures of courtes
Were most pryue with Mede ;"
the priests wish to live in London
"And syngen there for symonye for silver is swete."
See Dante's *Inferno* (c. xix.) for the punishment of the guilt of Simony.

P. 20, l. 640. *Ielacy.* Jealousy is personified in the *Temp. of Glas*, l. 148. See *Rom. of the Rose*, l. 3820 ; *Parl. of F.*, l. 252 ; *Quair*, 877.

l. 644. *Vsury.* Usury was the special sin of Avarice (v. *P. Pl.*, Pas. v., l. 240–52). All usury was prohibited as a sin by the Canon Law (Southey, *Bk. of the Church*, p. 187). It was the theory of the schoolmen that the taking of interest was unholy since money was not of itself productive. Dante consigned usurers to one of the lowest regions of Hell. The continued prejudice in England against the money lender is testified by Shakespeare's *Merchant of Venice*, and Bacon repeated the old theory, "It is against nature for money to beget money." Cf. a Roxbury Ballad (I., p. 426) :
"The Usurers follow,
That pawnes have in hand ;
With whoop and with hollow
They call for the Land
Which spend-thrifts pawne to them
While for cash they hye ;
To live to undoe them .
This bargaine they'l buy."

l. 648. *Boldnes | in Yll‖ with Foul | e Ry | baudy.* In this line the final *e* in foule seems to be pronounced. But Text B and the Prints read *Foule and Rybaudy.*

l. 655. *New-fangylnes.* The love of novelty seems to have been considered a special vice of the times. Lydgate in Min. P. (p. 71) speaks of "the serpent of newfangelnesse" and says (p. 60) :
"I-bannysshed have newfangelnesse
And put in his place perseveraunce."
Chaucer writes against "Women Unconstant":
"Madame, for your newe fangelnesse
Many a servaunt have ye put out of grace . . . .
To newe thing your lust is ever kene."
See also *An. and Arc.*, l. 141 ; *Leg. of G. Wom.*, Pr., l. 154. Nichol New-

fangle is the "Vice" in the interlude *Like will to Like* (1568). This is also one of Stubbes' "Abuses" (p. 31).

l. 666. *Idylnesse.* Lydgate calls Idleness the "Moder to vices" (Min. P., p. 88) and the "Chief porteresse" of the vices (Min. P., p. 68). In *Æsop* he says again that "Vice alle proceden of idelnesse." Cf. Chaucer, *Sec. N. Tale*, ll. 1-3:
"The ministre and the norice unto vices,
Which that men clepe in English ydelnesse,
The porter of the gate is of delyces."

l. 668. *but there was an [h]ost!* Considering the chief vices as roots and stems, the secondary branches and twigs become innumerable. Thus Chaucer enumerates in the *Pers. Tale* among the twigs from the root of pride inobedience, avaunting, ypocrisye, despit, arragaunce, impudence, swellyng of hert, insolence, elacioun, impacience, strif, contumacie, presumpcioun, irreverence, pertinacie, and veinglorie. This gives material and scope for incalculable growth and differentiation. Give the fancy play and in a moment one exclaims with Barclay (*Ship of Fools*, I., p. 4):
"For yf I had tunges an hundreth: and wyt to fele
Al thinges natural and supernaturall,
A thousand mouthes: and voyce as harde as stele,
And sene al the seven sciences lyberal,
Yet cowde I neuer touche the vyces all,
And syn of the worlde: ne theyr braunches comprehende:
Nat thoughe I lyued vnto the worlds ende."
For the abundance of vices of the time of Henry VIII., v. *The Hy Way to the Spitl-house* (Bartholomew's Hospital, London): description in Furnivall's ed. of *Capt. Cox, etc.* (Ballad Soc.) p. ci-ciii.—twenty-three sets of unfortunates. See especially the list of "unthrifts," p. ciii. Cf. Wyclif's list of sins in *Fifty Heresies and Errors of Friars* (ed., Arnold, III., p. 366). Cf. the vices that voyage in Barclay's Ship of Fools; also those satirized in Skelton's *Bowge of Court* and the list of rogues in the Miracle Play, *The Last Judgment* (Roxburge Club). For the species of rogues and vagabondes in Elizabethan England, cf. Thornbury, *Shaks. Engl.*, I., ch. viii.; Decker's *English Villanies*, Harrison's *England*, II., ch. xi., *passim; Three Tracts about Old Rogues*, ed. by Viles and Furn. (N. Shaks. Soc.); Stubbes' *Anatomy of Abuses* (N. Shaks. Soc.). These enumerations throw much light upon the practical life of the time. Many of the Commons in Lydgate's list are not known to us even by name.

P. 21, l. 673 *et. seq.* Langland groups "bakbiteres, breke-chestes, brawleres and chideres" (*P. Pl.*, Pas. xvi., l. 43).

ll. 674, 676. *fasers*=boasters, *crakers*=vaunters. See Skelton, *Garl. of Laur.*, ll. 188-9:
"Some lidderons, some losels, some noughty packis;
Some facers, some bracers, some make great crackis;"
Borde, *Bk. of Knowl.*:
"I wyll boost myselfe, I wyll crake and face;"
Barclay, *Ship of Fools*, I., p. 198:
"For greatest crakers ar nat ay boldest men.

l. 679. *scismatykes.* Cf. *Piers Plow.*, Pas. xi., l. 114-15:
"For Cryste cleped vs alle come if we wolde,
Sarasenes and scismatikes and so he dyd the Iewes."

l. 681. *coyn wasshers and clyppers.* For the evil of counterfeiting, etc., cf. Hoccleve's *Complaint*, Min. P., xxi.

l. 685. *tregetours.* For the pretentions of these tricksters see *Frank. Tale*, ll. 413-20:

>   "Which as the subtile tregetours pleyen
>   For oft at festes have I herd seyen,
>   That tregettoures, withinne an halle large,
>   Han made in come water and a barge,
>   And in the hall rowen up and doun;
>   Sometyme hath semed come a grym leoun
>   Som tyme a castel al of lym and ston,
>   And whan hem liked voyded it anon."

l. 691. *stalkers by night.* A proclamation was made in London in 1329 to the effect that no one should be so daring as to go wandering about the city after the hour of Curfew (see *Memor. of Lond.*, ed. Riley, I, p. 173; II, p. 482).

l. 692. *brekers of lofedayes.* Love-days were days fixed for settling differences by umpire. Cf. *Cov. Myst*:
>   "Now is the love-day mad of us foure fynially,
>   Now may we leve in pes as we were wonte."

A passage in Wyclif's Tracts (Works. ed. Arnold III, p. 322) throws light upon the custom. We see knights and yeomen kneeling in the castle chapel, a general gathering in the hall, statements from both sides, arbitration and reconciliation (Arnold).

l. 693. *getters.* Cf. Barclay, *Ship of Fools.*, I, p. 146:
>   "Ye wasters and getters by nyght."

In Bunyan's *Pilg. Prog.* is a schoolmaster who taught the art of "getting" either by violence or cozenage, flattery, lying, etc.

l. 694. *Tytyuyllys.* Any person with evil propensities (Collier). Douce derives the name from *Titivilitium*, a word used by Plautus. Collier suggests its derivation from *totus* and *vilis*. He appears in *The Mirroure of Oure Ladye* (E. E. T. p. 54) saying "I am a poure dyvel and my name ys Tytyvyllus." His office was to bring to his master every day one thousand bags of syllables skipped in reading and singing the divine service in the churches. He appears in this character in MS. Lansd. 762 (quoted by Wright):
>   "Hii sunt qui Psalmos corrumpunt nequitur almos:
>   Jangler cum jasper, lepar, galper quoque, draggar,
>   Momeler, for-skypper, for-reynner, sic et over-leper,
>   Fragmina verborum *Tutivillus* colligit horum."

He became a common figure in the plays as any evil fellow. He is one of the devils in the play of *The Last Judgment*, where he seems to be a churchman opposing the heresy of Wyclif. He is a fiend in a Townely Mystery (pp. 310, 319) and a lawless fellow in *Ralf Roister Doister*. He is a fiend in *Mankind* representing the sin of the flesh. Skelton (*Col. Cl.* l. 418) uses the phrase "and talkys lyke tytyuelles," probably here a tale-bearer, in which character he appears in *Rogues and Vag.* (N. Shaks. Soc. p. 15). In Stubbes' *Anat. of Abuses* he is a flatterer (p. 122). The word occurs again in Skelton's *Garl. of Laur.*, l. 642. See Collier, *Hist. Dr. P.* II, pp. 146, 297, 223; Dyce's notes on Skelton; notes to *Myrrour of O. Ladye*, p. 342.

l. 696. *carders*=card-players. For the punishment for cheating at play see *Mem. of Lond.* (ed. Riley, II, p. 395). "Turning the tables" was one method of cheating.

l. 696. *closshers.* This was a kind of game. Cf. Stubbes' *Anat of Ab.* notes p. 316: an act of Hen. VIII. — "noe manner of person shall . . . . kepe . . . any alley or place of bowlinge Coytinge, Cloyshe, Coyles, etc."

l. 697. *Tyburne.* The place of execution in London. Cf. Rowland's *A Fooles Bolt is soone Shot:*
>   "Of Tybourne (i. e. the gallows) common hye-way cannot fayle."

Harrison (*England* II, ch. 16) calls the halter a "Tiburne tippet." This was also the name of a prison in London. *Coloppys* means pieces of meat, used figuratively often for children (as in *I. Hen.* vi, v. 5). "Tyburne coloppys" may have been a slang phrase. Cf. *Cocke Lorelles Bote*, C. i. a.

l. 698. *double tollyng myllers* = those millers who tolled with a too "golden thumb."

l. 702. *brokers* = receivers of stolen goods etc. Cf. Stubbes' *Anat. of Ab.* Pt. II., p. 40.

l. 707. *sotyll ambidextres* = Jacks-of-both-sides. "Ambidexter is that jurous or embraceour that taketh of both parties for the giving of his verdict" (Cowell'r *Interpreter*). A tricksey character called Ambidexter appears in Bullein's *Dialogue against the Fev. Pest.* (E. E. T. p. 20), Cf. Middleton, *Fam. of Love*, V, 3 : "I'll play Ambidexter"; also Peele, *Sir Cly. and Sir Clam.*, sc. vi, l. 77. In an early American poem by Ebenezer Cook reference is made to
"an ambidexter Quack
Who learnedly had got the knack
Of giving glisters, making pills,
Of filling bonds and forging wills "—*Libr. of Amer. Lit.* II, 273. Stubbes in his *Anatomy of Abuses* speaks of "doble dealing ambodexters" (p. 141).

l. 708. *Sodomytes.* Used by Stubbes to signify fornicators (*Anat of Ab.* I. p. 145).

P. 22, l. 710. *wetewoldes that suffre syn in her syghtes.* A wittol was a tame "cuckold"—one who had knowledge of his wife's infidelity. Skelton, *Garl. of Laur*, l. 187, refers to "wetewoldis." Middleton in *Chast Maid of Cheapside* gives a picture of one. Cf. Shaks. *Mer. W. of Wind.*, II, 2 :
"But cuckold! wittol-cuckold! the Devil himself hath not such a name." Cf. *Loves's Labour's Lost*, v, 904–12 :
"When Daisies pied and Violets blew
And Cockow-buds of yellow hew
And Ladie-smokes al silver white,
Do paint the Meadowes with delight,
The cuckow then on everie tree
Mocks married men; for thus sings he.
Cuckow!
Cuckow! Cuckow! O worde of feare,
Unpleasing to a married eare."

l. 711. *abhominable.* This is the regular spelling of the N. E. abominable in O. Fr. and in English from Wyclif to the seventeenth century. This spelling is defended by Holofernes in *Love's Lab. Lost* against the "racker of orthography" who would say abominable.

l. 711. *auauntours.* Cf. Chaucer, *Pers. Tale*: "Avauntour is he that bosteth of the harm or of the bounté that he hath don."

l. 713. *vnthryftys.* Cf. Barclay, *Ship of Fooles*, I, p. 2 :
"But such Unthriftes as sue theyr carnal lust."

l. 714. *loselles.* Cocke Losel or Lorel was a generic term for a rascal. Cf. Browning, *Strafford*. III, 2, l. 170.

l. 717. *for to say.* The common M. E. usage. "For to fet," l. 1155.

l. 727. *I will auauntage take where I may.* Cf. the words of Legion in Bunyan's *Holy War:* "Therefore let us assault them in all pretended fairness, covering our intentions with all manner of lies, flatteries, delusive words."

l. 732. *mortall* = equivalent to "lethalis," deadly. Cf. *Æsop*, Fab. 4, l. 34, "Of mortal hunger."

l. 732. *shoure* = conflict, struggle. O. E. scûr. Commonly applied to the assault of battle. See line 1042.

l. 742. *to me ward.* Toward was frequently divided and the object inserted between the parts as here. Cf. II Cor. 3:4: "And such trust have we through Christ to God-ward."

P. 23, l. 748. *Ymaginacion.* Note the part played by Imaginative in *Piers Plow.* Pas. xii.

l. 760. *mowte.* Mowe and mowte are common in M. E. See l. 264 where mought rimes with fought.

l. 766. *lest and moost.* A common formula in Lydgate, Chaucer and other writers. Cf. *Ck. Tale,* l. 460:
"Faire they were welcomed bothe lest and meste."
Langland (*Piers Flow.,* Pas. ii, l. 45) has "the lasse and the more."

l. 773. *trayne.* Cf. Fairfax's Tasso, II, l. 89:
"So lions roar, enclos'd in train or trap";
Fairy Queene, Bk. I, c. iii, st. 24:
"By traynes into new troubles to have toste."
Milton has "wily trains" in *Comus,* l. 151. Shakespeare uses it once in this sense in *Macbeth,* IV. 3.

l. 773. *coltrop* = a pointed iron instrument strewn in battle fields to hinder cavalry. Cf. Beaumont and Fletcher, *Love's Pilgrimage:*
"I think they ha' strew'd the highways with caltraps,
No horse dares pass 'em."
It occurs in Middeton, *Women Beware Women.* Cf. the proper name Caultrap.

l. 776. *Vyce hys.* See "Vertew hys," l. 798 etc. The corruption of his for O.E.-ës, the genitive termination, is found as early as Layamon's *Brut;* "For Gwenayfer his love." "Ine was the forste mon that Peter his peny bigan" *Brut,* (B.) III., l. 285. The *Prayer Book* has "For Christ his sake." Cf. Stubbes' *Anat. of Abuses* (1583) p. 75: "Every poore Yeoman his daughter, every Husbandman his daughter, and every Cottager his daughter." This use occurs in Spenser, Shakespeare and Bacon and did not die out until the eighteenth century. Ben Jonson, English Grammar XIII, calls it "the monstrous syntax of the pronoun *his* joining with a noun betokening a possessor"; and yet Addison, *Spectator No. 135,* writes that "the same single letter (s) ... represents the *his* and *her* of our forefathers"; v. Marsh *Lectures* XVIII (Percival). In *Guardian No. 98* Addison writes: "My paper is the Ulysses *his* bow." The use extended to the feminine gender and the plural number (v. *Cent. Dict.* under *his²*).

l. 776. *purseuaunte.* Cf. Chaucer, *Ho. of Fame,* l. 1321: "The pursevaunts and heraudes"; *Flow. and Leaf,* l. 232: "Of heraudes and pursevaunts eke." Shakespeare has: "These gray locks the pursuivants of death" (*Henry VI,* II, 5, 5). Browning uses it in *Blot in the Scut.,* Act I, l. 4; and Tennyson in *Balin and Balan:* "A spangled pursuivant."

P. 24, l. 792. *foure dowty knyghtys* = the virtues called "Cardinal" in accordance with the Platonic Ethics. These virtues together with the theological triad appear as maidens in Dantes *Purg.* (c. xxix) accompanying the chariot of the Church. This pageant of the advance of Virtue suggests that of the last five cantos of the *Purgatorio.* No doubt, such scenes occurred in the street processional plays. Note the pageant in the *Anti-Claudianus* with Reason as charioteer. (There is a vicar in *Piers Plow.* who said the only cardinals he knew were those sent by the Pope.)

l. 808. *Pacyence.* In *Piers Plow.* Patience is described as a tree which grows in the heart and bears fruit of Charity. The tree is supported against the winds of the world, the flesh, and the devil by three props denoting the Trinity.

P. 25, l. 815. This line seems to be corrupted in the *MS.* which reads "was trapure was gay." *Trapure* refers to the "trappings" of the steed. Cf. *Flow. and Leaf*, ll. 244-5:

"With cloth of gold and furred with ermine
Were the trappores of here stedes stronge,
Wide and large, that to the ground dide honge";

Lydgate, Min. P., p. 118:
"Trappours of golde ordeyned were for stiedis";
Hawes, *Past. of Pleas.*, p. 132:
"Wyth haute courage betrapped fayre and gaye
Wyth shyning trappers of curiositie."

l. 824. *to steuyn.* Stevene is always employed by Chaucer as a noun. It has here a verbal use probably from the necessity of the rime. There was, however, the older verb from stefnen (cf. *M. E. Dict.*, Strat.-Brad.). Douglas has (II., p. 225, l. 8): "towart the port thai stevin" = directed their ship; but this is from the Icl. stefna = prow. Chaucer has this set of rimes in *Kn. Tale*, ll. 1720-21; *Troil. and Cris.*, III., ll. 1723-25; *Leg. of G.W.*, ll. 1218-19.

l. 844. *Pouerte.* Poverty was a highly praised virtue in the Church. It is said in *Piers Plow.*, Pas. xiv., that this virtue preserves men from the Seven Sins, for it (1) is hateful to Pride, (2) has few responsibilities, (3) does not win wealth falsely, (4) is the gift of God, (5) is the mother of health, (6) is without peril of robbery, (7) is a source of wisdom, (8) deals fairly with others, (9) is without care. Feigned Poverty is one of the Vices, l. 657.

P. 26, l. 854. *Konnyng with hys genalogy.* That is to say the Seven Arts and Sciences. The seven sciences as originally distinguished were Mathematics, Geometry, Astronomy, Music, Ethics, Physics and Metaphysics. The seven arts were: Grammar, Dialectics, Rhetoric (the trivium) and Arithmetic, Music, Geometry, and Astronomy (the quadrivium). These are mentioned familiarly by all the learned writers of the Middle Ages. They were characterized also in the plays and pageants and such objectification gives meaning to the processional of the poem. In Lydgate's description of the King's entry into London there is an account of a spectacle representing the Seven Sciences. The name of Priscian is associated with Grammar ("the roote of alle connyng"), Aristotle with Logic, Cicero with Rhetoric, Boethius with Music, Pythagoras with Arithmetic, Euclid with Geometry, and Albumasar with Astronomy ("alder-highest"). In *Piers Plow.*, the sciences appear as sons of the Clergy, serving the Lord of Life in a castle (Pas. xiii). See Gower, *Conf. Aman*, Lydgate's *Pur le Roy*, *Chestre Plays* (Wright, p. 241), Hallam, *Lit. of Europe*, etc.

ll. 867-870. The Magical and Black Arts. The specific "Black Arts" were commonly five: Necromancy, Pyromancy, Geomancy, Hydromancy, and Aerimancy, signifying divination by means of the dead, fire, the earth, water, and the air respectively. These species are indicated by Huge de S. Victore (see Skeat's Notes to *Piers Plow.*, p. 246). Gower *Conf. Aman.*, III., p. 45, describes these five kinds in detail; see also Lydgate's *Secrees*. As to the merits of the magical arts, opinion was divided. The Black Arts were almost universally denounced in this period in England. Alchemy and Physiognomy were, however, often employed. It seems that there was a revival of Magic, and especially of Alchemy, during Chaucer's and Lydgate's lifetime. But we find that sorcery, soothsaying and magic were punished in London as early as 1382, the affirmation being that "the art of magic redounds against the doctrine of Sacred Writ"; the punishment was exposure upon the pillory (*Mem. of Lond.*, ed. Riley, II., pp. 462, 472, 518). A statute forbidding the practice of Alchemy was passed in 1403. The art was revived again at about the end of the century, so that Henry VI. appointed three Royal Commissioners to investigate the subject. Their report is dated 1456 (see *The Antiquary*, Sept. 1891, for documents illustrating the revival of Alchemy at about the middle of the fifteenth century). We find that Alchemy was condemned by Gower (*Conf. Am.* II., p. 88); Alchemy and other arts by Langland (*Piers Plow.*, Pas. x., ll. 207-15); the magical arts in general by Chaucer (in *Ch. Yeo. Tale*, and *Pers. Tale*) and Lydgate (in the present instance and *Secrees* st. 82-84 — though favorable to physiognomy, st. 353-54, and in *Story of Thebes* [fol. 390], where he condemns Bishop Amphiorax to hell as the mede of his idolatry and magic) and Barclay (*Ship of Fools*, II., pp. 18, 191, 219). As a matter of fact, Alchemy flourished in spite of condemnation and belief in it continued far into the seventeenth century (see *Faery Queene*, I., c. i., st. 36-37 and Sir Th. Browne, Works I., ch. x.). In Ward's *O. E. Drama*, Introduction to Marlowe's "Dr. Faustus," the general attitude of the M. Ages toward magic and magicians is shown. See *Secrees*, notes, p. 93-95.

l. 868. *Glotony.* This must be a mistake of the scribe for Alchemy.

l. 870. *Pawmestry.* Divination by the lines of the hand.

l. 882. *Ches.* Cf. *Æsop*, Fab. 5, l. 71:
  "The crane chase a surgeon to be";
Temp of Glas., l. 214, 336:
  "Would freli chese."
Note *leese* l. 1100.

l. 886. *ware of contagious geere.* Contagious geere = ?

P. 27, l. 887. *lere.* "Lere" here means learn; "lerne" in l. 957 means teach. Cf. *Temp. of Glas.*, l. 297, 1021 = learn:
  "Fro dai to dai that I myghte lere";
idem, l. 656 = teach:
  "Than cometh dispeire and ginneth me to lere."
Cf. *Story of Thebes*, fol. 378:
  "The which beasts as the story leres."

l. 895. *secte.* Cf. *Rom. of the Rose*, l. 5745:
  "Eke in the same secte or sette."

l. 896. See note on l. 1997.

P. 28, l. 925. *then I reherse can.* Cf. *Temp. of Glas.*, l. 560: "as I reherse can" and often.

l. 932. *Macrocosme.* I interpret this to mean Microcosm from the interpretation by Doctrine, st. 262. For the conception of Microcosm see *Secrees*, ll. 2313-17:
  "In beeste nor thyng vegitable,
  No thyng may be vnyuersally
  But yif it be founde naturally
  In mannys nature. Wherfore of oon accoord
  Oold philisoffres callyd hym the litel woord (worlde)."
See also Stubbes, *Anat. of Abuses*, p. 111:
"And therfore, wheras in making of other things he used only this Woord, FIANT, be they made or let them be made, when he came to make Man, as it weare advysing himselfe and asking councell at his wisdome, he said FACIAMUS HOMINEM, let us make Man; that is a wonderful Creature: and therfore is called in Greek MICROCOSMOS, a litle world in himself. And truely he is no lesse, whether we consider his spirituall soule, or his humaine body, etc."
For a fuller account of Man, the Microcosm, assailed by Vices and defended by Virtues, see Fletcher's *Purple Island*, the most dreadful of all the Holy Wars.

l. 939. *hygh weyes fyue.* All the old books make much of man's five senses,

the high-ways of Mansoul. Note the use made by Bunyan of this conception in *Holy War:*
"The famous town of Mansoul had five gates at which to come, and out at which to go; and these were made likewise answerable to the walls, to wit, impregnable, and such as could never be opened nor forced but by the will and leave of those within. The names of the gates were these: Ear-gate, Eye-gate, Mouth-gate, Nose-gate, and Feel-gate."

l. 941. *blyue.* Cf. Chaucer, *Bk. of the Duch.* l. 152:
"Go now faste, and hy thee blyve;"
Æsop, Fab. 4, l. 206:
"With ravenous feete, wynged to flee blyue."

P. 29, l. 957. *lerne hem a new daunce.* A common saying with Chaucer and others. Cf. *Rom. of the Rose*, l. 4300:
"For she knew alle the olde daunce."
Cf. Chaucer, *Troyl and Crys.* II. l. 554; *Dr. of Ph. Tale*, l. 79; *Cant. Tales*, Pr. l. 470. Cf. Gower *Conf. Aman.*, I., p. 260:
"Now shalt thou singe an other songe."

l. 974. *dubbyd.* Cf. *Piers Plow.*, Pas. i., ll. 102-3:
"For Dauid in his dayes dubbed knightes
And did hem swere on here swerde to serue trewthe euere."
In *Ad. Dav. Dream* (E.E. T., l. 76) "dubbing" is a substantive and means decoration.

P. 30, l. 998. *Reson.* Reason is a common personification. See *Rom. of the Rose*, 3034, 3193; Lydgate's Min. P., p. 219; *Piers Plow.* Pas. xv., xvi.; Dunbar's *Gold. Targe*, 151, etc. In *Piers Plow.* Reason has many names: anima, animus, mens, memoria, ratio, sensus, conscientia, amor, spiritus. He plays an important part in the poem.

l. 1009. One instance of a double negative. Cf. *Æsop*, Fab. 4, l. 53:
"I may no favour do to nowther side."

l. 1012. *hyng in hys balaunce.* A very common figure. Cf. *Temp. of Glas*, ll. 641, 348; Chaucer, *Troyl. and Crys.* II., l. 466:
"And ek myn emes lyf is in balaunce."
In Barclay's *Ship of Fools* is a wood-cut showing the world and things eternal in a balance. Cf. Spenser's figure in *Faerie Queene* V., ii., 30-49.

l. 1012. *ambyguyte.* Chaucer has amphibologyes, *Troil. and Cris.*, iv., l. 1406.

P. 31, l. 1023. *sewe the felde.* Lydgate probably had in mind the parable of the Sower. Langland has a parable of the ploughman in Pas. xix.; there the weeds of vice grow in the field but they are uprooted by the harrow of the Law.

l. 1038. *swage.* I define as "discharge" but find no authority for it except the context.

l. 1038. *gonnes.* The first mention of guns or "gonnes" as being in use in England is found in an inventory of munitions of war in a London document dated 1339 (see *Mem. of London*, ed. Riley, I., p. 205). These "gonnes" were made of brass or "latone" and fired "pellets of lead," using gunpowder. Cf. Chaucer *House of Fame*, III., l. 553:
"Swift as a pellet out of a gonne,
When fire is in the powder ronne";
Lydgate's *Story of Thebes*, fol. 392:
"Noise more hideous then thunder
Of gonne shot."
The word was also employed to designate a machine that cast stones. Cannon is mentioned in Barbour's *Bruce* (1375) Bk. XIX., l. 399. Cannon had been used in Florence in 1326.

P. 32, l. 1063. *abew*=a beu. Gower has the phrase in *Conf. Aman.*, III., p. 356:
"Er thou make any such assaies
To love and faile upon thy fete
Better is to make beau retrete."
The word beau was commonly used in address as in *Rom. of the Rose*, l. 800:
"What do ye there, beau sir?"
Sir Gawain, E.E. T., l. 1222:
"Nay, for sothe, beau syr";
also *House of Fame*, l. 643. Cf. *Rich. Rede.*, Pas. iii., l. 1:
"Now leve we this beu brid."

l. 1063. *lytyll tyne*. Cf. Skelton, *Garl. of Laur*. l. 505:
"A lytyll tyne stande backe";
Heywood, *Dialogue:*
"For when prouender prickt them a little tine."
The two words generally occur together. See l. 1283.

l. 1066. *by lyklynes*. Cf. *Temp. of Glas.*, l. 18; Chaucer, *Am. Compl.* l. 15 *Cl. Tale*, II., l. 200, etc.

l. 1089. *lowte*. Cf. *Æsop*, Fab. 2, ll. 17–18.
"Whan sulphur toward the dawenyng
Lowtith to the oryent";
Piers Plow., Pas. iii., l. 115:
"Knelynge, Conscience to the kynge louted."
See also text, ll. 1439, 1925, vnderlowte 1273.
Cf. Browning, *Ring and Book:*
"I have louted low."

P. 33, l. 1094. *Perséueraunce*. The accent as in Chaucer.

l. 1095. *hogy*. Cf. Marlowe, *Tamb. the Gt.:* "my hugy host." This was Dryden's usage.

P. 34, ll. 1142–6. The way of repentance is made clear by Chaucer's Parson: "Now shalt thou understonde what bihoveth and is necessarie to verray parfyt penitence; and this stondith in thre things, contricioun of hert, confessioun of mouth, and satisfaccioun." The first, said Patience in *Piers Plow*. (Pas. xiv.), saves men, the second slays sins, the third uproots sin altogether. Contrition and Confession appear as two horses that bear ripened grain to the house of Unity (*Piers Plow*. Pas. xix.). They are good dames in Hawes' *Past. of Pleas.*, giving sure passage to Purgatory to Graunde Amour. They are characters in the Moralities. The trinal stairs in Dante's *Purgatorio* (c. ix.) refer to these stages of repentance. All these figures refer to the creed of the Church as expounded for instance by Thomas Aquinas in his great work *Summa Theologica* (III. p. 90).

l. 1147. *fro poost to pylour*. Cf. Barclay, *Eclogues:*
"From post unto piller tost shall thou be."

l. 1154. Despair appears in *Temp. of G*. l. 656. He was a common figure in the mediæval imagination. Cf. Spenser's treatment of Despair. (See a paper by Dr. F. I. Carpenter reported in Univ. of Chicago Cal. Aug. '95.)

l. 1158. *Alpha and Oo*. This occurs in the *Creation*, sc. I., York Plays, in the address of the Deity:
"I am Alpha and O."

P. 35, l. 1167. *borow*=verbal. Cf. Chaucer, *Ck. Tale* l. 204:
"For he hath slayn my two sones, but if God hem borwe";
the old play, *World and Child:*
"Some good word that I may say
To borow man's soul from blame."
See also *Piers Plow*. Pas. iv, l. 108–9.

This word was often used as a noun as in *Tem. of Glas*, l. 1145:
"And as for him I will bene his borow,"
and in the phrase "to borow" (=for a security).

l. 1169. *tenebrus.* Cf. Hawes' *Past. of Pleas.* p. 15, 74:
"Auster gan cover with clowde tenebrus";
"The night was wete, and also tenebrous."

l. 1185. *fly.* This is the reading of MS. B. A has sty from stigen, to ascend.

P. 36, l. 1204. *bettyr late then neuer.* Cf. Chaucer, *Ch. Yeo. Tale*, l. 399:
"For bet than never is late."

l. 1226. *sothe.* Cf. Chaucer, *Parl. Fou.*, l. 578, "sothe sadde"=sober truth.

l. 1232. *as a pleyer.* Collier in a note on this passage (*Annals of the Stage*, p. 31) refers to player as an actor, interpreting the line to mean that Sensuality must change his character like an actor. But "to drawe a draught" is used of games as chess. Thus Chaucer (*Bk. of the Duch*, l. 682) has
"I wolde have drawe the same draughte."
In a work described by Collier (*An. of Stage*, p. 63) entitled *The Church of Yvell men and women* players refers to gamesters, dicers, etc.
"Player" would seem to mean here "gamester"; though it is possible that "draught" may be used here figuratively for "character" as Collier suggests.

P. 37, l. 1242. *finaunce.* Cf. Skelton, *Erle of Nh.*, l. 195:
"With thy bloud precious our finaunce thou did pay";
the same line occurs in Percy's *Reliques*, I, p. 125.

l. 1255. Reason in Microcosm. Cf. description of Reason in the *Romaunt of the Rose*, ll. 3193 *et seq.*, where she warns against the follies of Love. Chaucer's Parson says:
"For it is soth, that God, and reasoun, and sensualité, and the body of man, be so ordeyned, that everich of these four thinges schulde have lordschipe over that other, as thus: God scholde have lordschip over reasoun, and reasoun over sensualité, and sensualité over the body of man."
Cf. Lydgate Min. P., p. 219:
"Sith thu were wroughte to be celestial,
Let reson brydle thy sensualite."

l. 1256. *recreaunt.* This was a word which Knights uttered in acknowledging defeat. "Yelde hym recreaunt" = yielded himself as a defeated knight. The oath taken by a combatant ran thus: "Je suis prest de le prouver de mon corps contre le sien, et le rendre mort ou recreant . . . et véez çy mon gage." The customary form of demanding surrender was: "And but thou yeeld thee as overcome and recreaunt thou shalt die." Cf. *Sir Gawayne*, E. E. T., l. 456:
"Therfore com other recreaunt be calde."
Piers Plow. (Pas. xv, l. 133) has "yelde hym creaunt" (as a believer?); "creaunt" is sometimes used for recreaunt in the sense explained above.

l. 1267. *astert.* Cf. Chaucer, *Fr. Tale*, l. 294:
"He seith, he may not fro his deth asterte."

P. 38, l. 1268. *Nature.* Nature was given especial personification by Alanus de Insulis in his *Planctus Naturæ* (Wright ed., Rec. Ser., pp. 431–456). Chaucer in the *Parl. of Foules* describes her as a Queen surrounded by the animals of the earth and air (ll. 298–301, etc.). In Langland's dream Nature appears and shows the wonders of the world (Pas. xi, l. 311–25). She was an empress in the pageant that welcomed Henry VI. to London (*Pur Le Roy*). See the *Faerie Queene* VII, vii.

l. 1274. *shoo clowte*=shoe-cloth. Cf. Skelton, *El. Rum*, ll. 143-4:
"Some wyth a sho clout
Bynde theyr heddes about."
Browning his "clouted shoon" (Ring and Book, p. 321).

l. 1299. *blere*. Cf. *Rom. of the Rose* l. 3912:
"That almoost blered is myn yhe";
Chaucer, *Maun. Tale*, l. 148:
"Far al thy waytyng, blered is thin ye."
See also *Rv. Tale*, l. 129; *Piers Plow*. Pr. l. 74; *Rox. Ballads* I, p. 163; Milton's *Comus*, ll. 153-6:
"To cheat the eye with blear illusion";
Shaks. *Tam. of Shrew*, V, i:
"While counterfeit supposes blear'd thine eyne."

P. 39, l. 1311. *astonyed*. Cf. *Tem. of Glas*, l. 24:
"I wex astonyed."

l. 1317. *howe a deuyll way!* Cf. Chaucer, *Ml. Tale*. Pr., l. 26:
"Tel on, a devil way!";
idem, l. 527:
"And let me slepe, a twenty devyl way";
Ch. Yeo. Tale, Pr. ll. 229-30:
"And al the cost on twenty devel waye
Is lost also";
Leg. of G. Wom., VI, l. 292:
"A twenty devel way the wynde him dryve."

l. 1327. *longeth*. Cf. *Secrees*, l. 1029:
"Of all such vertues as longe to a kyng."

P. 40, l. 1340. *Resydyuacion* = back-sliding. The term occurs again in Skelton, *Col. Cl.* ll. 523-5:
"And of resydeuacyon
They make interpretacyon
Of an aquarde facyon."

P. 41, l. 1384. *wysshe*. Cf. Chaucer, *A. B. C.* l. 155; *Ho. of Fame* ll. 489-91; *Temp. of Glas* l. 637:
"So wisse me now what me is best to do";
Piers Plow. Pas. v, ll. 540-562:
"I shal wisse you witterly the weye to his place."

l. 1386. *as I gesse*. Cf. Chaucer, *Bk. of Duch*. l. 35; *Compl. of M.* l. 195; *Parl. of Fou*. ll. 160, 200, 223; *Cant. Tales*, Pr. l. 82; *Knight's Tale*, l. 192; Lydgate, Min. P., p. 54. Cf. Dunbar, *Gold. Targe*, l. 230:
"God Eolus, his bugill blew I gesse."

l. 1403. Death and dread. Among the Roxburge Ballads (I, p. 312) is one which runs as follows:
"Lament your sinnes, good people all, lament,
You plainly see the Messenger is sent,—
I meane grim Death, and he doth play his part;
He stands prepar'd to strike you to the heart."
This is accompanied by the cut of a hideous skeleton with a dart. Cf. *Piers Plow*. Pas. xx, ll. 198-200:
"And as I seet in this sorwe I say how kynde passed,
And deth drowgh niegh me, for drede gan I quake,
And cried to kynde out of care me brynge."

P. 43, l. 1448. *vre*. This word occurs in French law — *mis en ure* (Kelham). Its use was maintained in England through the 16th century. I find it in an early American poem, Wigglesworth's *Day of Doom* (1662):
"The best of men had scarcely then
Their Lamps kept in good ure."

l. 1455. *sesyne.* A law term denoting the ownership of property. To take seizen refers to the ceremony of taking possession of one's freehold. Cf. R. of G. *Chr.* Reign of Wm. l. 528:

"Ac wende him out of Normandie anon to Engelande
Vorto nime hastiliche seisine of is lande."

See *Morte Arthur* (Th. MS.), l. 3589.

l. 1463. *fyn fast shut.* I make fyn an adverb with the force of very or completely. The word finliche in the phrase "finliche well" (= very well) occurs in *Sir Bevis of Hamtoun* l. 4052; also afin with the same meaning in l. 2577: "The beschop was glad afin." Chaucer uses fyn as an adj. in *Troil. and Cris.* V. 421: "of fyne force" (= of very need). Cf. our use of clean = completely, as in "clean laid aside," and of pure as "the pure death" (= death itself).

P. 44, 1479. *herber wallyd round about.* Doctrine's arbor is probably in imitation of the Garden of Mirth in *Rom. of the Rose*:

"And when I had a while goon,
I saugt a gardyn right anoon,
Ful long and brood, and every delle
Enclosed was, and walled welle,
With highe walles enbatailled,
Portraied without and wel entailled
With many riche portraitures."—ll. 135–141.

Cf. the Tower of Doctrine in Hawes' *Pastime of Pleasure*, written in imitation evidently of Lydgate's arbor: Graunde Amour is taught wisdom by learned dames, the Seven Sciences. All these may be suggestions of the Noble Castle of Learning in Dante's Inferno (c. iv) with its scholastic walls.

l. 1483. *Wytte.* In the homily of the *Sawles Warde* man is described as a house whose master is Wit. Wit's wife is named Will.

l. 1491. *perfyte.* Cf. *Secrees*, ll. 365, 387, 273: "In parfight clernesse."

l. 1509. *dalyaunce.* Dalyaunce in Lydgate seems always to refer to speech. See Schick's quotations, notes p. 91. In the *Pilgrimage of Man* "longe dalyaunce" translates the French "long parlement." Cf. *Temp. of Glas*, l. 291:

"Of port benygne, and of *daliaunce* (address);"

Æsop, Fab. 6, l. 93:

"That we togydre may have oure daliaunce;"

Min. P., p. 71:

"Countrefeteth in speche and daliaunce;"

Secrees, l. 2706:

"Lawhyng visage is good in daliaunce."

l. 1512. *myn ey gan I dresse.* Cf. *Temp. of Glas*, l. 850:

"Gan cast hir eyen."

P. 45, ll. 1515 *et seq. on tho walles was made memory*, etc. Douglas evidently imitates these pictures of sacred history in his account of the reflections seen in the mirror of Venus (Works I., pp. 57–59)—another poetical device of the same kind. See Introd., p. lvii.

l. 1538. *Iudyth.* Judith is often mentioned in M. E. Lit. Cf. Chaucer, *M. of L. Tale*, 841; *March. Tale*, l. 122; *Monks Tale*, ll. 561–584; *Piers Plow.*, Pas. xvii., l. 21, etc. The account of the O. E. epic of Judith was probably known by the side of the version in the Vulgate.

P. 46, ll. 1562 *et seq.* These pictures are drawn from the frescoes on monastery walls whereon it was customary to present the saints with their traditional attributes. Lydgate's descriptions represent late traditions—those of the 13th and 14th centuries (note the attribute of St. James = the scallop shell, given him after the 13th century). The attribute of Peter was the key;

Paul held a sword; James the Great was a pilgrim with a long staff, wearing a cape with a scallop shell on his shoulder or hat, etc. Other pictures were the "Martyrdoms" which represented the manner in which the saints were slain: Thomas by a spear, Philip on the cross, James the Less by a club, Bartholomew by flaying, Simon and Jude, always together, by a sword and club, etc. There will be remembered in this connection Albert Dürer's picture of St. Thomas who is seen holding a lance, and Angelo's Last Judgment where Bartholomew appears holding his skin in one hand and the knife with which he was flayn in the other. Many other pictures will be recalled—and this is a necessary process in reading Lydgate—of the Apostles and Fathers as here displayed. For the emblems of the Apostles and Saints cf. Jameson, *Sacr. and Leg. Art.* Cf. the *Ormulum* V. i., p. 201 and note; *Curs. Mun.*, p. 1218; Lyndesay's *Monarche*, ll. 2279 *et seq.*

P. 47, l. 1583. *Beede.* One does not meet with many late references to Baeda. He is mentioned however, by Dante in *Par.* c. x., l. 131; and by Wyclif (*Works*, I., p. 35; III., p. 477).

l. 1584. *Orygene.* An Alexandrine Greek, born A. D. 185. Bitter controversy arose regarding his views on the final salvation of men, the transformation of man's earthly body at the resurrection, etc. His "errors" are contained chiefly in his work, περὶ ἀρχῶν. A private "error" is also recorded of Origen to which reference here may be made. See Butler's *Lives of Saints*, ix., p 360.

l. 1589. *Sybyll.* "The pictures of the Sybils are very common, and for their prophecies of Christ in high esteem with Christians."—Sir Th. Browne. In the account of Varro the sybils numbered ten.

l. 1608. *houyd.* Cf. *Chorl and Bird*, 187: "Hovyng above his hedde" (said of a bird).

l. 1614. *gall.* Gall-trees were those that, like the oak, bear bitter galls. Spenser has "trees of bitter gall" (*Faery Queen*, II., vii., st. 52).

P. 48, ll. 1618 *et seq.*
The whole discourse of Doctrine is written in the light of Catholic doctrine and practice. There is a certain kind of ingenuity exercised in the handling of the materials, but beyond a skillful presentation of doctrine there is not the least display of poetic genius in all this part.

P. 49, l. 1657. *made her beerdys on the new gete* = changed their purpose. Palsgrave defines "new get" as "guise nouvelle." Cf. Chaucer, *Cant. Tales,* Pr., line 682:
"Him thought he rood al of the newe get;"
Ml. Tale, l. 136: (a kirtil)
"Schapen with goores in the newe get;"
Skelton, *Magnif.*, l. 458:
"The courtly gyse of the newe iet."
Those who cut their beards in the latest fashion had a place in Barclay's *Ship of Fools* (I., p. 35). Cf. the phrase, "To make one's beard"=to deceive; as in Chaucer, *Reeves Tale*, l. 176:
"Yet can a miller make a clerkes berd."
Cf. *Ho. of Fame*, l. 689; *W. of B. Tale*, Pr., l. 361.

P. 50, l. 1714. *habundaunce.* So in Chaucer's *Fortune*, l. 29.

l. 1718. *gryffyng.* Cf. *Secrees*, l. 2373:
"Which gryffyd on stokkys haue many braunchys."

P. 51, l. 1728. Cf. *Æsop*, Fab. 7, ll. 64-5:
"Men may at the ie se a pref
Of this matere."

ll. 1737 *et seq.* The Times. In the Calendar of the *Cursor Mundi* there are seven ages: (1) from Adam to Noah; (2) from Noah to Abraham; (3) from Abraham to David; (4) from David to Solomon; (5) from Solomon to the birth of Christ; (6) from the birth to the death of Christ; (7) from the death of Christ to the Day of Doom, the period of Antichrist.
Cf. also Wyclif, *Works*, I., p. 99.
Gower has a reading of the Times similar to Lydgate (Prol. *Conf. Am.*), agreeing especially in the Time of War.

P. 52, l. 1772. *that ys to sey.* Very common in Lydgate. Cf. *Temp. of Glas*, ll. 311, 426, 512, 715, 1124, etc.

l. 1784. *prynte hit in thy mynde.* A favorite phrase with Lydgate. Cf. Min. P., p. 36.

P. 53, l. 1805. *cast in a boon.* Cf. Chaucer, *Kn. Tale*, l. 319:
"We stryve, as doth the houndes for the boon."

P. 54, l. 1829. *the lesse worlde.* This is Milton's "less universe" (*Par. Reg.*, iv., l. 458). Said Sir Th. Browne (*Relig. Med.*): "That we are the breath and similitude of God, is indisputable and upon record of Holy Scripture; but to call ourselves a microcosm, or little world, I thought it only a pleasant trope of rhetoric, till my near judgment and second thoughts told me there was a real truth therein."

l. 1844. *dampnacion.* So Chaucer in *Pd. Tale*, l. 38; *A. B. C.*, l. 167.

l. 1852. *inwarde wyttes.* Man was regarded as having five outward and five inward wits. Cf. *World and Child*, Dods, I., p. 273:
Age   "Of the five wits I would have knowing.
Pres.   Forsooth, sir, hearing, seeing, and smelling,
       The remenant tasting and feeling:
       These being the five wits bodily,
       And, sir, other five wits there been.
Age.   Sir Perseverance, I know not them.
Pres. Now, Repentance, I shall you ken,
       They are the power of the soul:
       Clear in mind, there is one
       Imagination, and all reason,
       Understanding and compassion."
Hawes, in *Pastime of Pleasure*, enumerates the five inward wits as common-wit, imagination, fancy, estimation and memory. The five senses perform the outward offices, being simply receptive gates, but the wits perceive and judge. From this distinction arose the figure of the senses as gates, or as highways of the soul.
"Thet inewyt hys the dore-ward,
The doren wyttes fyve" — Shoreham, Per. Soc., p. 55.
"For tho (the five wits) be properly the gates,
Through which as to the hert algates
Cometh all thing unto the feire,
Which may the mannes soule empeire" — *Conf. Am.*, I., p. 52.
The inward senses were then the faculties of the mind. Thus Lydgate says (*Temp. of Glas*), ll. 380-1:
"With al my reson and alle my ful mynde, and five wittes."
The Five Senses were personated in Middleton's *Triumph of Truth* (1613). They appeared in character at the King's entry into London in 1603 and again at the Lord Mayor's Pageant in 1681 (Bullen).
The different senses are enumerated in Ælfric's Homilies, O. E. Homilies, Sawles Warde, etc. Cf. *Piers Plow.*, Pas. i., ll. 15-16; Wyclif's Tracts (III., p. 117); *Tale of Mel.*; *An Orysoun for sauynge of the fyve wyttes* (Vern. MS. E. E. T., xvii); *Interlude of the Four Elements;* Lydgate's Min. P., p. 253; *Faery Queene* (II., xi., st. 7); Fletcher's *Purple Island;* Bunyan's *Holy*

War, etc. Cf. a modern book entitled *The Five Gateways of Knowledge*, by Dr. Geo. Wilson, and *Lect. and Addresses*, by Sir W. Thomson, on the *Six Gateways of Knowledge*.

P. 54, l. 1855. *stremes*. Cf. *Temp. of Glas*, ll. 702, 582:
"For with the stremes of hir eyen clere."

l. 1858. *sauns*. Commonly found in the phrase "sauns faille," as in Chaucer, *Ho. of Fame*, ll. 188, 429; *Man of L. Tale*, l. 403; the *Court of Love*, l. 117 ("withouten faille," l. 710); Rob. of B. *Chron.*, l. 4507. *Piers Plow.* (Pas. xii, l. 286) has "saunz reule;" Skelton, *Why Come*, l. 426, "saunz aulter remedy."

l. 1860. *blyn*. Cf. Rob. of B. *Chron.*, l. 2263:
"Evere to brenne and nevere to blynne;"
Percy, *Reliq.*, III, p. 46:
"On thy striking doe not blinne."

P. 55, l. 1872. *wyre*. Cf. Chaucer, *Ho. of Fame*, l. 979:
"Tho gan I wexen in a were;"
Rom. of the Rose, l. 4468:
"Withoute deceyte or ony were;"
Piers Plow., Pas. xi, l. 111; xvi, l. 3; *Temp. of Glas*, ll. 651, 906 and see Schick's notes p. 104. Cf. Dunbar's *Man, sen thy Lyfe is ay in Weir*.

l. 1886. *daryng as a dastard*. Said in irony.

l. 1887. *Come of* = make an end. Probably our modern slang phrase "come off." It was in common usage in M. E. Cf. Chaucer, *Troil. and Cris.*, II, 310:
"Com of, and tel me what it is."
Temp. of Glas, l. 1272:
"Cometh off at ones, and do as I haue seide."
See Schick's notes, p. 119, for further references; also Skelton, *Magnif.*, l. 103:
"Come of, therefore, let se."

l. 1887. *thy wytte stant a crooke*. See also ll. 1918, 1932. Cf. Chaucer, *Ho. of Fame*, l. 621:
"Although that (wit) in thy hede full lyte is;"
Lydgate, *Chorl and Bird*, Min. P., p. 191:
"Thy brayne is dul, thy witte is almoste gone;"
Piers Plow., Pas. i, l. 138:
"'Thow doted daffe,' quod she, 'dulle arne thi wittes;'"
and cf, Emerson, *The Sphinx*:
"Dull Sphinx, Jove keep thy five wits."

l. 1897. *tonne*. Lydgate has again (Min. P., p. 176) the rime tonne, sonne, and in *Secrees*, ll. 249–50. Referring to Diogenes Lydgate says:
"His paleys was a litel poore tonne."

P. 57, l. 1952. *as blak as a coole*. Other objects of comparison with blackness were raven, crow, the devil, jet, ink and soot. Cf. *Conf. Am.*, II, p. 335:
"With fethers blacke as any cole."

l. 1953. *cropyn in a mouse hoole*. Cf. Skelton, *Why Come*, ll. 289–91:
"Our barons be so bolde,
Into a mouse hole they wolde
Rynne away and crepe."

P. 58, l. 1997. *my wyt ys soo thynne*. See l. 896. Middle Engl. writers were fond of acknowledging the weakness of their wits. Thus Chaucer confesses in the Prol. of the Tales (l. 746) "My wit is short." His Marchant said (l.

438) "My tale is doon, for my wit is thinne." Again the poet writes (*Ho. of Fame*, ll. 1179-80:
"Ne can I not to yow devyse (Temp. of Fame)
My wit ne may me not suffyse;"
and to describe the beauty of his lady (*Bk. of the Duch.*, l. 898):
"Me lakketh bothe English and wit."
Lydgate was even more self-depreciatory (for references see *Temp. of Glas* Introd. p. cxl-cxli and *Secrees*, p. xx).
"Make his wittes thynne" occurs in *Ch. Yeo. Tale*, Pr. l. 189; cf. R. of B, *Chron.* l. 113.

P. 59, l. 2008. *knette*. See line 991 knyt, 1186 knet. Cf. *Temp. of Glas*, l. 1230, "The cnott is knytt."

P. 60, l. 2065. *God knoweth and nat I.* An allusion to Paul's saying, II Cor. xii, 2-3.

l. 2070. *take the best, etc.* Cf. Chaucer, *N. Pr. Tale*, l. 623:
"Takith the fruyt and let the chaf be stille;"
Conf. Aman. I, Pr. p. 32:
"The chaf is take for the corne;"
Lydgate's Min. P. p. 149:
"Cheese we the roosys, cast away the thorn;"
idem, p. 173:
"Wedyde the cokkelle frome the puryd corne;"
Secrees, l. 734:
"As vndir chaaf is closyd pure corn;"
idem, l. 1224.
"Woord is but wynd; leff woord and take the dede;"
Story of Thebes fol. 370:
"Avoiding the chaffe . . .
Enlumining the true piked graine."

P. 61, l. 2079. *three enymyes*. The World the Flesh and the Devil were figuratively spoken of as foes or robbers or wild beasts or adverse winds etc. In O. E. Homilies (Morris p. 241) they are described as foes and again as robbers. According to Boccaccio the three beasts which hindered Dante's progress represented these forces. In *Piers Plow.* (Pas. xvi) these are winds that blow against the tree of Patience. Chaucer's *Tale of Mel.* reads "Thou hast doon synne ageinst oure Lord Crist, for certes the thre enemyes of mankinde, that is to saye, thy flessche, the feend, and the world, thou hast y-suffred hem to entre into thin herte wilfully, by the wyndow of thy body, and hast nought defended thiself sufficiently agayns here assautis, and here temptaciouns, so that they have woundid thi soule in fyve places, that is to sayn, the dedly synnes that ben entred into thin herte by thy fyve wittes."
"And thus it falleth
That thorugh the fende and the flesshe and the frele worlde
Synneth the sadman a day seuene sythes" (*P. Pl.* Pas. viii, l. 38-44).
The Devil was thought to work by Pride, Wrath and Sloth; the World by Covetousness and Envy; the Flesh by Gluttony and Lechery. Hawes gives a similar exhortation in *Past. of Pleas:*
"Than in your mynde inwardly despyse
The bryttle worlde, so full of doublenes,
With the vyle flesshe, and ryght sone aryse
Out of your slepe of mortall hevynes;
Subdue the devill with grace and mekenes,
That after your lyfe frayle and transitory,
You may than live in joye perdurably."

l. 2087. *guerdoun*. A favorite word of Lydgate's. Cf. *Æsop*, Fab. 3, l. 64; Fab. 5., ll. 21, 25, 35; Fab. 6., ll. 145, 165; Min. P. p. 76, "a gwerdonles guerdone"; *Temp. of Glass*, ll. 806, 1139; *Secrees*, l. 900, etc.

l. 2105. *benygne Ihesu.* Cf. Lydgate's *Testament* Min. P. p. 236: "O gracious Ihesu! benygne and debonayre." No one can question the piety of these monkish writers. Cf. Hawes' closing, the *Past. of Pleas:*
"Nowe blessed lady of the health eternall,
The quene of comfort and of heavenly glory,
Praye to thy swete sonne whiche is infinall,
To geve me grace to wynne the victory
Of the devill, the worlde, and of my body,
And that I may my selfe well apply
Thy sonne and the to laude and magnifie."

Skelton, looking back upon such writers, especially upon Lydgate and his *Assembly of Gods*, acknowledges their authority — those poets

"Whyche full craftely,
Vnder as couerte termes as could be,
Can touch a trouth and cloke it subtylly
Wyth fresshe vtteraunce full sentencyously;
Dyuerse in style, some spared not vyce to wryte,
Some of moralyte nobly dyde endyte."
—*Bowge of Court, Pr.*

To conclude, the significance of Lydgate in the history of literature I understand to be this: Taking his work in its entirety he seems to embody the forces that were shaping England during the late Middle Age in a more conspicuous manner than any other Middle English author. Chaucer stands out, of course, the supreme genius of the period, original and creative, the glory of the Court, the herald of the Renaissance. After Chaucer, in point of creativeness, ranks Langland the mystic, the scholar, the churchman, the prophet of the Reformation. Now the progress of literary history is often most clearly marked, as Mr. Gosse well maintains, in the less monumental figures of any period. The very genius of Chaucer and Langland removed them somewhat from the effects of environment. With Lydgate there is not much question of personal force. What is valuable in his work arises from his lack of originality and very incapacity as a poet. He is the product of his age — at one time yielding himself to the Romantic tendency, spending his youth in pleasure, writing ballads, romances, plays and histories for the King and Court. Then the love of Mother Church detains him, he assumes the cowl, and lives and dies at Bury St. Edmund. As a result of living in his environment no other early English author can equal him in the scope of his interests. He copied and translated everything that came to him in his hand. His work embraces ballads, lyrics, epics, allegories, fables, moral romances, social satires, histories, philosophical and scientific treatises, hagiologies and devotional manuals. The Romantic and the Scholastic blend in him in this remarkable manner. Because of his contemporaneity his rewards accrued to him in his lifetime. He was patronized by the Court and lived in the favor of his fellow-poets. For a century his fame was maintained, and his influence was even stronger than Chaucer's upon Burgh, Hawes, the Scottish poets, and laureate Skelton—his fame and influence passing with the traditions that gave them effect.

In the matter of language Lydgate is perhaps more typical of his period than Chaucer. Chaucer's whole linguistic system is for his time forced and artificial. Middle English does not have the regularity and certainty which Chaucer's usage seems to imply. Not a one of his successors could support his literary dialect. James's Quair, purposely composed in the Chaucerian manner, is artificial to the extreme. Lydgate's poetic incapacity compelled him to fall back upon the current speech. In short, in this, as in all other respects, Lydgate was the immediate product of his environment. He wrote not for all time but for an age.

CATALOG OF PERSONS.

(The numbers refer to lines except those marked st.=stanza).

LYDGATE.

The poet performs a twofold function; he is one of the prime movers in the vision (v. especially his fear of Death, st. 277-286) and at the same time the conscious teller of the story, never forgetting the "gentle reader." (*a*) As an actor: goes forth to the lake's side and dreams, st. 1, 2; accompanies Morpheus to the Court of Minos, st. 3-5; attends the banquet given to the gods, st. 27-87; a spectator on the field of battle, st. 88-210; at the school of Doctrine, st. 211-290 (fears Death, st. 277-286); returns to his bed, st. 291, 292; awakes and writes st. 293-296.

(*b*) References to himself as narrator, st. 76, 81, 160, 171, 214, 222, 228, 229, 230, 294-301.

THE DIVINITIES (AT THE ASSEMBLY).

Apollo, the God of Light, the giver and director of the banquet, st. 24, 25, 27, 28, 30, 32, 34, 35, 36, 37, 55, 73, 103, 189; interpretation by Doctrine, 237.

Atropos, the God of Death; is met by Discord, st. 60; makes complaint to the gods, st. 61-71; is promised aid against Virtue, st. 72-75, 81-87; threatens the gods, st. 138; is angered at the success of Virtue, st. 188-192; seeks the Lord of Light, st. 198-199; is called Death, st. 201; is made master of Microcosm, st. 203, 207-209; vanishes, st. 210; interpretation by Doctrine, st. 257-260; makes Lydgate to fear, st. 277-279; the fear of Death explained, st. 280-288.

Aurora, the Goddess of the Dawn, the companion of Apollo at the banquet, st. 37, 55.

Bacchus, the God of Wine, at the banquet, st. 51.

Cerberus, the Porter of Hell; brings Eolus to the Court, st. 6, 79; to the banquet, st. 27; is sent to summon Vice, st. 87-88; porter of Hell, st. 167.

Ceres, the Goddess of Corn, at the banquet with Cupid, st. 42; said to be influenced by Phœbe, st. 52; interpretation by Doctrine, st. 245.

Cupid, the God of Love, at the banquet, st. 43.

Diana, the Goddess of the Wood and the Chase, complainant at the Court of Minos, st. 6-11, 22, 80; dismisses the case to attend the banquet, st. 25-27; is persuaded by Apollo to forgive Eolus, st. 28-34; at the banquet with Mars, st. 38-39; interpretation by Doctrine, st. 235-239.

Discord, the Goddess of Strife, comes to the banquet but is given no seat and departs in anger, st. 59-60; conspires with Atropos, st. 60-62; interpretation by Doctrine, st. 257-260.

96   *Catalog of Persons.*

Eolus, the God of the Winds, a prisoner at the Court of Minos, st. 6–26, 76–80; judgment is suspended for the banquet, st. 28–35; is forgiven, provided he give aid to Atropos against Virtue, st. 75, 81–84; interpretation by Doctrine, st. 233–234.

Fortune, the Goddess of Chance, at the banquet, st. 46; interpretation by Doctrine, st. 246.

Isis, the Goddess of Fruit, at the banquet, st. 48; interpretation by Doctrine, st. 246.

Juno, the Goddess of Riches, at the banquet, st. 40.

Jupiter, the God of Wisdom, at the banquet, st. 39.

Mars, the God of War, at the banquet, st. 38; agrees to assist Atropos, st. 73–74.

Mercury, the God of Language, at the banquet, st. 53; agrees to assist Atropos, st. 74.

Minerva, the Goddess of War, or of Harvest, at the banquet, st. 50.

Minos, the Judge of Hell, in Court, st. 4, 6–26, 79–80.

Morpheus, the Shewer of Dreams (dwells in Fantasy l. 35); leads Lydgate to the Court of Minos, st. 2–5, 79, to the palace of Apollo, st. 27; is sent to warn Virtue, st. 103–107; is given care of the five gates of Microcosm, st. 184–186; conducts Lydgate to the School of Doctrine, st. 210–212, 223, 231, 268, 270, 277; interpretation by Doctrine, st. 265; leads Lydgate to his bed, st. 290–292.

Neptune, the God of the Sea, complainant at the Court of Minos, st. 6–7, 12–20, 80; dismisses the case to attend the banquet, st. 25–27; accepts Phœbe as arbitress, st. 34–35; at the banquet, st. 49; said to be ruled by Phœbe, st. 52; agrees to aid Atropos st. 73; is requested by Phœbe to forgive Eolus and complies, st. 82–83 interpretation by Doctrine, st, 235–239.

Othea (Athena), the Goddess of Wisdom at the banquet, st. 44; counsels the gods, st. 75; is referred to, st. 82.

Pan, the God of Shepherds, at the banquet, st. 47; serves as minstrel, st 58; interpretation by Doctrine, st 246.

Phœbe, the Goddess of Waters, the Moon the mistress of Neptune, st. 35; a the banquet, st. 52; entreats Neptune st. 81–83.

Pluto, the God of Hell, father of Vice, st 86–87; at the Court in Hell, st. 4, 6–24; dismisses the Court for Apollo' banquet, st. 24–27; declares the complaint against Eolus, st. 29; a the banquet, st 45 (how Eolus came into Pluto's power, st. 76–79); send for his son Vice to overthrow Virtue 85–87; commands Vice, st. 138; "O in Pluto's name," l. 1077.

Saturn, the God of Cold, at the banquet st. 40, 41; agrees to assist Atropos st. 74.

Venus, the Goddess of Love, at the banquet, st. 54.

POETS AND PHILOSOPHERS.

(WAITERS AT THE BANQUET, ST. 56–58; INTERPRETATION BY DOCTRINE=
FEIGNERS OF FABLES, ST. 241–249.)

Albert, 398.
Arystotyll, 390.
Aueroys, 394.
Auycen, 394.

Dorothe, 391.
Dyogenes, 391, 1397, 1399.
Esculapion, 396.
Euclyde, 398.

Catalog of Persons.

Galyen, 395.
Hermes, 393.
Ipocras, 395.
Messehala, 392.
Omere, 397.
Orace, 397.
Orpheus, 400.
Ouyde, 397.

Plato, 392.
Saphyrus, 393.
Socrates, 392.
Sortes, 393.
Sychero, 390.
Tholome, 391.
Virgyle, 397.

THOSE SLAIN BY ATROPOS WITH HIS DART (ST. 64–69)

Achilles, 474.
Alexaunder, 464.
Artour, 466.
Cesar, Iulius, 465.
Charles, the Noble, 467.
Cirus, 474.
Cosdras, 473.
Dauid, 466.
Ector of Troy, 463.

Godfrey of Boleyn, 469.
Hanyball, 473.
Hercules, 472.
Iason, 472.
Iosue, 466.
Iudas Machabee, 468.
Nabugodonozor, 470.
Pharao, 471.
Sypio, 473.

THE MORALITIES.

Virtue, Christ's Champion (l. 1103). Atropos complains to the gods that Virtue escapes his dart, st. 69–70; the gods conspire to conquer, st. 72–75, 81–87; is warned by Morpheus to prepare for the battle with Vice, st. 103–105; gathers his hosts, st. 107–133; hastens to the field Microcosm, st. 135; charges his men to be guided by Grace, st. 136; gives knighthood to fourteen captains; sends embassadors to Freewill; engages in battle, st. 148–162; is compelled to retreat, st. 152; returns to the field, st. 160; overthrows Vice with the help of Preseverance, st. 162; is rewarded and blessed by Predestination, st. 168–169; thanks God for the victory, st. 170; is sought for by some of Vice's host, st. 171–174; seeks recompense from Freewill, st. 174–179; puts Reason and Freewill in charge of Microcosm, st. 180; charges Sensuality to be guided by Sadness, st. 181–183; gives to Morpheus the care of the five gates, st. 184–186; returns to his castle, st. 187; (Apollo informs Atropos that Virtue is not in his jurisdiction, st. 190); sends messengers to Microcosm, st. 197; prepares the field against the coming of Death, st. 204–207; is exalted above the firmament, st. 210; interpretation by Doctrine, st. 261–266; the moral, st. 297–301.

Virtue's host, st. 109–132, pauses under the Sign of the Rood, st. 149; is protected by the Shield of the Holy Trinity, st. 150.

Imaginacion, messenger of Virtue, 748, 757.

Messengers=
  Prayer, 1377.
  Fastyng, 1377.
  Penaunce, 1377.
  Almesdede, 1378.

Baptyme, the leading captain, 951, 1081, 1090, 1105, 1198, 1211, 1216.

Perseueraunce, captain of the reargard, 1094, 1115, 1125, 1129.

Constaunce, 1128.
Knights, guides of Virtue's car=
    Ryghtwysnes, 795, 1385, 1394, 1401, 1418.
    Prudence, 796.
    Streyngth, 797.
    Temperaunce, 798.
Seven chief captains=
    Humylyte, 801, 1142.
    Charyte, 804, 1435.
    Pacyence, 808.
    Lyberalyte, 811.
    Abstynence, 814.
    Chastyte, 818.
    Good Besynesse, 821.
Embassadors sent by Virtue to Freewill=
    Reson, 998.
    Discresion, 998.
    Good Remembraunce, 998, 1452.
Minor captains dubbed knights by Virtue (14)=
    Feythe, 986, 1082, 1089, 1105, 1196, 1208, 1210, 1435.
    Hope, 986, 1082, 1089, 1105, 1196, 1435.
    Mercy, 986, 1194.
    Trouthe, 986.
    Ryght, 986.
    Resystence of Wrong, 987.
    Confession, 988.
    Contricion, 988.
    Satisfaccion, 988.
    Verrey Drede of God, 989.
    Performyng of Penaunce, 989.
    Perfeccyon, 990.
    Konnyng, 990.
    Good Dysposicion, 990.
The minor captains led by Grace; 1st group (57)=
    Grace, 853, 948.
    Trew Feythe, 828.
    Hoope, 828, 986, 1082, 1089, 1105, 1196, 1435.
    Mercy, 828, 986.
    Peese, 828.
    Pyte, 828.
    Ryght, 829.
    Trowthe, 829, 986.
    Mekenesse, 829.
    Good Entent, 829.
    Goodness, 830.
    Concorde, 830.
    Parfyte Vnyte, 830, 1082, 1105.
    Honest Trew Loue, 831.
    Symplycyte, 831.
    Prayer, 832, 1377.
    Fastyng, 832, 1377.
    Preuy Almysdede, 832, 1378.
    Artycles of the Crede, 833.
    Confession, 834, 988, 1143, 1429.
    Contrycion, 834, 988, 1145, 1429.
    Satysfaccion, 834, 988, 1146, 1429.
    Sorow for Synne, 835, 1430.
    Gret Repentaunce, 835, 1430.
    Foryeuenes of Trespas, 836.
    Good Dysposicion, 836, 990, 1431.
    Resystence of Wrong, 837, 987.
    Performyng of Penaunce, 837, 989, 1148, 1377, 1432.
    Hooly Deuocion, 838, 1431.
    Good Contynuaunce, 838.
    Preesthood, 839, 1424, 1426.
    Sacramentes, 839; the Sacrament of Eukaryst, 1428, 1439; Holy Unccion, 1444.
    Sadnesse, 840, 1233, 1265, 1279, 1349, 1355, 1361, 1374, 1380, 1436.
    Commaundementes, 840.
    Sufferaunce in Trowble, 841.
    Innocency, 841.
    Clennesse, 842.
    Continence, 842.
    Virginite, 842.
    Kyndnesse, 843.
    Reuerence, 843.
    Curtesy, 843.
    Content, 844.
    Plesyd with Pyteous Pouerte, 844.
    Entendyng Well, 845.
    Mynystryng Equyte, 845.
    Hooly Indyfferency, 846.
    Laboryng the Seruyce of God to Multyply, 847.
    Refuse of Rychesse, 848.
    Perfeccion, 849, 990.
    Parfyte Contemplacion, 849.

Catalog of Persons.

Relygyon, 850.
Profession well kept in Memory, 850.
Verrey Drede of God, 851 (989).
Holy Predycacion, 851.
Celestiall Sapience, 852.
Goostly Inspiracion, 852.
Minor captains led by Cunning; 2d group (17)=
    Konnyng, 854, 872, 876, 931, 990, 1105.
    Gramer, 855.
    Sophystry, 855.
    Naturall Philosophy, 856.
    Logyk, 856.
    Rethoryk, 856.
    Arsmetry, 857.
    Geometry, 857.
    Astronomy, 857.
    Canon, 858.
    Cyuyle, 858.
    Musyk, 858.
    Theology, 859.
    Physyk, 859.
    Moralizacion of Holy Scripture, 860.
    Poetry, 861.
    Drawyng of Picture, 861.
Minor captains; 3d group (9)=
    Moderat Dyete, 885.
    Wysdom, 885.
    Euyn Wyght & Mesure, 886.
    Ware of Contagious Geere, 886.
    Lothe to Offende, 887.
    Louyng ay to Lere, 887.
    Worshyp, 888.
    Profyt, 888.
    Myrthe in Manere, 888.
Commons with Virtue, numbering one-tenth of Vice's host=
    Doctours, 897.
    Prestes, 899.
    Confessours, 899.
    Declarers of Holy Scripture, 900.
    Rebukers of synne, 901.
    Fysshers of fowles, 902.
    Lovers of clennes, 903.
    Dyspysers of veyn & worldly ryches, 903.
    Prelates (pesyble), 904.
    Gouernours (iustyciall), 904.
    Founders of churches, 905.
    Peeres (mercyfull), 905.
    Reformers of wrong, 906.
    Merchauntes (well menyng), 908.
    Artyfyceres (trew), 908.
    Vyrgyns, 909.
    Innocentes, 909.
    Matronys (hooly), 910.
    Contynentes, 910.
    Pylgryms, 911.
    Palmers, 911.
    Laborers (trew), 911.
    Hooly Heremytes, 912.
    Goddes Solycitours, 912.
    Monkes, 913.
    Freres (well dysposyd), 913.
    Chanons, 914.
    Nonnes, 914.
    Professours (feythfull), 914.
    Coniugatoures of worldly people, 915.
    Louers of Cryst, 916.
    Confounders of yll, 916.
    All that to godward yeue her good wyll, 917.
    Mayntenours of ryght, 918.
    Verrey Penytentes, 918.
    Distroyers of errour, 919.
    Causers of Vnyte, 919.
    Performers of mercy and pyte, 921.
    Contemplatyf peple, 922.
Vyce, son of Pluto, st. 86, 87; summoned by Pluto to do battle against Virtue, st. 87, 88; leads towards the field of Microcosm, st. 137-139; is charged by Pluto to overthrow Virtue, st. 138; dubbs fourteen knights; sends embassadors to Freewill, st. 144; sends Sensuality into the field to scatter evil seeds, st. 146-147; engages in battle, st. 149-150; is reinforced by Freewill, st. 151-152; causes Virtue to retreat, st. 152-155; is overthrown by Virtue, st. 160-162; leaves the field by a private gate and meets with Despair, st. 165; is driven to torment by Prescience, st. 166-168;

100   *Catalog of Persons.*

    interpretation by Doctrine, st. 261–266; moral, st. 297–298.
Vice's host, st. 89–103.
Oryginal cryme=
    Messenger of Vice, 776, 781, 950, 955.
Seven chief captains=
    Pryde, 621.
    Enuy, 622.
    Wrethe, 624.
    Couetyse, 626.
    Glotony, 628.
    Lechery, 630.
    Slowthe, 631.
Embassadors sent by Vice to Freewill=
    Temptacion, 1004.
    Foly, 1004.
    Sensualyte, 1004.
Minor Captains dubbed Knights by Vice (14)=
    Falshood, 974, 643.
    Dyssymulacion 974, 636.
    Symony, 975, 636.
    Vsure, 975, 644.
    Wrong, 975, 645.
    Rebawdy, 975, 648.
    Malyce, 976, 640.
    Deceyte, 976, 647.
    Ly, 976, 644.
    Extorcion, 976, 637.
    Periury, 977, 644.
    Diffidence, 977, 652.
    Apostasy, 977, 657.
    Boldnesse in Yll, 978, 648.
The Minor Captains (75)=
    Sacrylege, 636.
    Symony 636, 975.
    Dyssimulacion, 636, 974.
    Manslaughter, 637.
    Mordre, 637,
    Theft, 637.
    Extorcion, 637, 976.
    Arrogaunce, 638.
    Presumpcion, 638.
    Contumacy, 638.
    Contempcion, 639.
    Contempt, 639.
    Inobedience, 639.
    Malyce, 640, 976.
    Frowardnes, 640.
    Gret Ielacy, 640.
    Woodnesse, 641.
    Hate, 641.
    Stryfe, 641.
    Impacience, 641.
    Vnkyndnesse, 642.
    Oppression, 642.
    Wofull Neglygence, 642.
    Murmour, 643.
    Myschyef, 643.
    Falshood, 643, 974.
    Detraccion, 643.
    Vsury, 644, 975.
    Periury, 644, 977.
    Ly, 644, 976.
    Adulacion, 644.
    Wrong, 645, 975.
    Rauyne, 645.
    Vyolence, 645.
    False Iugement, 646.
    Obstynacy, 646.
    Dysseyte, 647, 976.
    Dronkenes, 647.
    Improuydence, 647.
    Boldnes in Yll, 648, 978.
    Foule Rybaudy, 648, 975.
    Fornycacion, 649.
    Incest, 649.
    Auoutry, 649.
    Vnshamefastnes, 650.
    Prodygalyte, 650.
    Blaspheme, 651.
    Veynglory, 651.
    Worldly Vanyte, 651.
    Ignoraunce, 652.
    Diffydence, 652, 977.
    Ipocrysy, 652.
    Scysme, 653.
    Rancour, 653.
    Debate, 653.
    Offense, 653.
    Heresy, 654.
    Errour, 654.
    Idolatry, 654.
    New Fangylnes, 655.
    False Pretense, 655.

Catalog of Persons.

Inordinat Desyre of Worldly Excellense, 656.
Feynyd Pouert, 657.
Apostasy, 657, 977.
Disclaundyr, 658.
Skorne, 658.
Ielousy, 658.
Hoordam, 659.
Bawdry, 659.
False Mayntenaunce, 659.
Treson, 660.
Abusion, 660.
Pety Brybery, 660.
Vsurpacion, 661.
Horryble Vengeaunce, 661.
Idylnesse, 666.
Captains refused by Virtue who enter the service of Vice (st. 124–126)=
Nygromansy, 867.
Geomansy, 868.
Magyk, 868.
(Glotony), 868.
Adryomancy, 869.
Ornomancy, 869.
Pyromancy, 869.
Fysenamy, 870.
Pawmestry, 870.
The Commons with Vice led by Idleness=
Bosters, 673.
Braggars, 673.
Brybores, 673.
Praters, 674.
Fasers, 674.
Strechers, 674.
Wrythers, 674.
Shakerles, 675.
Shaueldores, 675.
Oppressours, 676.
Crakers, 676.
Meyntenours of querelles, 677.
Lyers, 677.
Theues, 678.
Traytours, 678.
Herytykes, 678.
Charmers, 679.
Sorcerers, 679.
Scismatykes, 679.
Symonyakes, 680.
Vsurers, 680.
Multyplyers, 681.
Coyn wasshers, 681.
Coyn clyppers, 681.
Vsurpers, 682.
Extorcioners, 682.
Bakbyters, 683.
Glosers, 683.
Flaterers, 683.
Murmurers, 684.
Claterers, 684.
Tregetours, 685.
Tryphelers, 685.
Feyners of tales, 685.
Lurdeyns, 686.
Pykers of males, 686.
Rowners, 687.
Uagaboundes, 687.
Forgers of lesynges, 687.
Robbers, 688.
Reuers, 688.
Ryfelers, 688.
Choppers of churches, 689.
Fynders of tydynges, 689.
Marrers of maters, 690.
Money makers, 690.
Stalkers by nyght, 691.
Euesdroppers, 691.
Fyghters, 692.
Brawlers, 692.
Brekers of lofedayes, 692.
Getters, 693.
Chyders, 693.
Causers of frayes, 693.
Tytyuyllys, 694.
Tyrauntes, 694.
Turmentoures, 694.
Apostates, 695.
Relygyous dyssymulers, 695.
Closshers, 696.
Carders, 696.
Hasardoures, 696.
Tyburne coloppys, 697.
Pursekytters, 697.
Pylary knyghtes, 698.
Double tollyng myllers, 698.
Tapsters, 699.
Hostelers, 699.

102   Catalog of Persons.

Hoores, 700.   Enchauntours, 706.
Baudys, 700.   Renegates, 706.
Blasphemers, 701.   Ambidextres, 707.
Ipocrytes, 701.   Sekers of debates, 707.
Brothelles, 702.   Pseudo prophetes, 708.
Brokers, 702.   Sodomytes, 708.
Swerers, 702.   Quelmers of chyldren, 709.
Dryuylles, 703.   Fornycatours, 709.
Dastardes, 703.   Wetewoldes, 710.
Dyspysers of ryghtes, 703.   Auouterers, 711.
Homycydes, 704.   Auauntours of syn, 711.
Poyseners, 704.   Clappers, 712.
Morderers, 704.   Makers of clamours, 712.
Skoldes, 705.   Vnthryftys, 713.
Caytyffys, 705.   Vnlustes, 713.
Clappers, 705.   Luskes, 714.
Idolatres, 706.   Loselles, 714.

IN THE FIELD OF MICROCOSM (MS = MACROCOSM).

The Field: is named Microcosm, 932; in the midst = Conscience, 934, Synderesys, 937; its lord = Freewill, st. 143; approached by five highways open to the Vices and Virtues, st. 135; interpretation by Doctrine, st. 262, 265.

The battle: the field, first entered by Original Crime, st. 111 = driven out by Baptism, st. 112; sowed with evil seeds by Sensuality, st. 146-148; the battle between the vices and virtues, st. 148-162 (won by Perseverance, st. 157-162).

Freewill, Lord of Microcosm, st. 143; receives embassadors from Virtue, st. 143, from Vice, st. 144; gives an ambiguous answer, st. 145; takes the part of Vice, st. 151-152, 155; repents and seeks the counsel of Conscience, st. 163; is sent to Humility, Confession, Contrition, Satisfaction and Penance, st. 164; appears before Virtue, st. 174; blames Sensuality, st. 175-176; in recompense yields Microcosm to Virtue, st. 178-179; is made bailiff under Reason, st. 180.

Prescience, sent from above the firmament by Alpha and Omega (v. l. 1158, 1176, 1467) to punish Vice, st. 166-167.

Predestinacion, sent to reward Virtue, st. 168-169; they vanish, st. 170.

Vice's host; scourged by Prescience, st. 167; some seek Peace, Mercy, Faith, Hope, Baptism, Confession, Conscience, Circumcision, st. 171-174.

Sadnesse, takes Sensuality prisoner, st. 177; is given the guidance of Sensuality in Microcosm, st. 181, 183, 193; with Reason clears Microcosm of the evil weeds of Sensuality, st. 195; with Reason prepares the field for the coming of the Lord of Light, st. 206.

Reason, rules in Microcosm, st. 180, 187, 193, 195, 197, 206.

Nature (has jurisdiction over living creatures, st. 65, 69, 190; has "carnal might," l. 1381) requires that Sensuality be given his liberty, st. 182; is powerless to help Atropos against Virtue, st. 194.

Morpheus, is given charge of five gates of Microcosm, st. 185-186.

Atropos, resolves to enter the service of God, st. 191; inquires the way to

Catalog of Persons.

Righteousness, st. 198, 199; is called Death, st. 201; is given power in Microcosm, st. 203, 207–209; vanishes, st. 210.

The Lord of Light, received in Microcosm, st. 204–206.
Resydyuacion, enters Microcosm but is repulsed, st. 192–195; interpretation by Doctrine, st. 266.

THE ACCORD OF REASON AND SENSUALITY.

Reason, an embassador of Virtue and ruler in Microcosm; Lydgate muses how he may make Reason and Sensuality to accord, st. 1; Reason is sent by Virtue as an embassador to Freewill, st. 143; has no fear of Sensuality, st. 176; is given charge of Microcosm, st. 180; has guard over Sensuality, st. 187, 193 (v. 266); is superior to Nature, st, 194; with Sadness clears Microcosm of weeds, st. 195; is directed by Prayer, Fasting, Penance and Almsdeed st. 197; shows Atropos the way to Righteousness, st. 198–199; with Sadness, cleanses the field against the coming of the Lord, st. 206; comes with Sensuality to Doctrine to clear up Lydgate's doubt, st. 276–279; Reason and Sensuality agree as to the fear of Death, st. 280–282; vanishes, st. 283; interpretation of the concordance by Doctrine, st. 287–288.

Sensuality, an embassador of Vice to Freewill, and an ally of Nature; Lydgate muses how he may make Sensuality and Reason to accord, st. 1; Sensuality is sent by Vice as embassador to Freewill, st. 144; sows evil seeds in Microcosm, st. 146–148, 153; is charged with corrupting Freewill, st. 176; taken prisoner by Sadness and brought to Virtue, st. 177; is placed under the guidance of Sadness, st. 180–181; his liberty plead for by Nature, st. 182; is denied freedom in Microcosm, st. 183; guarded by Reason, st. 187; meets with Residivation but can do no evil, st. 193, 194; his evil weeds cut down by Reason and Sadness, st. 195; enters with Reason the School of Doctrine to clear up Lydgate's doubt, st. 276–279; agrees with Reason as to the fear of Death, st. 281; vanishes, st. 283; interpretation of the concord by Doctrine, st. 287–288.

IN THE SCHOOL OF DOCTRINE, ST. 211–290.

(A FOUR-SQUARE ARBOR).

Wytte, chief porter, st. 212.
Teachers of the people=
    Dame Doctryne, st. 213–214, st. 229–231; as interpreter, st. 232–288.

Holy Texte, st. 215.
Glose, st. 215.
Moralyzacion, st. 215.
Scrypture, st. 215, the Scribe.

PICTURED ON THE WALLS:

1ST AND 2D WALLS: TIMES OF DEVIATION AND REVOCATION.

(The false gods are not here described).

Adam, 1521.
Eue, 1521, holding an apple.
Noe, 1522, in a ship.
Abraham, 1522, holding a flintstone.
Isaac, 1523, bound on a mount.
Iacob, 1524, sleeping by a ladder.
Ioseph, 1526, in a cistern.
Moyses, 1527, with two tables.
Aaron, 1528, } supporting Moses' arms.
Vrre, 1528,
Ely, 1529, in a burning car.
Elyze, 1530, clad as a hermit.
Dauid, 1531, with a harp and stone sling.
Ieremy, 1532.
Ezechiell, 1532.
Danyell, 1533, in a lion's den.
Abacuc, 1534.
Mychee, 1534.
Malachy, 1534.

Ionas, 1535, coming out of a whale's body.
Samuell, 1536, in a temple.
Zakary, 1536, by an altar.
Osee, 1538, } conspiring the death of
Iudyth, 1538, } Holofernes.
Salamon, 1539, dividing a child with his sword.
Melchisedech, 1543, offering bread and wine.
Ioachym, 1545, } at the golden gate.
Anne, 1545,
Iohn Baptyst, 1547, in a desert.
Sodechy, 1549, } with faces toward
Amos, 1550, } Sophony.
Sophony, 1551.
Neemy, 1552.
Esdras, 1552.
Ioob, 1553, as an impotent.
Thoby, 1554, as patient.

3D WALL=TIME OF RECONCILIATION.

Petyr, 1562, with keys.
Poule, 1563, with a sword.
Iames, 1563, with a scallop.
Thomas, 1564, with a spear.
Phylyp, 1565.
Iames the lesse, 1566.
Bartylmew, 1567, all flayn.
Symon, 1568.
Thadee, 1568.
Mathy, 1569, } drawing lots.
Barnabe, 1569,
Marke, 1570, a lion holding his book.
Mathew, 1571, like an angel.
Luke, 1573, a calf holding his book.
Iohn, 1574, with a cup and palm in his hand, an eagle holding his book.

Gregory, 1576,
Ierome, 1576,
Austyn, 1576, } as doctors.
Ambrose, 1576,
Bernard, 1578.
Anselme, 1578.
Thomas of Alquyn, 1579.
Domynyk, 1579.
Benet, 1580.
Hew, 1580.
Martyne, 1581.
Iohn, 1581.
Crysostom, 1582.
Beede, 1583.
Orygene, 1584.
Sybyll, 1589.
Andrew, 1595, with a cross.

Catalog of Persons.

4TH WALL=TIME OF PILGRIMAGE, OR DANGEROUS PASSAGE, OR OF WAR.
(See the battle of the vices and virtues.)

DAME DOCTRINE.

Dame Doctrine, interpreter of the vision, summons Lydgate to draw near, st. 231-232; interprets the imprisonment of Eolus = unbridled wealth increases misrule, st. 233-234; Minos =Judge of Cruelness, st. 235; the complaint of Diana and Neptune= the blindness of fools, st. 235-236; the dismissal of the court=forgetfulness of fools, 237-239; the gods at the banquet = false idols, st. 240-249; the Time of Deviation, st. 241-249 =from Adam to Moses; the poets and philosphers=feigners of fables, st. 249; Time of Revocation = from Moses to Christ, st. 250-251; Time of Reconciliation=time of Grace, st. 251-252; Time of Pilgrimage=time of war, st. 255; (the present battle between Vice and Virtue, st. 256); the complaint of Atropos=the constraint of friendship (Discord and Death) st. 257-260; the battle between Vice and Virtue=the moral struggle in the human soul, st. 261; Microcosm = the world of man, st. 262; Perseverance = continuance of good living, st. 263; Prescience and Predestination=rewarders of vice and virtue, st. 264; the five keys given to Morpheus = the five inward wits, st. 265; Residivation=return to sin, st. 266; the accord of Reason and Sensuality=in the fear of Death, st. 275-288; Doctrine vanishes, st. 290.

OTHER NAMES.

God, 1293, 1333, 1410, 1497, 1640, 1685, 1748, 1754, 1818, 2065, 2088; Lord God, 1930; Lord, 1819; 2093, Lord of Glory, 2098; Fadyr, 2104; Alpha and Omega, 1158, 1176.
Ihesu, 1121, 2105; Cryst, 1103, 1752, 1775; Son of Man, 1755; Crystyn, 1764.
Mary, 2105.
Devyll, 21, 1818, 2080.
Peleus, feast of, 413.
Phebus, the sun, 1, 361.
Pictagoras, 3.

CATALOG OF PLACES.

A lake, st., 1.
Lydgate's habitation, st., 2.
The Court of Minos in Pluto's realm, st., 4.
The Palace of Apollo, st., 27, 36, 107, 192.
The Palace of Virtue, st., 187.
The field of Microcosm, st., 134, 135.
The school of Doctrine, a four-square arbor, st., 212.
Fantasy, 35, the dwelling place of Morpheus.
Synay, Mount of, 1747.

GLOSSARY.

(For a fuller explanation of many words see the Notes.)

Abew, 1063. See *bew*.
Abhominable, adj., 711, abominable.
Aboorde, 248. See *borde*.
Abusion, sb., 660, abuse.
Abydyng, sb., 34, dwelling place.
Abyte, vb., 194, abides, remains.
Accusement, sb., 160, accusation.
Adryomancy, sb., 869, (Aero-? or Hydro-?) divination by air (or water).
Adulacion, sb., 644, flattery.
Afore, adv., 1120, before.
Afray, sb., 729, battle.
Aftyr, prep., 76, in accordance with; *aftyr*, adv., 1024, afterwards.
Agayn, prep., 100 and often, against. See *ayene*.
Aldyrs, 490, 579, gen. pl. of all, *althrys* 599.
Allyaunce, sb., 991, alliance.
All be, conj., 476, al-be-it.
Aloft, adv., 101, in the air, on high.
Altherlast, 186, last of all.
Aly, sb., 1810, ally.
Ambidextres, sb., 707, double dealing persons.
Ambyguyte, sb., 1012, ambiguity.
Anone, adv., 14, 1615, soon.
Apply, vb., 485, incline.
Aray, sb., 282, 296, dress.
Arere, adv., 962, to the rear.
Armure, sb., 931, armor, weapons.
Arow, 763 = a row, host.
Asaute, vb., 588; sb., *assawte*, 1049, assault.
Asay, vb., 980, try.
Asondre, adv., 66, asunder.
Aspyed, vb., 1368, spied.
Astert, vb., 1267, escape.
Astonyed, vb., 1311, astounded, dismayed.

Astyrlabes, sb. pl., 1896, instruments for taking altitudes of the sun and stars (astrolobes).
Ateynt, vb., 362, disgraced, afflicted with sorrow.
Atwene, prep., 2006, between.
Atwyx, prep., 1966, between.
Auaunce, vb., 954, advance; imper., *avaunt*, 1121.
Auauntage, sb., 727, 1033, advantage.
Auauntours, sb., 711, boasters.
Auaylyd, vb., 19, helped; *avale*, vb., 360, bow down — perhaps=to have force.
Auenaunt, adj., 885, agreeable, handsome.
Auentur, sb., 944, chance, adventure.
Auoutry, sb., 649, adultery; *auouterers*, 711.
Avowe, sb., 983, vow.
Auyse, vb., 866, advise; sb., 1352, advice.
Auysment, sb., 140, deliberation.
Awayters, sb., 1741, waiters.
Awter, sb., 1537, altar.
Ax, vb., 520, ask; *axyd*, 1383.
Ay, adv., 119, 256, 966, ever.
Ayene, prep., 19, and often, against. See *agayn*.
Ayeyn, adv., 63 and often, again.

Bake, sb., 1905, back.
Balaunce, sb., 1012, scale, decision.
Bankes, sb. 105, shores of the sea.
Banket, sb., 188 and often, banquet.
Batayll, sb., 753, 1010, etc., battle.
Baudys, sb., 700, bawds.
Bawdryk, sb., 285, belt.
Bayll, sb., 1259, bailiff.
Baytys, sb., 596, lures.
Be, vb., 115 and often, been.
Bedene, adv., 277, together, in order, or perhaps an expletive.

Glossary.   107

Beforn, adv., 819; *before*, 1792, before.
Begoon, vb., 441, suffered.
Begylyd, vb., 571, diverted.
Beheste, sb., 481, promise.
Behoue, sb., 1260, advantage.
Beleue, sb., 1679, belief.
Bende, sb., 1172, band, company.
Benedycyte, 1594, bless ye, equivalent to thank God.
Benygne, adj., 1224, gracious, benignant.
Beseene, vb., 275, 823, bedecked adorned.
Beseke, vb., 1929, beseech.
Beset, vb., 297, beset, studded with ornaments.
Beshut, vb., 1169, shut up.
Bespreynt, vb., 258, sprinkled.
Bestadde, vb., 1106, placed, sorely imperilled.
Besy, adj., 563, 746, 1811, busy, anxious.
Bettyr, sb., 882, better.
Betyn, vb., 105, beating (?) or beaten.
Bew, adj., 1063 (beu) good, fine.
Blere, vb., 1299, make dim.
Blyn, vb., 1860, cease from.
Blyue, adv., 941, quickly.
Bone, adj., 720, ready; *bowne*, vb., 716, prepared.
Boorde, sb., 1242, conversation; *boorde* 388, table; *aboorde* 248.
Boote, sb., 1351, help, succor.
Borow, vb., 1167, bail out, secure.
Boystous, adj., 127, 156, boisterous, noisy.
Brayde, vb., 499, started up.
Breched, vb., 325, dressed with breeches.
Breede, vb., 599, grow, breed.
Brennyng, vb., 1529, burning.
Brokers, sb., 702, receivers of stolen goods.
Brybores, sb., 673, robbers, beggars.
But yef, conj., 89, 490, unless.

Caltrop, sb., 773, an iron instrument scattered in battlefields to impede cavalry.
Carders, sb., 696, card players.
Carnall, adj., 1381, worldly, fleshly.
Carpe, vb., 402, play, speak; *carpyng*, 439.
Castaway, sb., 1274, something of no value.

Caytyffys, sb., 705, caitiffs.
Certeyne, adv., 112 and often, certainly.
Chamelet, sb., 320, camlet, a woven fabrik of wool and cotton, or of goat's hair and silk.
Chare, sb., 506, car.
Chases, sb., 58, open hunting grounds.
Chaunse, sb., 996, chance.
Chere, sb., 263, 284, face, countenance; greeting, 418, 423.
Chese, vb., 882, chose.
Chyders, sb., 693, scolds.
Chyne, vb., 536, to open in cracks or fissures.
Chyst, sb., 1300, chest.
Claterers, sb., 684, tattlers.
Clause, sb., 136, proviso.
Cloke, sb., 1503, cloak.
Closshers, sb., 696, "closh"-players.
Clowte, sb., 1274, clout, rag.
Cofres, sb., 273, coffers for money.
Coloppys, sb., 697. See note.
Columbyne, adj., 374, dovelike, like the flower (?)
Comfort, sb., 65, 532, pleasure; 206, confidence; 488, help, support; *comfortyd*, vb., 761.
Comon, adj., 1938, familiar.
Compace, sb., 1881, space.
Conceyte, sb., 1989, thought, idea.
Concordaunce, sb., 2005, agreement.
Condescendyd, vb., 1974, agreed.
Condycyons, sb., 322, states, circumstances.
Confound, vb., 506, destroy; 1042, ? pass; *confounders*, 916,
Coniecture, sb., 1694, opinion.
Coniugatoures, sb., 915, uniters.
Constreynyd, vb., 49, urged, compelled.
Context, adj., 1503, woven firmly.
Contumacy, sb., 638, resistence to authority.
Corner, sb., 35, secluded place.
Correccion, sb., 91, 486, correction, fine.
Cost, sb., 119, coast; 952, region.
Costlew, adj., 296, costly.
Couerture, sb., 1723, covering, concealment.

Glossary

Coueyte, vb., 1476, covet.
Counterfete, vb., 212, construct.
Cowchyd, vb., 287, 308, inlaid, laid in order.
Craft, sb., 1710, business, 1134 craftiness.
Crakers, sb., 676, braggarts, noisy fellows.
Croppe, sb., 620, stem of a plant.
Cropyn, vb., 1953, crept.
Cruell, adj., 41, 471, harsh, severe, cruel; *crewelnes*, sb., 1643.
Crysmatory, sb., 1444, a vessel for chrism.
Cryspe, adj., 374, fresh.
Culuer, sb., 1608, dove.
Curas, sb., 345, cuirass, breastplate.
Cure, sb., 59, 455, care.
Cure boyle, 617, hard leather; v. note.
Cyrcute, sb., 757, circuit.
Cysterne, sb., 1526, cistern.

Dalyaunce, sb., 1509, talk.
Dampnacion, sb., 1844, damnation.
Darkyd, vb., 1193, lay hid.
Dastard, sb., 1886, coward; pl. 703.
Date, sb., 425, date, time. See note.
Daungere, sb., 96, 527, 543, 2084, power; 165, 445 refusal.
Debonayr, adj., 1441, gentle.
Defaute, sb., 460, default; ? vb., 782.
Dele, vb., 146, deal, distribute; *deele*, 1634, have dealings.
Dell, sb., 1333, part; *dele*, 1027.
Deme, vb., 1068, think, judge.
Demenyng, sb., 269, demeanor.
Deputate, vb., 1641, appointed.
Dere, vb., 600, injure.
Dereygne, vb., 612, set in order, fight.
Desert, sb., 1288, merit.
Desperate, adj., 28, causing despair.
Desyreth, vb., 138, demands.
Disclaundyr, sb., 658, slander.
Disport, sb., 531, pleasure.
Do, vb., 54 and often, done.
Dolour, sb., 735, grief.
Domynacion, sb., 1911, domination.
Doole, sb., 487, dole, portion.
Dotyng, adj., 1394, foolish, childish.

Dowte, sb., 761, 1001, 1321, 1929, doubt; vb., 523.
Dowty, adj., 792, brave.
Draught, sb., 1232, drawing, move at chess.
Dresse, vb., 534, direct, reach, prepare; myn ey gan I dresse, 1512.
Dryuylles, sb., 703, idiots.
Dubbyd, vb., 974, conferred knighthood.
Dure, vb., 1777, last, extend; *duryd*, 751.
Duresse, sb., 1270, restraint.
Dynt, sb., 487, dint, stroke.
Dyscordyd, vb., 1973, differed.
Dyscrese, vb., 232, decrease.
Dysdeynyd, vb., 168, refused.
Dysgysyd, vb., 343, dressed, tricked out.
Dysport, sb., 67, 531, 671, pleasure, recreation.
Dyspurueyde, vb., 723, unprepared.
Dysseyte, sb., 647, deceit.
Dysvsyd, vb., 1400, disused, out of use.

Effecte, sb., 1617, 1916, conclusion, meaning.
Efte, adv., 560, again.
Eftsones, adv., 1007, immediately.
Egall, sb., 154, equal.
Eke, adv., 247, also.
Elles, adv., 33, else; *ellys*, 161.
Enbrowderyd, vb., 332, embroidered.
Enforme, vb., 785, inform.
Enhaunse, vb., 999, increase, raise.
Entent, sb., 108, purpose; 451, attention, effort; *thentent*, 1904.
Entresse, sb., 1941, interest.
Equyte, sb., 495, justice.
Er, Ere, adv., 8, 1558, before.
Eschew, vb., 961, avoid.
Estate, sb., 27, 424, state, place, rank.
Euerychoon, 1806, each one.
Euesdroppers, sb., 691, eves-droppers.
Euyll, adv., 38, in an evil manner.
Evyn, adv., 162, at the time; 202, evenly; adj., 886, even.
Execute, vb., 53, bring to bear.
Exorte, vb., 1488, teach, advise.

Fade, vb., 70, wither, decrease.

Glossary. 109

Fall, vb., 230, fall; 10, fallen, pp.; 124, befall; 558, happen; *fell*, 530, happened; *fyll*, 367, was fitting.
Fande, vb., 131, found.
Fantasy, sb., 35, 2050, fancy; *fantasyes*, pl., 1854.
Fare, vb., 810, proceed.
Fasers, sb., 674, hypocrites (facers).
Fauset, sb., 357 faucet.
Fawchon, sb., 283, falchion.
Fawcon, sb., 803, falcon.
Fayne, adj., 11, inclined, desirous.
Fee, sb., 995, domain.
Feere, sb., 1952, fear.
Feet, sb., 1064, deed.
Fell, adj., 434, cruel (many?).
Fendes, sb., 1412, fiendes.
Fenyx, sb., 810, phœnix.
Fere, 52, *in fere* = in company.
Ferre, adv., 102, 1613, 1627, 1913 far; *ferther*, 1932.
Feruent, adj., 1448, vehement.
Fet, vb., 544, bring, fetch.
Feynt, adj., 80, 359, weak, lacking color and energy.
Finaunce, sb., 1242, fine, forfeiture.
Flayn, vb., 1567, flayed.
Foly, sb., 1631, 2097, foolishness, sin.
Fone, sb., pl., 1748, foes.
Foom (?), sb., 104, foam.
Forteresse, sb., 187, palace; 303 figuratively as strong-hold.
Forse, sb., 1057, matter, consequence, *no forse* = no matter.
Forsothe, adv., 211, 581, in truth.
Foryete, vb., 239, forgotten.
Fowtyn, vb., 1826, fought.
Foyson, sb., 408, abundance, plenty.
Frese, sb., 325, a cloth.
Froward, adj., 1816, ungovernable; *frowardness*, 640.
Fructuous, adj., 900, fruitful, profitable.
Fury, sb., 53, judgment.
Fygure, sb., 1725, form of speech.
Fyn, adv., 1463, very.
Fysenamy, sb., 870, physiognomy.

Gaderyd, vb., 760, gathered.
Galaunt, adj., 296, splendid, gay.
Gall, sb., 1614, nut-gall.
Gan, vb., 202, 534, began, and used as auxiliary = did.
Gape, vb., 1316, desire, stand in expectation of.
Garnysshyd, vb., 377, adorned.
Gastes, sb., 754, guests, (cf. Lat. hostis) followers.
Gate, vb., 1836, won.
Gawdy, adj., 320, gaudy, perhaps dyed with weld.
Geere, sb., 886 ? riches (or ? jeer).
Genalogy, sb., 854, lineage.
Geomansy, sb., 868, divination by earth.
Gesse, vb., 1386, think, suppose.
Get, sb., 1678, 1657, fashion.
Getters, sb., 693, ? swaggerers or ? thieves.
Gladyd, vb., 383, made glad.
Glosyng, adj., 2081, flattering; *glosers*, sb., 683, flatterers.
Go, vb., 1396, gone.
Gonnes, sb., 1038, guns.
Goostly, adj., 852, spiritual.
Gramercy, 575, many thanks.
Greefe, sb., 47, harm; 216, sorrow.
Grogyng, sb., 217 (grochyng) grumbling, malice.
Grounde, sb., 304, reason, agency, 1690, place.
Gryffyng, sb., 1718, grafting.
Guerdoun, sb., 2087, reward.
Guy, vb., 1720, guide.
Guytornes, 970, (? guydons) cavalry flags.
Gyldyn, adj., 367, golden.
Gymlot, sb., 357, gimblet.
Gyse, sb., 1965, manner.

Habundaunce, sb., 1714, abundance.
Habylyte, sb., 1247, ability.
Habytacle, sb., 11, habitation.
Happyd, vb., 419, chanced.
Hasardoures, sb., 696, gamblers.
Haunt, sb., 1295, dwelling; *hauntyd*, 119.
Heede, sb., 10, head.
Heede, sb., 1815, care.
Hele, sb., 1853, health.
Hem, pr., 1636 and often, them.

Glossary.

Her, pr., 47, 65, 1635, their.
Herber, sb., 1479, arbor.
Hermyne, sb., 266, ermine.
Herowde, sb., 719, herald.
Heuynesse, sb., 186, slowness, 10 heaviness.
Heynous, adj., 962, hateful, reprehensible.
Hit, pr., 62 and often, it.
Hogy, adj., 1095, huge.
Holly, adv., 2014, wholly.
Hoole, adj., 967, whole.
Houyd, vb., 1608, hovered.
Howe be hit, conj., 1081, how-be-it.
Hulke, sb., 88.
Hy, vb., 765, hie; *hyghyd*, 941, hied.
Hydyr, adv., 604, hither.
Hygh, adj., 73, great.
Hygh-weyes, sb., 1460, high-ways.
Hyghyd, vb., 941, hastened.
Hym, pr., 128 and often, them; also him.

Impotent, sb., 1553, sick man.
Inconuenyent, sb., 415, inconvenience.

Iape, sb., 525, jest, mockery.
Iugement, sb., 161, the court sentence.
Iurysdyccion, sb., 1111, power.
Iust, vb., 1099, joust.

Karyk, sb., 88, cark, a kind of ship.
Kendall, adj., 356, describing a kind of cloth.
Keruell, sb., 87, caravel.
Knowleche, sb., 529, knowledge.
Knyt, vb., 991, united; *knet*, 1186; *knette*, 2008.
Konnyng, sb., 854, wisdom.
Krany, vb., 536, crack into fissures.
Krauers, sb., 534, crevice.
Kynde, sb., 1647, nature; 1544, kind.
Kyrtyll, sb., 332, an outer garment.

Lak, sb., 369, lack.
Langoure, sb., 1853, languor.
Lappyd, vb., 126, wrapped.
Large, sb., 1239, liberty.
Largely, adv., 1637, freely.
Largesse, sb., 1327, liberty.

Lastyuyous, adj., 686, lascivious.
Laurer, sb., 791, laurel.
Lawe, vb., 404, laugh.
Leese, vb., 1100, lose.
Leme, sb., 1609, light.
Lere, vb., 887, learn.
Lerne, vb., 957, teach.
Lesynges, sb., 687, lies.
Let, vb., 1130, hinder; 251, avoid, neglect; 529, given; 956, let; sb., 319, hinderance.
Lewde, adj., 403, worthless, perhaps loud; sb., *lewdenesse*, 1633, free action.
Loft, see *aloft*.
Longeth, vb., 1327, belongs.
Loore, sb., 2074, wisdom, lore.
Lore, vb., 1309, lost.
Loselles, sb., 714, worthless fellows, lorels.
Lothe, adj., 881, loath.
Lowte, vb., 1089, 1439, 1925, bow, yield.
Lurdeyns, sb., 686, block-heads.
Luskes, sb., 714, lazy fellows.
Lust, sb., 1307, strength, desire; 1277, wish.
Lyeftenaunt, sb., 1254, lieutenant, representative.
Lyght, adv., 1201, lightly.
Lyke, vb., 225, please.
Lyklynes, sb., 1066, probability.
Lyst, vb., 1007, wished; 1291, wish.
Lythe, vb., 105, lies.

Mace, sb., 476, mace.
Malapert, adj., 503, impudent, forward.
Males, sb., 686, pockets.
Manaces, vb., 61, threatens.
Maner, sb., 69, kind of; on a *maner*, 5; any *maner* wey, 1735.
Marre, vb., 556, destroy.
Mastresse, sb., 243, mistress, governess.
Mawgre, prep., 1381, in spite of.
Mede, sb., 756, merit.
Medewes, sb., 259, meadows.
Mekyll, 92, "in as mekyll as"; mochyll, 1813.
Mene, sb., 1195, mediator; adj., 946, mean.
Mene, adj., 1720, mean, low.
Merueyle, sb., 103, marvel, wonder.

Glossary.

Messe, sb., 257, plate, table.
Mesure, sb., 84, degree, *out of mesure* = beyond due degree or bounds.
Meuyd, vb., 145, proposed; *meve*, 431, propose.
Meynt, vb., 361, mingled.
Meyny, sb., 853, followers, army; *meyne*, 774.
Monacorde, sb., 7, agreement.
Moo, 863, 1600; *more*, 1606, *moore* 1791.
Mood, sb., 1571, manner.
Mortall, adj., 732, 1450, deadly.
Mowte, vb., 1951, been able.
Mowthe, sb., 2060, mouth.
Multyplyers, sb., 371, 681, money makers.
Murre, sb., 329, murre, a cold in the throat.
Muryd, vb., 1460, enclosed, walled.
Myscheue, vb., 523, do harm; sb., *myschyef*, 620.
Myddes, sb., 934, midst.
Myte, sb., 1607, 1814, mite, thing of no value.

Ne, 1197 and often, not.
Nere, adv., 1, nearly.
Newe, adv., 562, newly.
Next, adj., 551, nearest.
Noonys, 502, nonce.
Nouelte, sb., 1705, new thing.
Noy, vb., 774, annoy.
Nygromansy, sb., 867, divination by the dead.

Obstacle, sb., 9, hinderance.
Odoryferous, adj., 336, fragrant.
Offyce, sb., 494, employment.
On, sometimes written *oo*, 117, one.
Onwarde, adj., 162, further.
On lyue, 1851, alive.
Oon, 6 and often, one.
Oonys, adv., 1127, once.
Opteygne, vb., 1353, obtain.
Or, conj., 752, ere.
Ordynatly, adv., 203, in good order.
Ordynaunce, sb., 245, decision, law.
Ornomancy, sb., 869, divination by birds.

Ospray, sb., 813, the fish hawk.
Ost, sb., 668, host; *hooste*, 1124, cf. Fr. ost.
Othes, sb., 502, oathes.
Ouches, sb., 297, jewels.
Outher, conj., 33, either; *owther*, 480.
Overstert, vb., 1593, ? overlooked.
Oweth, vb., 91, is under obligation, followed by an objective clause introduced by an infinitive, with *to*, as in Chaucer.

Pak, sb., 368, company.
Panter, sb., 822, panther.
Parable, sb., 1987, parable.
Parciall, adj., 153, partial.
Parde, 619, 1275, (par Dieu).
Party, adj., 316, partial, favoring one party.
Pase, sb., 632, step, way.
Passyd, vb., 368, surpassed.
Patent, sb., 496, written bond of office.
Pauyse, vb., 1640, used reflexively—bring to pause.
Pawmestry, sb., 870, divination by the hand.
Paynym, adj., 1679, pagan.
Penowns, sb., 970, small banners.
Pere, sb., 808, equal.
Perfyte, adj., 1491, perfect.
Permyssyue, adj., 1731, permitted.
Perpetuell, adj., 899, constant.
Pesecoddys, sb., 493, pea-pods.
Pety, adj., 827, inferior.
Peyne, sb., 746, 1811, pain, trouble.
Plenteuous, adj., 408, plenty, cf. O. F. plentevous.
Plesaunce, sb., 798, pleasure; *plesere*, 197.
Plyght, vb., 1473, pledge.
Polytyk, adj., 1742, wise.
Ponderously, adv., 9, heavily.
Posternes, sb., 1296, 1849, gates.
Poudryd, vb., 266, powdered.
Praters, sb., 674, trifling talkers.
Precept, sb., 1682, command.
Predicament, sb., 1329, in logic = a general class.
Prefyxyd, vb., 549, appointed.
Preparate, vb., 1467, prepared.

Presse, sb., 256, throng; 1755, torment.
Prima facie, 157, at first view.
Prophetyssa, sb., 1589, prophetess.
Proue, vb., 1728, test, determine.
Prykeryd, adj., 328, prick-eared.
Prynte, vb., 1784, impress.
Pryse, sb., 1354, contest.
Pseudo-prophetes, sb., 708, false prophets.
Purfylyd, vb., 266, trimmed.
Purpur, sb., 306, purple garments.
Purseuaunte, 776, messenger.
Puruey, vb., 75, provide; 946, *prevydyd;* 1029, *purveyde.*
Puruyaunce, sb., 956, 1433, provision, plan.
Put, vb., 761, 1090, bring to a condition of; *put out,* 1481, expel.
Pyke, vb., 1348, betake.
Pylary, adj., 698, pillory.
Pylow, sb., 12, pillow. Cf. Chaucer's *pilwe.*
Pylyons, sb., 1577, priests' hats.
Pyne, sb., 216, punishment.
Pyromancy, sb., 869, divination by fire.
Pyry, sb., 126, storm of wind.

Quelmers, sb., 709, killers, (infanticides).
Quod, 1477, said; 1210, quoth.

Rancour, sb., 235, enmity, malice.
Ray, sb., 550, striped cloth.
Recorde, vb., 272, remember.
Recouer, vb., 769, ? cover over, win.
Recreaunt, adj. 1256, defeated.
Redolence, sb., 1611, fragrance.
Reft, vb., 564, deprived.
Reherse, vb., 83, relate.
Reioyse, vb., 532, make glad.
Rekke, vb., 560, care, reck.
Relese, vb., 883, rehearse.
Reproche, sb., 71, reproach.
Rerewarde, sb., 1094, rear gaurd.
Resorte, vb., 63, return.
Respyte, sb., 170, postponement.
Resydyuacion, sb., 1340, back-sliding.
Retourne, vb., 100 (active), turn back.
Reuers, sb., 688, robbers.
Reyne, vb., 2086, reign.

Roode, sb., 1040, cross.
Route, sb., 388, 438, company.
Rought, vb., 1197, reached.
Rowne, vb., 12, consult with; *rownyd,* 142, consulted with; *rownyd,* 421, whispered; *rowners,* sb., 687, whisperers.
Russet, adj., 325, coarse.
Rybaudy, sb., 648, ribaldry.
Ryght, adv., 191, very.
Rynde, sb., 66, bark (tree).

Sabatouns, sb., 346, sabbatons, armorial coverings for the feet.
Sad, adj., 270, 390, 1561, earnest, serious.
Safe, conj., 402, except.
Safecondyte, sb., 89, 490, safe-conduct.
Sakcloth, sb., 290, sackcloth.
Sanctuary, sb., 1446, a sacred place.
Sauns, prep., 1858, without, (v. Nares' Glos.).
Sauerys, sb., 336, odors.
Sauoryd, vb., 338, smelled.
Scalop, sb., 1564, scallop-shell.
Scisme, sb., 411, division.
Se, pr., 376, she.
Secte, sb., 895, sect, kind.
See, sb., 365, seat.
Seere, adj., 1459, dry, withered.
Seethe, sb., 97, restoration.
Sekerly, adv., 787, surely.
Sentence, sb., 136, 458, decision; 1863, truth.
Sequelys, sb., 871, followers.
Sercote, sb., 276, surcoat, outer coat.
Sesyd, vb., 1744, ceased.
Sesyne, sb., 1455, possession (a law term).
Set, vb., 2016, settled.
Sew, vb., 219; *su,* 238, entreat; *sewyd,* 1198.
Sewe, vb., 1023, sowed.
Sewerte, sb., 449, surety.
Sewre, adj., 524, sure.
Shakerles, sb., 675 (?).
Shaueldores, sb., 675 (?).
Shent, vb., 1092, destroyed, shamed.
Shoures, sb., 322, gifts; *shoure,* 732, struggle.

Glossary.

Slepyr, adj., 1026, 1069, slippery.
Smokke, sb., 377, smock.
Sobre, adj., 1233, sad; 1660, sober.
Sodomytes, sb., 708, fornicators.
Soort, sb., 619, troop, company; *sorte*, 1489.
Soot, sb., 618, soot.
Sore, adv., 341, greatly.
Sothe, sb., 1226, truth.
Sotyll, adj., 1694, 1701, subtle.
Sought, vb., 788, went.
Sownde, vb., 1688, sound.
Sowneth, vb., 1302, tends, inclines; *sownyd*, 1987, seemed.
Spere, sb., 3, sphere; *speres*, pl., 1698.
Spreynt, see bespreynt.
Stadde, see bestadde.
Stale, vb., 2040, stole.
Stant, vb., 1887, stands.
Stede, sb., 340, place; 1129, steed.
Steuyn, vb., 824, proclaim, announce.
Stoute, adj., 313 — said of eyes; 439 — said of words: haughty, resolute, bold·
Strayte, adj., 45, strict; adv., 539' narrowly.
Strechers, sb., 674, ? liars.
Stremes, sb., 1855, streams.
Streyngthe, vb., 751, strengthen.
Streytyd, vb., 1633, restricted, put in bonds.
Styrt, vb., 566, started.
Superfluyte, sb., 1824, superfluity.
Superfyciall, adj., 538, pertaining to the surface,
Sustynaunce, sb., 336, support, living.
Sy, vb., 1058, saw.
Sygne, sb., 1442, miracle.
Sykerly, adv., 270, surely.
Sylogyse, vb., 19, reason, contend, argue.
Symonyakes, sb., 680, simonists.
Synderesys, sb., 937, syneresis.
Syngler, adj., 71, special.
Syth, conj., 1354, since.
Sythe, sb., 127, time.
Swage, vb., 1038, ? discharge.
Swemfully, adv., 1223, sorrowfully.
Swet, sb., 104, 2044, sweat. In 2044 said of body.

Take, vb., 59 and often, taken; *takyn* 1626.
Tane, vb., 2013, taken.
Tayll, sb., 754, company, number.
Teche, vb., 1701, teach; *taught*, 1231.
Tendre, vb., 135, consider, have a care for.
Tenebrus, adj., 1169, dark.
Than, adv., 89 and often, then.
The, pr., 52 and often, thee.
Then, conj., 1607, than.
Tho, pr., 447, those.
Thorough, prep., 70, on account of (preceded by where); *thorow*, 2061.
Thought, sb., 1234, 1360, 2051, anxiety, care; 1991, thought.
Thryd, 1776, third.
Thynne, adj., 1591, thin.
To, adv., 511 and often, too.
Tong, sb., 367, tongue.
Tonne, sb., 1897, tub.
Trapure, sb., 815, trappings.
Traunse, sb., 15, trance.
Trauayll, sb., 1971, work.
Trayne, sb., 773, snare.
Tregetours, sb., 685, jugglers.
Trespase, sb., 221, injury, offense.
Triumphall, adj., 2087, triumphal.
Trouthe, sb., 1473, troth.
Trow, vb., 957, believe; 1386, know *trowyd*, 432.
Try (out), vb., 2071, separate.
Tryacle, sb., 12, a medicine, (cf. treacle).
Tryfyls, sb., 1854, trifles, cheats.
Trypartyte, adj., 1031, divided into three parties.
Tryphelers, sb., 685, cheaters.
Tweyne, sb., 1966, two.
Tyburne, sb., 697. See note to this line.
Tyde, sb., 334, time.
Tylthe, sb., 1710, cultivation.
Tyne, 1063, tiny (generally preceded by little, as here).
Tytyuyllys, sb., 694. See note on line 694.

Vnbrydelyd, vb., 1630, unrestrained.
Vnderlowte, sb., 1273, servant.

Vndyrtake, vb., 233, 1390, 1411, be surety, promise.
Vnkynde, adj., 1023, unnatural, cruel.
Vnlustes, sb., 713, idle men.
Vre, sb., 1448, use, practice.
Vsyd, vb., 117, was accustomed to do.
Vtter, adj., 594, absolute.

Valewyng, vb., 1607, valuing.
Varyaunce, sb., 244, difference, dispute.
Vaward, sb., 602, van.
Verrey, adj., 918, 2002, true.
Veryly, adj., 2042, truly.
Vouchesafe, vb., 2019, granted.

Walewyng, vb., 557, wallowing.
Wanton, adj., 378, sportive; 1230, reckless; sb., *wantones*, 1362, 1635.
Ware, adj., 128, aware.
Wede, sb., 377, garment.
Wedyr, sb., 530, weather.
Welde, vb., 670, wielded.
Wele, sb., 56, 210, weal, prosperity.
Wende, vb., 739, 1623, go; see *wene*.
Wene, vb., 278, 985, think, suppose; *wenyng*, 1651, 1713; *wend*, 239; *wende*, 1344.
Weryd, vb., 379, wore.

Wetewoldes, sb., 710, tame "cuckolds."
Wex, vb., 1369, 1415, grow.
Whan, conj., 1, when.
Whedyr, conj., 24, whether.
Whereas, adv., 118, where.
Whereon, adv., 48, whereof.
Whew, sb., 1316, 2049, hue.
Whore, adj., 400, white; *whore-berdyd*= hoar-bearded.
Whyle, sb., 129, time.
Wood, adj., 1314, mad (also *mad* 347).
Woote, vb., 621, knows; *wete*, 1011.
Wrapped, vb., 1383, wrapped.
Wrethe, sb., 417, wrath.
Wrought, vb., 1882, done.
Wrythers, sb., 674 ?
Wyght, sb., 987, 1034, man.
Wyre, sb., 1872, doubt.
Wyse, sb., 51, manner.
Wysshe, vb., 1384, direct, recommend.
Wyt, sb., 896, wisdom.

Ydiote, sb., 1963, idiot.
Yef, conj., 56, 63, etc., if.
Yeue, vb., 17, 77, give.
Yuy, sb., 355, yew.
Ywys, adv., 879, 1056, certainly.

SPECIAL PHRASES AND PROVERBS.

All and some, 192, each and all, the whole matter.
In especiall, 116, 1445, 1599, especially.
By and by, 202, then; 302, 800, one after the other.
More and lesse, 306, 536, more or less; 1264, altogether.
Lest and moost, 766, 784, high and low degree. *Most or leste*, 480.
To or fro, 24.
Fer and wyde, 626.
Make and marre, 556.
For feyre or foule, 475.
For the nonnys, 502, for the nonce.
Out of mesure, 84, 102, beyond measure or reason.
What in the deuyllys date, 425, exclamatory.
Howe a deuyll way, 1317, exclamatory.

Croppe and roote, 620, the whole of anything.
Roote and rynde, 66, the whole tree.
Kepe noon in store, 151, keep nothing in reserve.
Not worth a peere (pear), 597.
Then a myte, 1607; *nat a myte*, 1814, *myte*=a small thing.
Rekke nat a strawe, 560.
Nat yeue two pesecoddys, 493.
Bryght as glas, 276.
Breched lyke a bere, 325.
Grene as any gresse, 334.
Here shone as wyre of goold bryght, 373.
As a goste came in wyndyng shete, 420.
Tomblyng as a ball, 557.
Harde as glas, 614.
Hard as horn, 618.
Blakker then soot, 618.
Slepyr as an yele, 1026.

As a castaway or a shoo clowte, 1274.
Close as in a chyst, 1300.
Coloryd as a crystall, 1603.
Darke as a myste or a feynyd fable, 1988.
Wyt ys oute where hyt went ynne, 1999.
Dreuyn to her wyttes ende, 1665.
My wyt ys so thynne, 1997.
Ferre ys fro the wytte and ferther good mende, 1932.
Thy wytte stant acrooke, 1887.
For feere I lookyd as blak as a coole. I wold haue cropyn in a mouse hoole, 1952-53.
Howe the game gooth, 426, how the matter stands.
Ledeth by the sleue, 1680, causes to follow submissively, cf. *toke me by the sleve* 14, 2033.
Cast in a boon (of contention), 1805.
Hit hyng in hys balaunce, 1012, it depended upon his decisions.
Of all maner greynes she sealyd the patent, 292; cf. "wenyng in her honde had leyn all power of cornys habundaunce" 1713-14; v. 449, ye seelyd my patent.
Take the mantell and the ryng, 267, vow perpetual widowhood.
Varyaunt Fortune, 318.
Taught to drawe another draught, 1232, taught to make another move—to do differently.
Lerne hem a new daunce, 957, teach them a new motion.
Fro poost to pylour was he made to daunce, 1147, he was driven from one thing to another without purpose.

Made her beerdys on the new gete, 1657, changed their minds.
The bende of your bowe begynneth to slake, 1243-44.
Put in prese, 1755, enter into torment.

He must nedys go that the deuell dryues, 21.
Where vertew occupyeth must nedys well grow, 1372.
A false myrrour deceyueth a mannys look, 1727.
Bettyr late then neuer, 1204.
Bettyr be dede than a lyve, 518.

He ys nat as he doth apere, 2083.
As good ys ynowgh as a gret feste, 2035.
Such as ye haue sowe must ye nedes reepe, 1244-45.
Bettyr were a chylde to be vnbore then let hyt haue þe wyll and for euer be lore, 1308-9.
Wealth unbrydelyd encreseth mysrewle, 1631.
Fooles ouercome ay wyse men, 1661.
Try out the corne clene from the chaff, 2071 = "take the best and let the worst be," 2070.

The manufacturer's authorised representative in the EU for product safety is
Oxford University Press España S.A. of el Parque Empresarial San Fernando de
Henares, Avenida de Castilla, 2 – 28830 Madrid (www.oup.es/en or product.
safety@oup.com). OUP España S.A. also acts as importer into Spain of products
made by the manufacturer.

www.ingramcontent.com/pod-product-compliance
Ingram Content Group UK Ltd.
Pitfield, Milton Keynes, MK11 3LW, UK
UKHW041906220426
12034UKWH00001B/5